Not That Anyone Asked

A Travel Memoir about Sex, Drugs, Love, and
Finding Purpose

Travis W. King

Tra lala lala,

[signature]

P.S. Thank you for coming to Earth Day!

CONTENTS

.

THE PREAMBLE IN THREE PARTS

DEDICATION

To my Dad, aka "Bob."

I went out and made myself interesting, Pops. Thanks for the advice.

"Go out and make yourself interesting" was the second-most-common piece of advice my Dad gave my brother and me growing up, after "wear your seatbelt." My Dad claims he was called the "flow-meister" in college, but nobody can either confirm or deny this—all we know now is that he is what you would call a bit of a worrier and has been as long as I've known him.

My first few years of traveling were sprinkled with frequent emails from my Dad asking: "Do you ever think you're going to use your master's degree?" "Aren't you getting tired of all the travel?" "What's your five-year plan?" He wasn't the biggest fan of the choices I was making in my late 20s and early 30s. My pursuit of the uncommon. He wanted to brag about me to his peers and colleagues the same way he bragged about my older brother, Austin, the lawyer and Harvard graduate. My younger son is "somewhere in Bolivia" wasn't something my Dad felt proud of.

It took time—years of actual evidence—for him to know that I would "be fine," showing up at Christmas every year, no matter how far away I was, with some worldly gifts and the same smile. A lifetime's worth of memories to unpack from the latest adventures. He saw I was happy. He softened.

It also took some mental gymnastics on his part I'm sure—pushing past the baby boomer generation's preconceived notions of what success looks like. Those ideas of success weren't mine, and I was chasing a different dream; I didn't want to die in a house with the most toys. I don't think it was one conversation or one photo he saw of me smiling in a foreign country that flipped a switch. I think it was likely the slow and steady stream of evidence mixed with a sincere questioning of his own assumptions of what a "good life" and a "good job" looked like.

Whatever pieces contributed to this puzzle he was working on, he eventually finished it, and then he took a step back to see what the picture was. When he adjusted his little Benjamin Franklin glasses on his cute wrinkled face, he would see that the picture formed simply read: "Your son is happy and free, he's seen more of the world than most people ever will, and it's in large part thanks to you." It would take years and thousands of miles for us to get there, but my Dad is finally proud of "his son, the world traveler," and that makes me happy.

Writing this book made me nervous because I knew he would read it, but I also knew that for it to be any good I had to be honest, be human, and tell every story. I hope this book makes him proud as well—drug stories and all.

I went out and made myself interesting, Pops.

HOW TO APPROACH THIS BOOK

For anyone who is lucky enough to have traveled extensively, we all have a story—and this is mine. Names have been changed to protect people's identities, but only if they wanted me to. Most of the names are actually real, as are the stories—as best as I can remember. If I'm using a pseudonym or just taking a wild guess, I'll be sure to include some version of "let's call them Timmy-Tim-Tom" to clarify. There might be timelines slightly out of order or details slightly off, but this is generally not done for dramatic effect, rather because I started writing this from my memory nearly seven years after my travel life began. The majority of the dialogue is entirely based on how I remember or imagine that conversation going and the nuances of the characters. This is a true story, as true as any story based on memory.

So pour a nice cup of Vietnamese coffee, or Japanese whiskey, or Chilean wine. Maybe pour mint tea from a great height, or take a shot of aguardiente out of someone's belly button. Maybe just crack a PBR or get a glass of water from the robot in your refrigerator door.

Whatever you choose, settle in, get comfy, and approach this book like you would a long-lost friend who's just returned home from a big trip with their eyes wide open—a new alpaca sweater on and stories swirling in their mind. Try to be that curious person who wants to hear those stories, however far from your day-to-day reality they might currently be.

Note: Unless otherwise noted, the photos in this book were taken by me or a total stranger who graciously offered.

THIS BOOKS HOPE

I've spent a fairly insane number of hours in transit—on buses, planes, ferries, and trains—and during that time I normally read. I've read a lot of books with travel at the heart. Some are great, some are preachy, some are hard to believe, some are repetitive, some smell like tobacco and leather, and some read like history books without the maps.

My hope is that this isn't going to read as either a "how-to" travel book or a series of Instagram captions where everything seems perfect. I don't want to imply that anyone living a stable life back home should feel like they've messed up or to reiterate the cliché that "travel is the only thing you buy that makes you richer." (Now picture me at Angkor Wat, bowing to a monk.) Whether or not you've had the opportunity to travel—and whether or not you've taken that opportunity—I hope you see part of yourself in these misadventures, successes and struggles. I hope that, in my stories, you find parts of yours.

Whether you have twenty or zero country patches sewn onto your imaginary backpack, I do hope this leaves you wanting to get out there and see more of the world, to explore the corners of the map you wondered about as a kid. I remember as a ten-year-old being blown away that there was a place called *Komodo Dragon National Park*, which I found in one of my Dad's National Geographic magazines. A couple of years back I took a boat there and saw it—lizards, sharks, rays, and all. It was even cooler than I imagined it in my ten-year-old mind. Whether the variables of your life allow you to book a flight to see Komodo Dragons, or rather you go exploring with your kids deep in the woods near your house, I want to stoke your desire for adventure, your fire for something new.

———

For my generation—the one that went from long curly phone cords to the iPhone in ten short years, the one who will hold an average of around eight jobs before turning 30—the societal and familial pressure I faced to be *a success* was likely not unique.

It's natural that our parents would want our lives and careers to resemble theirs, the same way we hope our babies carry our features and show off our DNA, but the world is changing fast and I wasn't interested in chasing someone else's idea of success. This book is as much about figuring out what my purpose is, what a good life is, and what success looks, feels, and dresses like for me, as much as it is about travel.

Alongside all of the new countries, rare moments, and characters that come with well-lived days, I hope to make you pause and think. I hope to make you reconsider long-held assumptions and personal beliefs, especially those that have started to feel more like facts than opinions, those ideologies that have come to feel like the temperature in your mind—like water to fish.

I hope this book opens the windows and allows a cool breeze to flood the hallways of your brain.

CONTINENT ONE:
SOUTH AMERICA

CHAPTER 1: WISCONSIN & ARUBA

G rad School was finishing and I started telling people I was leaving. My placement at the neighborhood center through school was wrapping up, the lease on my house had a few months left, and I didn't have a girlfriend, dog, or goldfish; I saw the world's window open, and so I just started telling people I was leaving.

I was back in the place of my childhood, Milwaukee, Wisconsin, wrapping up a master's degree in nonprofit management at Marquette University as a Trinity Fellow. The Trinity Fellowship is a selective graduate program, admitting about ten fellows a year, full of do-gooders and future U.S. Consulates. I'm not entirely sure why, but that's what a surprisingly high percentage of my classmates would become.

When you get close to finishing any sort of degree, people around you will start asking, "How's the job hunt?" "Any jobs lined up?" and "You want me to put you in touch with Fred?" I was 28 and had made every major next-step decision based on what seemed to make the most sense for my career, but one day I thought, *"When do I get to make a big decision for my life—for me, for my happiness, and not for my career?"* Once that seed had been planted, I couldn't uproot it.

I figured that my degree was something I could tuck away into a drawer like a memento from my YMCA Summer Camp days, something no one could ever take away from me. If I wanted to pull it out and dust it off, I could still use it down the road. The questions kept coming, and there came a day when I just started replying, "I'm going to South America."

While I was grateful for the degree, for this golden checked-box on my resumé, I was disenchanted about higher education. My previous life experiences had revealed to me a universal truth that's been haunting higher ed for years—*true learning is experiential.*

At the start of my final semester in grad school I was able to get an independent study approved for which I formed a volunteer committee; together we planned and executed a neighborhood wide clean-up. The clean-up was a fierce competition, the prizes were legit and the after-party had free pizza, local rappers, and news crews in attendance. Not only was the event a huge success—with several thousands of pounds of litter removed from the west side of Milwaukee, near 35th and Lisbon Avenue— but I also grew into my adult self through the project. I learned and obtained tenfold more than I had in all of my coursework combined. By the end, I believed I could turn garbage into gold and dust into magic.

After the success of the independent study, I thought of the trip I had begun planning in my mind as a self-funded bonus semester. Curriculum unknown, reading to be assigned later, syllabus purposefully full of holes.

I started telling everyone and anyone who would listen that I was going to South America. Even people I met in passing or at a bar who probably thought, *"Wow, that guy's an over-sharer!"* I just kept saying it. I was telling people I wanted to learn more about myself and the world. I wanted to learn more Spanish. I wanted to be a farmer. I wanted to unlock universal secrets.

My simple plan was to volunteer with World Wide Opportunities on Organic Farms (WWOOF) all around South America, drinking the same coffee I had harvested earlier that month while studying the future-tense conjugation of new verbs. It was going to be an enriching, educational, and totally new experience. I was going to peel back the globe's layers and learn about it's soil and people. And I already had my ticket out: thanks to a Spirit Airlines screw-up a few years earlier, I had a free round-trip flight anywhere they flew.

Pro tip: If you don't absolutely need to be somewhere, and an airline asks for a volunteer to come to the desk before boarding starts, go up there!

I fancied myself a bit of an explorer from a young age. I was a child constantly in motion, curious about what was down every street, optimistic about what creepy crawler might be under every rock or log. I spent evenings as a kid lying on our rickety basement bench press, thumbing through old National Geographics. For years, I had been telling myself, I would have traveled more, I would have needed a passport for some big trip or another, but I've been busy with volunteering, work and school. In between all of that, I had also been busy and fairly successful in trying to see as many of these 50 odd states as possible, which I reasoned, incorrectly, was important to do as a first step before going somewhere with different-looking money. I had excuses, but the world didn't care. It beckoned, and I knew it was now or never to really meet her.

International travel was always at the top of my life to-do list, and I often wondered if I was mistakenly attributing the lack of doing it to a lack of time. Maybe instead I'd been lacking enough motivation or courage to actually take a risk and do something scary. It's a lot easier to blame time, or lack thereof, since that seems more out of our control when our lives are filled with so many "urgent" things. So I always kept mine full—one professional endeavor linked to an educational one, always the right next choice for the most approved path.

That way, I never had to face myself and wonder why I didn't do the thing I said I wanted to, the thing that scared me and called me in equal measures. I had the perfect excuse—*too busy*. When I saw my window open, when I could feel the healthy pieces of grad school that had been making my plate full being digested in my stomach, I was determined to make sure I wasn't fooling myself. *When do I get to do something for myself, I'm almost 30*, I thought on loop, bolstering my courage.

I told my ten year-old self that I was finally going, and then I told many more people. I said my South American plans out loud so many times that I had to go. I booked a flight to Aruba, which I chose after looking at a map of Spirit's routes. It was the place farthest from the United States that Spirit flew at that time. Before leaving, I remember talking to one of my closest childhood friends, Kevin, who asked, "What are you going to do when you get there?"

"Well, I'm going to drink coffee while learning Spani..." I started to tell him, standing in my kitchen, just off Downer Avenue on the east side of Milwaukee.

He cut me off, shaking his head, and said, "No, I know you want to farm and stuff, I just mean, like, when you get to the airport in Aruba, what are you going to do?" I told him I didn't know but that I wasn't really worried about that part.

I was smart, strong, and trying my best to be fearless.

i. Honeymooners in Paradise

I was in fact entirely lost and helpless when I exited the airport in Aruba, and, while I was doing my best to keep my confusion internal, one of the airport security guards looked at me and then said in a calm, straightforward tone, *"You look lost."*

I was. I sat outside on a bench with a disconnected phone that was about as helpful as a climbing rope, and I pondered which way to start aimlessly walking.

I am strong and fearless. *Come on Trav*, strong and fearless!

I should also point out that, at this early point in my travels, I refused to take taxis, especially from airports, and Uber wasn't even a thing yet.

As I was sitting there debating whether I should just bite the bullet and pay for a taxi, a woman sat next to me, noticed my backpack, my face, my clear confusion, and asked, "Do you need a ride?"

I looked at her like she was a mind-reading gypsy, and I was probably a little too eager to accept. As we walked to throw my stuff in her car, we started chatting.

Anna was from Germany but teaching at a school in Aruba and was at the airport waiting to pick up her boyfriend. I was a lost puppy with a backpack.

We hung out while waiting for her boyfriend's flight to land, and after chatting and getting to know each other she said, "You know, I've got a spare bedroom at my flat if you want to just crash there. You can take a spare key and use the room for as long as you want. I've got to teach during the day, and my friend is here, but you can come and go as you please."

This was my first real taste of travel serendipity. Had I planned where I was staying or even how I was getting into the city, I would have certainly never met Anna. I would have never spent a free week on Aruba running around drinking at beach bars with honeymooning couples, taking free rides on pirate-themed party boats, chasing iguanas, and slowly figuring out how to get to South America.

I arrived in Aruba with about $9,000 in my savings account, earned through a combination of bouncing at a hipster bar (read: sitting on a particular stool while reading grad school assignments), pedi-cabbing most nights I wasn't bouncing (read: biking around portly drunk Wisconsinites to festivals and bars for tips), and other savings from my work at the neighborhood center throughout grad school. Also, I had my share of a little nest egg one of my grandmothers left behind for me, my siblings, and my cousins.

Nine thousand dollars was simultaneously the most savings I'd had at any point in my adult life, but also not so big a figure that I couldn't see the pinhole sized light at the end of my savings tunnel. I was grateful for the free bed, knowing that my savings could only stretch for a certain number of nights in hostels. How many nights, how many months, I had no idea.

One evening during my week in Aruba, I worked through the last of my duty-free whiskey and wandered the beach looking for action of some kind, surrounded by baby strollers and honeymooners in paradise. I had to pee for the fourth time in an hour. I decided to meander into the calm and dark ocean until it was up to my chest, so I could let it all out. Everything felt like a wonderful choice until I looked down into the clear water to notice that I was getting a notification on my iPhone. It died in a bag of rice, and I bought a burner smart phone, a Samsung, the very next day. I was a week into my first big trip and determined to not let this drunken phone misfortune rattle me. I thanked my grandma in my mind for the new phone as I swiped my credit card, and I was ready to get off of Aruba.

————

On a map, it looks like you could swim from Aruba to Venezuela. It's about 15 nautical miles away. Since it was the closest country in South America, and I clearly hadn't done any proper research, Venezuela was my aim. That is, until a certain old man said a single sentence to me.

I was asking all the big boats in the Marina where they were headed, hoping to catch a ride. He was a Venezuelan man, working at the Marina, and asked me where I was hoping to go.

I told him, pointing, "Venezuela, it's just right there."

He told me he was from Venezuela, then urged (in slow motion), *"If you go to Venezuela, you're playing with your life."*

Every now and then, life provides moments that feel straight out of an action movie where time bends and the music stops. His expression was fierce, his sincerity was palpable, and my plans had just changed. I often relied on following my gut while globetrotting over the next years, but advice from a local like this was always a trump card. No Venezuela—it was out. I booked a flight to the Caribbean coast of Colombia.

As I had told everyone back home, after making it to South America, I immediately got knee-deep in the farm scene. The farming days were the best, exactly how I imagined them. Early mornings, strange smells, all that good, sweet farming.

Just kidding—I only wanted to take a moment for you to think I did the thing I said I was going to do. Instead, I quickly found out that's not really how the traveling I was interested in works. You can have every intention to do a certain thing, but, once you open yourself up to the world and the possibility of serendipity, the choices are more often than not taken out of your hands. Traveling for me was all about adaptation, going with the flow. One domino slowly tapping the next, sometimes curving, sometimes failing altogether and needing a restart—a little push in the right direction. Once it starts, it all feels a bit like it's left in the universe's hands.

Needless to say, where I ended up wasn't close to a farm. In fact, I didn't farm one day over the next five months.

A few years later, however, I did work at the world's largest organic dragon fruit farm on Maui for several months. We'll get to the farming days eventually.

CHAPTER 2: COLOMBIA

I walked around the small town of Riohacha extremely thirsty. I recited over and over in my head, *Yo quiero agua... yo quiero agua*. I had taken a year of high school Spanish, so I could say, in theory, "I want water."

I walked up to a woman at a small stand selling snacky things (Yo quiero agua, yo quiero agua) and when I got up to her (Yo quiero agua), I looked at her, ("Yo..."), I opened my mouth, ("............"), I continued to look at her some more, my face flushing in embarrassment, and then I shook my head and turned around to walk away.

I was thirsty for the next few hours until I worked up the courage for a more successful second attempt, where I was able to grab the water and place it down before a shopkeeper. I handed him a new, strange, colorful piece of paper, signifying that I wanted the water. The shopkeeper took my note of some worth and returned several of a different color, which he certainly could have kept.

I eventually used my impressive language skills to organize transport for myself from Riohacha, west along the Caribbean coast to Santa Marta, a more well-traveled destination. I was hoping to find my footing. I was really hoping to have a conversation in English.

After several very body-language-heavy Spanglish conversations, I took a nervous half-day van ride and was dropped in the middle of Santa Marta, with some real questions starting to swirl in my mind about whether I had made the right decision.

I was in Colombia, a place I was made to feel nervous about visiting. I didn't really know where I was. I didn't know a soul. I didn't know how to speak much Spanish or how to find a farm. I wasn't really feeling smart, strong, or fearless. I was lost—even worse—I was keenly aware of how alone in the world I was.

I wandered around trying my best to look the part of a confident traveler. I stopped in at a café and used its WiFi to Google "hostel" and saw one close by, called *The Dreamer*. I clipped my backpack across my chest and wandered there with my last few drops of optimism.

When I got through the gate, I stepped into a large open space with a bar, a pool, and 20 or so backpackers from all over the world drinking beers, splashing about, and laughing as the sunlight rained down on their carefree faces. I checked into a dorm, threw my stuff on my bunk, and changed into some board shorts.

After getting a beer from a nice Scottish kid working at the bar, I slipped into the pool. I met an English guy named Mick, then eventually the group of friends he knew at the hostel. They cooked a family-style dinner that night, and we made plans to go visit a coffee plantation the next day. The energy was so inclusive and open. I was hooked—I was a born backpacker, and I knew it after my first hour at my first hostel. I was a hostel-loving, globe-trotting, party-pushing, card-carrying, backpacker.

————

I spent the next ten days or so with this group of new friends, camping at Tayrona National Park, surfing, partying our faces off, and falling in love with my new lifestyle. I had sex under the stars on a secluded beach with a Dutch girl I met at The Dreamer, as a heat lightning storm went off in the distance. The dark silhouette of her body and long hair was framed by perfectly shaped palm trees leaning toward the water against a clear sky of countless stars. It was my first travel-sex experience, and it was on a beach in one of the most beautiful national parks in the world. You could do worse.

Our little travel crew made it to Cartagena, where we shared a few final and insanely hot days together. We partied hard, we floated in a mud volcano, we partied some more, and I—for the first of many times— hooked up in a hostel bathroom, bending a German girl over a broken sink. It was incredibly sexy sex and still plays in my memory at times. If you frown at that scene out of disgust or disapproval, well, to use one of my favorite Southeast Asian expressions: *"Never try, never know."* I realized then that I had never been with two different women within so short a period of time, but they both felt right. *Maybe this is just part of traveling,* I thought.

We gathered together for a final drink at Café del Mar, a world-famous spot to catch the sunset. I gave Mick and everyone some really earnest hugs, and we promised to stay in touch. I questioned whether I would ever again meet such good people to share my travels with, and, as I walked away from the crew, loneliness and doubt started to creep back in. Maybe I just got extremely lucky with this group? Maybe now is when I should seek out the inevitable isolation of farm life?

About a block after exchanging hugs, I turned a corner and nearly bumped into a woman about my age. As I apologized, I noticed she had a Green Bay Packers t-shirt on, which is essentially a religion in my home state of Wisconsin. We chatted for five minutes about how two Wisconsinites ended up bumping into each other on a random street corner in Cartagena.

She was teaching in Cartagena, and I was once again a happy, traveling puppy with a backpack.

This was the second big lesson I learned early on. People may come and go, but there are good people around every corner in the world. If you're lucky, some might even be Green Bay Packers fans, and others still might become your closest friends and loved ones.

i. Milk with Dinner

I am a Wisconsin boy and proud of it. I really do travel with a Green Bay Packers jersey just to wear it for a certain sixteen (hopefully more) Sundays every year, and I know this is a seemingly stupid use of precious space—but it barely feels like a choice. Wisconsin is a beautiful state filled with "salt-of-the-earth" people, humble and kind folks who drink glasses of milk with dinner. I loved growing up there.

It was full of soccer tournaments, summer camps, playing punk rock drums in suburban basements, and all the other things that fill childhood— first kisses, social stresses, being bullied, peer pressure, and shaping my identity as a new human in a huge world. I wouldn't exchange my childhood for anyone else's, except for one part.

My Mom passed away when I was ten, and, if I'm being totally honest, I'm still processing it. My Mom was sick in most of my childhood memories, battling through rounds of chemo and putting on both a wig and a smile for her two boys, although certainly in a great deal of pain and discomfort most of the time. I remember feeling embarrassed that my Mom was in a wig, and that sense of embarrassment still stings today. I wish I could apologize for that, but obviously I can't. I do talk to my Mom in my mind at times, and, when it feels like the universe winks at me, I thank my Mom, certain that she orchestrated that fateful encounter or delayed flight.

I remember attending my Mom's funeral feeling like I was watching a service for someone else in a movie, entirely detached from the reality of it in an attempt to be strong for my Dad who just lost the love of his life and the mother of his two boys. Lots of people from our suburban Milwaukee community came to the funeral along with most of my fifth-grade class.

Standing in the reception area after the ceremony, watching the scene from above and pretending it was all a work of fiction, David, one of the kids in my class, came over to me and asked in a straightforward, curious way, "Why are you not crying?" I just looked at him and said, "I don't know, I guess I don't want to," and walked away holding back tears. I cried that night in my bed for hours, wondering if the nebulous ball of pain that swelled in my chest would ever dissipate, wondering why it hurt to swallow. I cried myself to sleep like a toddler with a temper tantrum and the next morning I decided, at the age of ten, that I would never judge anyone for how they processed something difficult or grieved a loss. I kept that along with two other foundational life lessons that I trace back to my Mom's passing.

The first: that there is no God. I believe in energy, souls, karma, the possibility of reincarnation, and all types of hippie notions, but you can't convince a ten-year-old who lost his Mom that there is a divine creator who has a "plan for everyone." If so, why would the plan for my Mom—a beautiful person who committed her life to raising two boys and improving special education for troubled kids—end with an incurable and progressive disease that would take her away at age 43? You can't explain it—I still can't and neither can any religious person I've ever had this conversation with, outside of just repeating, "It's god's plan." Well then, *fuck god*. I can say that because I know nobody is listening and because it's been 25 years and I still feel the same way. This isn't some conclusion that felt right in the heat of the moment and faded, it just feels like the truth.

The second thing is that, with the absence of a higher power determining my fate or a "this leads to that" life-planning paradigm, I decided that I wouldn't live in fear. My Dad became increasingly worried about life, having the sole responsibility of getting two boys safely into adulthood on his shoulders. When you have a parent who worries incessantly, you have to decide whether to adopt that same fear or push back dramatically in the other direction. I decided to do my best to never worry—to let the chips fall where they may. My Mom played life safe and was taken, my Dad worried about everything as the last adult left in the room, and somewhere along the way I decided that, whatever happened, I would be fine with the result. I would do every drug, drive every two-wheeled toy, say yes to everything that scared me, and put myself in uncomfortable situations deliberately just to remind myself that I was still here—that I still get to enjoy this one chance at life.

I wonder if this desire to feel a wide range of emotions relates to why I put my wallet somewhere different every time I get home, just to panic and then find it on top of the fridge an hour later feeling simultaneously overjoyed and annoyed with myself.

Staying in Wisconsin, or in the United States, would have been the safe thing for me to do. But this equal and opposite reaction from my Mom's passing and Dad's subsequent worry shot me out into the world.

———

My Mom's illness affected me a great deal, but so did a lot of other aspects of growing up in Milwaukee. When someone asks where I'm from, I say, "The States," then, "Wisconsin," then, "Milwaukee," always in that order, watching the person's face morph from neutral to confused more often than not. It's not the answer people are hoping for. I would love to just say "California" and have everyone be like, *"Aw, that's cool."*

I'm really good at describing Milwaukee in relation to Chicago, which is what 95% of the world needs to place Milwaukee on a map in their mind. But I hate the *where-are-you-from* question in general. I avoid asking it at all costs.

Here are some other things that I was and am.

If you're into Myers Briggs personality traits, I'm a pretty classic ENFP (Extrovert, Intuitive, Feeling, Perceiving), which probably helps explain why I think my travels and perspective on them are interesting enough to write down and hopefully interesting enough for you to read and enjoy. It's also why I've been a camp counselor and group leader for most of my adult life.

If you're astrologically inclined, a *Mercury-is-in-retrograde* type, I'm a Scorpio, which I don't want to admit is a good fit for me, which is exactly what a Scorpio would say (at least according to Sunny, one of my exes). I'm competitive, confident, passionate, opinionated, and I love sex. I know everyone likes sex, but I'm pretty sure I like it more than you. *I win.*

If you're looking at me in a photograph, I'm probably the guy wearing a stupid patterned shirt or tank top, no shoes, sticking his tongue out, eyes wide. Wherever I am, you can bet I'm never the stoic big guy just standing normally in the back row.

If you're doing trippy drugs, I'd like to be there. I have a great constitution when it comes to mind-altering substances, and I take pride in making sure everyone is on a good frequency. The only bad trip I've had in my life was during my senior year of college when I had to play drums during a jam session with five of my college professors and I was out of my mind on mushrooms. It was not my fault (read: it was sort of my fault) and still gives me sweaty palms and a clenched butthole when I think about it.

If we're at a house party, I'm the guy playing drinking games, DJing, or playing an acoustic guitar—sometimes rightly, sometimes very wrongly, assuming everyone loves average, live, acoustic covers. Sometimes I'm doing all three of those things I love at once. I've been described as both "extra" and "like dating a Labrador puppy"—the former by kids I've worked with, the latter by romantic partners.

In high school, I set the single-season scoring record in soccer and won the superlative *most dreamed about*, together with my girlfriend at the time— let's call her Leslie. We were photographed together for the yearbook, and a thought bubble was transposed above each of our heads featuring the other in it.

That same winter, I tore my ACL during an indoor game, crushing my division one soccer dreams. Shortly after surgery, I crutched in on Leslie at our Senior Prom after-party hooking up with her ex on a white leather couch in my Russian friend Boris' basement. She dumped me a few weeks before prom, so she wasn't necessarily cheating, but this still resulted in my first time puking from drinking.

During this time I also stressed daily about the acne on my face, back, and neck, and did side bends in the mirror every time I brushed my teeth because, as I discovered, I had a genetic propensity to be chubby. I used to fall asleep thinking about Cinnamon Toast Crunch, Golden Grahams, and the other sugary cereals signing their siren song from the kitchen cupboard, my mouth watering onto my pillow. Now I fall asleep thinking of freshly brewed coffee. We grow up and change, but more often in scope, scale, and taste than disposition.

Junior year I ballooned to 235 pounds (107 kilos for you non-pound folks) between soccer seasons due to a friend who got a job at Schlotzsky's Deli, a loosely run pizza and sandwich joint. All the Cinnamon Toast Crunch certainly didn't help my physique either. I hung out with the punk rock crew. I had two ten-gauge bull-ring earrings, I sewed NOFX and Rancid patches onto my backpack and hoodies, and I played the shit out of a double bass pedal in a screamo hardcore band called *Will Denied*. We released one five-song EP called *Crossing the Rubicon*.

So yeah, high school was confusing, heartbreaking, full of throat-choking laughter, sleepless nights of anxiety, late nights with Conan O'Brien, followed by 6:40 a.m. alarms and a pressure to *do better*, to *be better*.

It was a mixed bag; a beautiful and formative one. I tried admirably to be cool, to fit in. I tricked everyone—my athletic ability being my biggest cover. In truth, back then none of us were cool or uncool, hip or bogus, gnarly or square—we were kids trying our best to keep it together.

During the first chapter of my professional life, when I worked with youth for almost ten years, one writing activity I would facilitate to help kids build their sense of self was called an "I am" poem. The only instruction is to simply begin every line of the poem with "I am."

I am a brother and a son.
I am from Milwaukee, Wisconsin.
I am a straight, white, middle-class man with all of the related privileges.
I am a traveler and constantly seeking the new.
I am extremely competitive and thankfully coordinated.
I am a "try hard" and a people pleaser.
I am "results-oriented" and restless with a new idea.
I am a musician who is good at most instruments and amazing at none.
I am an extrovert who craves connection and doesn't shy away from attention.
I am extremely present, and I value each hour of the day.

For many years now, I've either avoided the where-are-you-from question altogether and gone with another question ("What kitchen appliance would you be?"), or, if I am genuinely curious about someone's "background," which is what I think we want to know when we ask about their geographic origin, I'll ask, *Where are you from, and how did you get here?* It forces the connection of their oldest dot to the most current and gives that person the freedom to answer it with as much or as little context as they choose. This could lead to someone telling you their entire life story or simply responding, "On an airplane, dummy."

I came up with this accidental icebreaker one night with the help of two Dutch guys I had just met in front of my favorite bar in Cape Town called *House of Machines.* I asked them where they were from (I could place Europe but wasn't sure exactly where) and then, immediately after they said Holland, I followed up with, "And how did you end up here?" They traded off giving a circuitous, tandem explanation, which largely covered both of their life paths, and in that few minutes I got the actual answers to the questions we're all really trying to ask each other. *Who are you? Why are you here?* Give me some context on how we ended up sharing a moment together at this bar in Cape Town, *please.*

I hope that this gives you a better sense of who I am than the typical, *"Yeah, Milwaukee. Yeah, it's the city where That '70s Show takes place. Yeah, it's where Harley Davidsons are made too."*

ii. Mugged & Confused

When I got back to my hostel in Cartagena after bumping into my fellow Wisconsinite, one of my roommates was also packing, and as we chatted we realized we were on the same flight to Medellín departing in a few hours. That's how I met Simon. He was from Latvia and traveling through South America, which is all I knew about him on the way to catch our flight. *"Where are you from?"* doesn't get you too far.

We checked into the same dorm room in the same hostel in Medellín, and, once we dropped our bags on our bed, a tall dreadhead immediately offered us a line of blow. That's how my few days in Medellín started, and ultimately I felt lucky to leave relatively unscathed.

Medellín was a blur, including one night that I'll never forget and never fully remember. A bunch of new friends from the hostel were all out together in Zona Rosa, drinking heavily, taking turns locking ourselves in the bathroom stall to sample the Colombian energy powder. At some point, things get a little fuzzy, but I remember there being one guy in our group who wasn't a good drunk. He was entitled, angry, and picking fights with everyone. I remember feeling a sense of responsibility to make sure he didn't get his face punched in by the locals. I was only 28, but still the oldest guy in our group by years.

This aggressive "bro" was still out and actively trying to get his face punched late into the night, and at around three o'clock in the morning I realized that: I had met this guy only a few hours ago, I didn't even know his last name, and it wasn't my job to keep him safe. Simon had bailed a while ago, and I told a local guy who worked at the hostel that I was ghosting. Not my monkey, and Medellín was certainly not my circus.

I only had a ten-minute walk home, through a little park, then a couple blocks to my hostel. In the middle of the park, I stopped to unwrap a sucker that I had in my pocket.

The wrapper was stubborn. It was very stuck to the sticky sucker. I kept picking at it—my drunken fingers trying their best to act sober. *Come on stupid wrapper.*

As I drunkenly fought this wrapper, my butt was forced down onto the step I was standing in front of by two strong sets of hands on my shoulders, and two broken bottles were shoved into my neck. Little hands started to dig into my pockets. My phone was pulled out, and, before they could find my wallet, I pulled it out, took out the cash from it and threw it in a cloud, then held the wallet close to my chest.

These two sets of strong wiry hands, which I now realized belonged to kids, scrambled to pick up the cash, then took off into the darkness of the park, likely just as scared as I was. I might have weighed more than the two of them collectively, and if I had to guess I would say they were 14. I sobered up pretty quickly in those 30 seconds, threw the sucker on the ground and made a beeline for the hostel.

When I made it back, close to 4 a.m., there was still a big group of people up (read: on drugs). They tossed me a beer as I began to tell them what happened. Right as I started the story, Simon burst into the room shirtless and all scratched up.

My story could wait. Simon told us the tale of his evening while panting and laughing simultaneously. How he went home with a classy-looking, older woman and ended up jumping out of her second-story window when her boyfriend came home while Simon was both in her bed and in her. It was just a normal night in Medellín. At least we were all still alive and still laughing as we told our stories.

Before I had boarded my one-way flight to Aruba, cocaine held a place in my mind that was closer to heroin or meth than to weed, a drug to be considered only by those who had no regard for their own futures. This belief was partially cultural, directly shared by my Dad, and molded a bit by the D.A.R.E. program, but I also developed it partially as a witness.

I had a friend as an undergrad at St. Norbert College who indulged in cocaine so much that he skipped the "peeing in bed" party phase and went straight to pooping in bed—with his girlfriend lying right next to him. He also skipped right past struggling to find any type of balance in college, instead dropping out in pursuit of short-term highs and more cocaine. He was a walking anti-drug ad, a coke-fueled Icarus who flew full-speed into the sun, and he led me to stay away from the stuff throughout college.

Even after graduating from St. Norbert and moving to Madison, Wisconsin, I can recall nights at house parties when someone would offer me a line, and I would think, *Whoa, that's a serious drug.* I would sometimes partake, because *I'm no nerd*, but I would also pass judgment in my mind about the type of person who would bring cocaine to a house party.

Cocaine was serious, cocaine was expensive, and cocaine could ruin your life. Somehow, in less than a month in South America, those long-held beliefs started to get replaced by new ones. *Cocaine is normal, cocaine is cheap, and cocaine is from here.*

iii. Shaman Fucking Bullshit

One of the guys with whom I'd been partying in Medellín was a loose, young Irish lad named Brian. We got on well, but I was still pretty shocked when, after I told him my plans to escape town the following day for Salento, he declared, "I think I'm going to come with you." It wasn't really an offer or a discussion—it was stated as though I was simply being told he would join me.

I was open to the company and had no way of knowing that his decision to join me on the journey to Salento would lead to our traveling together for the next five months. Salento was a small town on the way to Bogotá that was famous for being home to the world's tallest palm trees. They were cool, and very tall, but not quite as memorable as our hostel's group trip to do ayahuasca with a local shaman.

The owner of our hostel grew up in the States and had recently opened a popular place in the middle of the Colombian countryside. We didn't know when we checked in, but its popularity was due in part to twice-weekly trips to a local shaman with whom he had developed a relationship over the years.

Without much thought, Brian and I said we were in for the following night's ceremony, took the night off from drinks, and started consuming only water and bananas based on others' advice and a quick Google search about ayahuasca. Since this experience, I've met a lot of travelers who have planned, sought out, and fasted their way to experience ayahuasca somewhere in South America—for us, we stumbled into it, open to everything.

The next night, we paid our host to participate (roughly $60) and loaded into a van to head out to the shaman's property. When we arrived in the evening, there were candles lit, mattresses laid down around the perimeter of the property, and one area with a semicircle of chairs facing a group of musicians, assistants, and ceremonial artifacts. As the ten of us looked around, scanning the bizarre setting for what was to come, we knew we had gotten off the typical backpacker's trail somewhere a few giant palm trees back.

The ceremony started, music played, and the shaman chanted, sang and began inviting people one at a time to drink the opaque, brownish ayahuasca out of a little clay bowl. It tasted like an earthly, poisonous witches' brew, full of minerals and mysteries. The atoms of the portal to the next dimension slapped my cheeks and rang my uvula like a cowbell.

After ingesting the brew, we were led to our own mattresses where we were instructed to *lie down and wait for the effects of the medicine.* We were told multiple times by the shaman and our host from the hostel, "The ayahuasca shows you what you are ready for; it works in different ways for each person, based on how open you are to experience it."

Lie down, wait, but don't sleep, and don't overthink. I was tired, and immediately began the struggle to ward off sleep. Shortly after, I had to fight off pooping my pants.

I started into a routine of seeing some strange, shadowy figures while my eyes were half-closed, telling myself not to sleep and not to freak out, and then having to spring into action to pee water out of my butt, every 20 to 30 minutes.

On one of these trips to the bathroom, I encountered one of the shaman's pets. A humongous vulture tied up to a rope came across my path, and only some higher power kept me from squirting ayahuasca water from my butthole into my trousers. I dodged the bird, relieved myself, and carried on with this lovely routine.

After about two hours of this, at around two in the morning, one of my new travel mates from the hostel, let's call her Amy, was clearly having a rough time and not the good type of *"trip"* we were each hoping for.

The shaman had sent two of his female assistants over to her mattress to help talk her through the experience, to aid her through this rough patch. After fifteen minutes of things only getting worse, it became evident to the shaman that he needed to intervene. He invited Amy to a chair in the middle of the semi-circle where the evening began. Most of us who were awake rose from our scattered bare mattresses and made our way over to see what was happening.

He began again to sing and chant, but this time as he sang he started taking large pulls of rum from a leather satchel and spitting them into Amy's face as he circled around her. Watching, I thought to myself *she doesn't seem to like this.*

He then took a large gem and began to rub it all over her skin, under her shirt, all over her body. *She seems even less amused.*

He then took a long batch of stinging nettles and used them as a switch, to whip the bad spirits out of Amy. *Owww, she definitely doesn't love this part.*

At some point, after getting spit on, man-handled with a crystal, and then beaten with poisonous foliage, Amy sort of came back into herself for a moment. She looked around the semi-circle, which at this point everyone had gathered around as spectators rather helplessly, and said in a long loud slow groan, *"This is F U C K I N G B U L L S H I T..."*

For me, it wasn't total fucking bullshit—it was mostly peeing from my butt and a bad night of sleep. I had minor hallucinations, but nothing profound, as you often hear is possible with ayahuasca.

———

On the way to the shaman's house as the sun was setting the night before, the hostel owner asked our van full of excited travelers what we were hoping for. After a prolonged silence I said, "I hope it's a positive trip and just a cool experience in general." To this, the hostel owner made a very stern point to remind me, and everyone else, that *this was a medicine,* and that we should not be hoping to have a trip, but a *cleansing*.

I was made to feel like a child with the wrong answer in second grade. Wrong, Travis. Does someone else want to try? He might as well have pulled the van over to the side of the road as he scolded me.

The next morning, after the sun came up, I went to the toilet one last time, and waved to the vulture, now looking way more strange and misplaced than scary. I also found a humongous tortoise living in a dirty fountain. The sunlight had transformed the shaman's house into what one might call a "drug den." Mattresses everywhere, people struggling to come to, and the sunlight making everyone question the evening before.

Brian, Amy, and everyone else were piling into the van, and as I approached our host, holding the van door open, he asked me, "So, how was everything?"

"I didn't really have too much of anything happen, to be honest, just a lot of peeing from my butt," I joked.

The hostel owner looked disappointed and replied, "What?! *I tripped my face off.* Next time, make sure you puke. *It really helps!*"

iv. Horse Tour or Special Tour

Brian and I saw the palm trees, drank the sacred poison, and rolled to Bogotá for a few drug-fueled nights of partying. Bogotá has some amazing sights and some really memorable street art in La Candelaria, but we had an itch to get to San Agustín.

San Agustín was not on our travel agenda for any particular reason until we met a weathered backpacker in Salento who told us about a "special tour." A tour where you go through the entire process of making your own cocaine—and, at the end, you get to keep it.

Since I had been ingesting this powdery disco drug since coming to South America, I thought it was only prudent to know exactly what I was putting up my nose, and maybe why it was so damn fun—so fun I'd seen it mess with people's psyches and ruin lives. I was taking it all with a very *when-in-Rome* mentality, and when in Colombia, I figured, *you should do drugs!*

Our directions from the weary traveler were too simple to be promising. We were told, "Go to the town square in San Agustín, and wait for a small, squat man in a baseball cap to offer you a horse tour. He'll have some photos of the horses, and once you're speaking, you ask, '*Special tour?*'"

With these directions in mind and the idea of visiting the area's ancient rock sculptures as a backup plan for how to spend a few days, we bused down to San Agustín.

We checked into a hostel run by a wily old ex-pat and overrun by nature, and we familiarized ourselves with the surroundings. We found the small town square and made plans to try our luck the next afternoon. Brian and I also met a Singaporean girl at the hostel named Marla—who made me a bracelet later on in our relationship. I'm still wearing that bracelet as I type this.

Marla was keen to try her luck as well.

The next day we added a flannel-wearing Canadian to our crew and ended up back in the twenty by twenty meter square, trying to act casual—like there was nowhere else we'd rather spend an afternoon. Forty minutes went by, and no small, squat man in a baseball cap. We told ourselves we'd wait another ten minutes.

Ten minutes expired, still no small, squat man.

We were getting ready to search for the old stones and discussing what we should do to salvage our time, when a voice from behind us asked, "*Horse tour?*"

I must have seemed like a huge horse lover when I quickly turned and snapped off a response, "Horse tour! ... Yeah, we could probably do a horse tour."

Our prospecting guide flipped through some pages in a binder of backpackers smiling on horses with rolling green hills behind them while we feigned interest. After about five pages of childlike collages, we asked the question we came to San Agustín for—"Sorry, *but is there a special tour?*"

A smile flashed across our new friend's face, and he flipped to the back of his binder. The last few pages were of travelers, from the neck down, processing leaves in yellow basins and cooking something mysterious over a regular four-top burner.

He asked how we'd heard of the special tour, and after we told him of our run-in at the hostel in Salento, he flipped open a much smaller book filled with a list of names. We found our friend's name and said pointing at the scribble in the book, "*Yeah, that's the guy we met.*"

In a flash, it became a negotiation.

We settled on something around $75 per person for the four of us.

The guide instructed us to meet him at a bar at 7 p.m. on the outskirts of town. We would share a beer, chat about the day as people do, and leave from there.

The rest of the afternoon we spent wondering what our lives were, what was going on, if we should actually go to the bar, if this was a setup. Of course, we went.

After finishing one beer with the sun quickly setting, we thought maybe we were simply set up to spend our money at a mate's bar until a now-familiar voice from behind shouted, "AMIGOS! *Vamos!*"

We finished our second beers in a hurry and followed our guide to his truck, where we all loaded into the back. He shouted, "Todo bien?," and then took off from the bar. The truck quickly left the small town, driving down dirt roads into the hills, where the city lights vanished. Three minutes into the drive we could barely see each other, but I knew we were all thinking the same thing—*this is how you die in Colombia.*

We bounced around in the back of the truck, trying to keep track of the turns in the darkness, making a mental map of how to run these winding roads with a blindfold on if the situation called for it. As our minds raced and we nervously giggled and reassured each other, the truck came to a halt behind a poorly lit, small home. Our guide came around the back and told us to follow him. He was still smiling, still playing the part of a guide. It was mildly reassuring.

———

Over the gate of the truck, through some mud, through a back door and past a kitchen table where a young kid ate cereal, we found ourselves in a garage where a second guide awaited us.

Above us, chickens squawked and pooped from rafters. In front of us were huge branches of coca leaves piled up. There were also four large yellow basins and many other mysterious jugs and containers of liquids.

"The process starts by stripping the branches of their leaves into a basin," our guide explained. He carried on, describing in detail what he was adding to the leaves to extract the element that made Pablo millions. He also explained to us that, at the height of the Medellín cartel, he was one of Pablo's top scientists. He stated this without any sense of pride; it was a statement of fact, to demonstrate his credibility.

Gasoline, cement, and some rarer compounds were added to the basin. This final liquid was hard to come by, and we were told that it was the primary reason for the high price of the final product. We all thought silently: *the price is actually very reasonable here in Colombia.*

After rolling a cylindrical rock over the leaves and through the soupy liquid for around ten minutes, we drained the liquid into a clear plastic bag. Held at an angle, the sediment of the liquid pooled in one cone-shaped corner, which was then poked with a needle, and that thicker sediment was drained into yet another bag. This process was repeated one final time, and our guide-turned-scientist held aloft the final bag and exclaimed, "NOW, we cook!"

We followed him into the kitchen, where I was glad to see that the child had rinsed and put away his cereal bowl. The gelatinous milky substance from the final bag was spooned into a single large, silver ladle. The front burner of the four-stovetop range was turned on, and we were instructed, "NOW, *cook!*"

We took turns holding the ladle over the burner, taking pictures of each other from the neck down—one of the only rules of the evening. It felt like the only rule in all of Colombia.

After some time, the milky, viscous liquid hardened into a grey crust and was scooped out onto a small white saucer. The scientist took the back of a teaspoon and proceeded to break up the grey crust. Despite his cocaine-cooking resumé, it did not look like any of us had expected, and I began to doubt the process.

Once it was ground up enough, the grey crusty dust was heaped onto a single tablespoon, and the scientist revealed the next step—"NOW, *we put it in the light!*"

We followed him into one of the children's rooms, with pink walls, where he had a blue bucket screwed to the white ceiling around an ordinary house light. There was a fist-sized hole cut into the side of the bucket. He said, "NOW, *someone time me for three minutes!*"

He slid a chair under the bucket as I pulled out my shitty burner phone.

The spoon stayed in the hole for three minutes as I watched the seconds pass. We snickered while secretly still doubting the process. When my count hit three minutes, the scientist pulled the spoon out of the hole to reveal a Scarface-sized pile of pure white Colombian cocaine.

Snickering turned to full out laughter as we went back to the kitchen and stood around the table as he spread the cocaine out. Without asking, he took out a razor, divided four massive lines, and handed a rolled-up bill in our direction. Brian went first, and I could see the hair on his neck stand up as his body rose from the table—his eyes huge, his pupils racing to the edges.

We each did our line and were handed the rest in a small bulging plastic bag. The horse-tour-guide-turned-cocaine-scientist told us how to walk home, and after we thanked him we exited the way we came in. Our bulging eyes could see the twinkle of the small-town streetlights off in the distance.

———

I don't fully remember, but I'm pretty sure we floated home.

Back at the hostel, we each told our life stories in under ten minutes with small cats from the hostel lying on our chests. We came up with countless brilliant restaurant, travel, and small business ideas. We figured it all out. *Everything.* Brian shaved my head. The cat purred. We laughed and laughed. The sun came up in what felt like 30 minutes after we got home.

Maybe it was becoming *someone who made his own cocaine* mixed with the love of telling this story, but early on in South America my idea of cocaine, perception of the people who do it, and relationship with the drug all walked into a house of mirrors. I didn't know what to think about any of it but justified imbibing *"in this moment"*—and *"that moment"* turned out to be most nights. Five or six nights a week we partied, and the partying in Colombia came with cocaine the way it comes with whiskey in Wisconsin.

In the years that followed, I came to realize more and more that cocaine is in a lot of people's pockets. It's been startling year after year to realize how much bigger the circle is of *"those who sometimes do cocaine."* It's a lot of people. My thirteen-year-old self would, I think, be proud of this journey, alright with me partaking in illicit drug use as a part of it, and absolutely blown away by how many people do blow. All the adults you know who are not Republicans have probably done blow, and of those who are Republicans—it's closer to 100%. They tend to have the money, and cocaine is fun. Also, everyone famous you've ever heard of has done blow. Tom Hanks *loves blow.*

The next afternoon, when we finally woke, we played Apples to Apples in the grass near some pretty cool old rocks that were carved hundreds of years ago. It was a great day, but I don't ever tell the story of that day.

v. Leslie

I was certain I was going to marry my very first crush. Leslie and I dated when we were 13, again at 18, and then again at 25. We had an extremely close group of friends (read: the exact same friends), friends we spent summers growing up alongside at Camp Minikani, and all the awkward school years and "phases" that came in between. The same camp. The same schools.

We went through all of our growth moments, childhood triumphs, and every single first with each other. Overthinking everything together. Life was vast and stretched out before us, and, however uncertain it was, it felt like a foregone conclusion that our paths would be intertwined; Leslie's life and mine would eventually end up as one path, doublewide. It felt like the universe had intervened and chosen my partner for me. I was smitten. I was deeply in love. I wanted to grow old with Leslie. I was done thinking of any other outcome—that was until she called me after a year of long-distance to end it.

I was 25 and in New Orleans at my first *"real,"* professional job, running a group home called Boys Hope New Orleans. She was a teacher in Madison, Wisconsin. After seeing each other at a party when I was back from serving in AmeriCorps, we made out on a futon, eventually slept together, and ultimately got back together officially. It ended the same way it ended when we were 18; it was her choice, and I was destroyed. For six months, I wasn't the same guy.

As much as that sort of deep heartbreak is a pain I hope I never experience again, it did teach me a lot. I will never marry someone who seems good enough, compatible enough. I'll never just settle for a satisfactory partner to trudge through the remaining years with. I'll either remain unmarried or find a love like that again. One where you would gladly jump in front of a bus for the other person. One where your partner's happiness trumps your own in every waking moment. A love that you're proud of: *that is lesson number one.*

It's a nice sentiment to think that you're the author of your own story, but it's not a complete thought. The whole idea fails to mention that the most important part of our stories are the characters—and that we can't control them. They can leave, die, become drug addicts, or break your fucking heart. Leslie also taught me this. My response to learning it has been to guard my little heart box.

I've been in love seven times since Leslie, but I've never said it out loud. I promised myself I never would and that, the next time I did, it would essentially be a proposal. Relationships have two ultimate outcomes: they end or you get married. In the case of lifelong marriage, somebody dies first anyway—so I guess those end as well—but you get the point.

I've chosen to take the weight that the words *"I love you"* add to a relationship out of the equation, and that way, when they end, the next six months of my life aren't so fucked up that I can't taste food. It's worked so far. Some might say that I'm limiting my capacity to feel, but I still feel. I'm my father's son, and he tears up at every children's movie preview ever, so trust me—*I feel deeply.* I love deeply. I just make the active choice to avoid stomach-cramping heartbreak and to keep everything a bit lighter.

It also taught me that impermanence is something nice to make peace with. It's the reason Buddhists rake out their Zen gardens. Nothing stays the same forever, and sometimes, as soon as you're done making the perfect lines throughout a beautifully manicured garden, it rains. Sometimes when you're madly in love with your high-school sweetheart, living in New Orleans for your first real job and trying to make long-distance work, the phone rings.

———

Part of me still wonders how much of my pursuit of the uncommon was to prove to Leslie that she made the wrong choice when she picked up that phone, rather than proving to myself that I was brave enough—a narrative I was more comfortable sharing with friends and family. How much of my *"why"* is simply because of a girl who made me sad?

For every person who has truly had their heart put through cupid's wood chipper, I reckon that hurt is a factor that molds your future in the same way the sun impacts your vision. It's always there, always driving you to prove your worth beyond a doubt to that unrequited love, to their parents, to everyone who knows you both, and to the whole fucking world for that matter. After putting together the pieces of a pulled pork heart, the future becomes a testing ground to prove to everyone, especially yourself, that they made *the biggest mistake of their life.*

Ohhhhh, you want to date that beekeeper with a ponytail, well did he ever make his own cocaine?! I don't think so!

I don't think it was entirely because of Leslie, but I never entered into anything that resembled a relationship while I was living in the States after that breakup. My second year in New Orleans, my two years in grad school back in Milwaukee—*nothing.* I had a lot of random (and not so random) hookups, but I was always hesitant to make it anything more than that, anything more than fun nights and semi-awkward mornings sometimes strung together for months.

Especially in Milwaukee, with my parents' house fifteen minutes away, I felt like any type of relationship tethered me to my deepest roots. Like it would become entirely how my oldest friends and family perceived me. I would quickly go from hooking up with someone, to being "Travis and [lady friend]," to being a married homeowner with three kids in a blink— without ever wanting for that to happen, stumbling forward like a baby with a big head into someone else's version of a proper adult life.

In the same way that travel allows you to reinvent yourself if there are pieces you want to change, stories you don't want told, or perceptions you want to shake, travel allowed me to take more chances on love. If I liked someone, I wasn't shy to engage in something meaningful. That person wouldn't be tied to my childhood and life story—they wouldn't meet the friends I've had since I was in diapers. They would meet my travel buddies, they'd meet *fucking Brian.* It all felt a lot less serious and a lot more possible, and it all started with Lisa.

Brian and I had crossed the border from Colombia to Ecuador, and we found Simon again in Quito. We also met a girl named Ali at the free hostel breakfast.

Ali was our eventual tie to Lisa, and her two other Australian friends.

CHAPTER 3: ECUADOR

B rian and I spent our first full day in Quito negotiating the public bus out to the equator, *La Mitad Del Mundo*, which cuts a line through northern Ecuador, just above Quito. We spent two hours with two girls we met on the bus, wandering around the bright Disney-like development with souvenirs, snacks, and little anthropomorphic statues galore.

The focal point of the park, which we happily paid to enter, was a massive temple spire situated in the middle of a giant compass rose, the thick yellow East and West lines representing the equator itself. Brain and I took photos lying on the equator, straddling the equator, doing headstands on the equator, and other positions we thought would make our two new, cute female travel mates laugh.

Upon leaving the grounds through a huge gate, a middle aged man with a fedora stopped me and said, *"did you see the real equator?"*

"Yeah, of course," I said looking back at the massive spire. "We took, like, 100 photos," I finished, in a tone that implied *"psshhaa, duh man."*

"No, not that equator. The **REAL** equator, *man,*" he fired back, with an expectant glance.

He knew we were very sure we had just been to the equator. There was a sign. It was a thing. He also knew that what we just took over 100 photos of was not the actual equator. It was simply where the government had built a park to attract tourists, but the true equator is a real natural place, a physical phenomenon, a thing birds feel, and it was nearby. He could also see we were listening as soon as he started squeezing all of this conspiracy theory tasting juice.

We had the time, so we ended up taking our new friend's advice, and walking half a kilometer down the road, looking for a sign to a museum— *Museo de Sitio Intiñan.*

Once in line, I found out the couple in front of us was from the United States—Wisconsin, actually—after the oft-mumbled, "So, where are you from?"

"I'm from Milwaukee; that's wild," I told them, incredulous to meet fellow Wisconsinites at the earth's leather cowboy belt.

"We're from Milwaukee too, well the North Shore to be specific."

"No way, me too, I'm from Fox Point," I responded.

"GET OUT OF HERE!," these wholesome love birds told me. They told me to *get out of here*, to just disappear, because they really couldn't believe it. They had also lived in Fox Point, Wisconsin, a place you've never heard of, for years.

I told them the street I grew up on, and they knew it—they lived two streets away. They described the two big dogs that they took for walks daily to me, and I knew them. I could picture these two with their huge muts walking past our house, through the big bay window of my family's ranch style house. I didn't, and still don't, understand how this occurred. I don't really understand anything, the more I think about it, so I guess it fits the pattern. It belongs in the finger painting of humanity.

Once we got into the museum, I knew the man in the Fedora was a good soul, that he was genuinely trying to benefit our day. We learned about a small fish that can swim up a human dick, hence the ropes tied around the fake dicks on the fake people in the museum exhibit. We learned about tarantulas, guinea pigs and ancient tribal ways. Finally, it was proven to us that we were on the equator—that it was an actual place of real wonder, not just a line on a map; not something the flat earthers can deny once witnessed.

Our guide placed a basin of water on the equator at the museum, and then moved it one foot to the right. He crushed up a dry leaf from the ground, sprinkling it into the basin, then pulled a plug from the bottom. The water drained counter-clockwise, the leaves swirling in giant circles before exiting through the hole. He repeated this process, with the basin one foot to the left of this yellow line on the ground, and the leaves swirled in the opposite direction. Like a magician, knowing his crowd was enthralled, knowing the hook was in our mouth, he put the basin right on the line, then slowly yanked the plug from the bottom, and the leaves all went directly towards the drain, spilling out onto the true equator.

Fifteen minutes later, I earned a certificate for balancing an egg on the head of a nail. I was proud as fuck of the certificate, blown away by the undeniable reality of the equator, and so curious about everything I didn't fully understand, everything yet to still learn.

As we bounced along in the back of the bus towards Quito, I thought to myself, *this is the type of stuff I want to be learning, to be experiencing.* Two hours at this museum was a more powerful learning experience than anything I had been a part of in nearly 20 years of formal education.

I had only been gone on my bonus semester for about a month, but I could feel myself gaining wisdom, the type not taught in schools. Small flowers and mushrooms were blooming in the garden of my mind. I knew for myself that the earth was round, and it felt good to not have to take anyone's word for it. Better still, to never again have to argue with anyone who doesn't agree on the shape of the thing we're all standing on.

The next morning, after eating a quick hostel breakfast of bread, jam, and butter (the definitive "free breakfast" at a hostel in South America), we struck up a conversation with an American girl named Ali, telling an animated tandem version of our adventures to the equator. She was game to ditch her two friends from home and join Brian and me.

Her friends weren't traveling the way she wanted to, and Brian and I must have been pretty charming breakfast company. We were open to a third amigo, and frankly we were flattered. Simon, my Latvian travel mate from Medellin, had also made it to Quito and was keen to ramble south.

Throughout Colombia, we had talked about hitchhiking parts of Ecuador, and maybe it was the boost of confidence we got from Ali's ditching her lifelong friends to join our little merry band, but we decided that we would try to thumb our way south from Quito to Baños de Santa Agua, Ecuador's outdoor playground.

Simon, Brian, Ali, and I made signs from cardboard and waited on the side of the road near a gas station. Eventually, after only 15 minutes, we piled into a truck bed full of oranges, and I told the driver in my broken Spanish that we'd give him some gas money. *Tenemos dinero para petrol, senor!*

As the truck pulled off, the four of us shot smiles back and forth at each other as we tipped from side to side, bumping shoulders under the sun in the back of the truck while oranges rolled at our feet. Five weeks ago it was a struggle to get water, but now I was managing to lead a random group of new friends on a hitchhiking adventure through the countryside of Ecuador—*LIFE!*

Like so many aspects of life, confidence is key. I was like a toddler who had graduated from barely being able to feed myself to a teenager who could make wicked macaroni and cheese. Ultimately, it's just cooking noodles and stirring up all the shit in the box, but having the confidence to try it is the most important part.

Also, like most things in life, confidence can go too far and get to your head. Traveling is not a competition—*it's a gift.* Enjoy it, and try not to spend one second convincing yourself or anyone else that you're doing it the *"right way"* or better than the person next to you.

I've met many travelers who will try to "out-backpacker-you" in the first few minutes of a conversation.

"Have you been here?"

"You've never been to *HERE?!*"

"You've got to go to this secret place over *HERE*, and not on the backpacker trail!"

"Oh, I've been there for a considerable amount of time, and when I was there, this crazy thing happened to me with this local person."

Cool story, would-be-backpacker-friend. Way to skip, hop, scoot and brag right past trying to relate on an equal level with someone else who's doing essentially the same thing you are. If we're talking at this hostel bar in Ecuador, we're at least in the same ballpark.

These are also the same people who normally have strangely strong opinions about eating at a fast-food restaurant or ordering spaghetti bolognese in Thailand. For me, if you're craving pasta or a McDonald's breakfast—eat it. *Who cares?* You've probably had your share of pad thai and rice, and sometimes your tummy wants what it wants. The body craves what it craves.

These are also normally the same people who will give others a hard time for how much they're traveling with.

"Whoa, *you're carrying all of that!*"

"I've only got this…"

"What do you even have in there?"

"I just have a carry-on…"

Way to go, *here's a fucking Egg McMuffin!* Unless this other person is asking you to carry their stuff for them, leave them alone. Quit bag-shaming people. How often someone wants to do laundry versus how much they're willing to lug around is a personal choice, and the amount of stupid conversations I've heard about it over the years is an enormous waste of time.

These *travel sheriffs* who have a long list of "no-no's" about how one should, or more accurately, should *not* travel, I imagine are the same people who in high-school identified more with their dislikes than likes. Not liking things in adolescence was cool, coy and safe. Strongly liking things was too audacious. Not liking boy bands, or Drake, or Taylor Swift, or Celine Dion, or any pop music, or football, or any sports at all, or anyone or anything at all—*that was safe*. Having an opinion can get you teased—kids are mean—so kids wise up. Then some of those kids grow up and mistake identifying with things they dislike or disapprove of as a personality. It appears to be a solid position, *hating pop music*, but this trait of judging first out of fear of judgement is weak and dug out. It's as hollow as a cheap chocolate Easter bunny upon close examination.

This whole diatribe also bleeds into the often-had hostel conversation of *the difference between a tourist and a traveler*, or a *true* backpacker, and it might have sounded above like I'm defending "the tourist" because *"a real backpacker never eats spag-bol in Thailand!"* But I think the choice of what goes in your mouth or how many kilos you want to carry around doesn't really get you there. We'll try to tease it out later on, but, as you see, I have some thoughts on the subject.

i. Doing This Better Than Anyone Else Ever

There was plenty of time to contemplate the crazy transformation I had undergone in six short weeks. The wind was so loud in the back of the truck that we couldn't really speak, just smile, stare, nod, slap each other's legs, and give flashing looks that said, *Life can be such a crazy adventure if you're open to it, right?* I picked up an orange from the truck bed and ate it, smiling wildly as the juice dripped down my chin.

We eventually made it to Baños, and found a dingy room that was perfect for all four of us. It was two twins and a queen bed, which Brian and I shared in perfect harmony, comfortable as kin. The next morning we were up for adventure.

Turns out, ten hours of unbridled adventure in Baños costs around $55. Starting at around 9 a.m. we went bungee jumping off a bridge, zip-lining across a gorge, rappelling down a series of waterfalls, and driving little dune buggies through the *"Ruta de Cascadas,"* the waterfall route, where we stopped to drink a beer along the way as the sun began to set.

"Brian, how much did we pay for the waterfall rappelling thing this morning?," I yelled as I totaled up the price we each spent on the whole day. Knowing we got to Baños for only a few dollars in gas money, I really had to stop myself from thinking, *I'M DOING THIS BETTER THAN ANYONE ELSE EVER IN ALL OF HUMAN HISTORY!*

I did find myself thinking about how lucky I am as I slowly settled into my travels. I might be the luckiest guy ever. Ultimately, if you've had the opportunity to backpack in a foreign country without an overly strict budget or timeline and end up on an adventure like this one with brand-new friends in a town you had never heard of—*you are incredibly lucky.*

I also try to be aware of my privileges. Being a big, white, American male who is prone to smile, I generally get smiles right back from anyone I meet around the world, even as they call me "mzungu" (read: "whitey"— but not offensive) in Nairobi. I can run at night carrying my iPhone. I can talk to pretty much any stranger I'd like and not be met with suspicion. I can walk into any bar or restaurant in the world and be greeted with a smile and the assumption that I have money to spend. My passport grants me incredible ease of entry to most places I've been.

These all have their exceptions, but speaking in generalities, traveling for me is easier than it is for most—not to mention simply being alive at this point in history when it's possible to have a world map and an entire universe of information in your pocket.

Above and beyond these privileges, my greatest one of all is knowing my true bottom is only ever having to ask my parents for help. That's as far into the abyss as I can fall—back into Fox Point, Wisconsin. I realize how fortunate I am for that mental safety net; I know many don't have that freedom. My drive to not fall into the safety net is fierce, but knowing it's there allows for the freedom a trapeze artist feels mid-flight. My father's propensity to worry, coupled with the knowledge that he would always help me up if I fell, worked like the two opposite ends of a powerful magnet and pushed me spinning out into the world, a steel dreidel on a map.

———

Being in a fortunate position alone does not cause an open-ended, life-changing adventure. The other half of this equation is that I bought the first flight (read: used my Spirit airlines credit) and then worked up the courage to get myself in that flying silver tube headed for foreign lands. As easy as it seems to me now to just pick up and go, I remember exactly what that lost puppy felt like, and I'm pretty good at spotting the lost puppies now. They are without a doubt my favorite people to initiate a conversation with at a hostel or on a bus.

Looking back, these years of my life directly correspond with the time that I really got comfortable in my own skin. I think that, for men at least, in your late 20s and/or early 30s this happens for a lot of us. I stopped asking myself big life questions, and I started really liking myself—loving myself actually, which resulted in caring less whether other people did. I developed into a much more confident, positive, and present person. I was also spending most of these years backpacking and meeting people in their early 20s and could see that most of these lost puppies were often more than slightly nervous about being in South America or the sketchy seafood they ate earlier; they were often anxious in general and wondering if they were *"okay."* You can almost see a 19-year-old who isn't self-assured at a party thinking, *Am I partying right? Is this cool what I'm doing? Now I'll look at my phone because cool people look at their phone.*

I love chatting up these people, to just give them that sense that it's normal to be thinking too much about all of that heavy stuff, and to hopefully reassure them that they are perfectly *"okay."* That ultimately "what you do" with your life matters so much less than "who you are" as a person in general. How you show up in your communities and relationships. How you treat people. Whether you add to or take away from the good vibes in whatever room you're in. That all that matters infinitely more than *"what you do."* We just don't have the right vocabulary or cultural norms to ask each other "who" or "how" so we go with "what."

So whether you're a twenty-something who is overly self-conscious with worry about what you're doing with your life, or a retiree hung up on regrets from long ago—*stop*. It's like the people on the hostel couch reading the Lonely Planet about the city they're in, and after you've been out for hours exploring markets and smiling at random strangers, they're still on the couch reading about *"what to do"* when you return. *You're overthinking it.*

Go do anything in this town besides lay on a hostel couch and read about what there is to do in this town. Don't get to retirement and use the years the same way you did your lunch hour. Don't pay to get into the water park and wimp out at the top of the ride. Don't worry that the window is open after you've already left the house. Don't stop half way then later wish you'd finished the book.

ii. Touch the Snow

After Baños we made new signs and carried on with our hitchhiking adventure—giggling in the back of another truck on our way to Chimborazo, the tallest peak in Ecuador. (Fun fact: it also happens to be the farthest point from the center of the earth because of our planet's oblong shape—*SCIENCE!)*

We got dropped off at the base of the mountain and trekked into the park with all of our stuff. We dropped it off at a ranger station and started our way up the mountain, with no intention of making it to the top. We made a goal to simply *touch the snow.* An hour later, we were making snow angels and crafting a small snowman. The scenery was grey and white, rocky and otherworldly, so drastically different from the lush rolling hills dotted with waterfalls near Baños, just a few hours away.

When we made it back down, our run of good hitchhiking fortune continued as we found another truck willing to stop for some weary travelers. We were in the truck for about thirty minutes when our good fortune failed and it started to rain. The speed of both the rain and truck combined to make it feel as though push pins were falling from the sky, and there was no hiding. Our driver, let's call him Ernesto, pulled off the road to check on us after a few minutes and several hundred push-pins. He pointed out Chimborazo in the distance, and we all thought simultaneously, *We know, we were just up there.* We smiled and nodded, wondering just when exactly we were going to get sick from the truck-bed water-torture situation.

Ernesto then pulled three black ponchos out from under his driver's seat and handed them out to us. I've never been as grateful for a piece of plastic. Then he brought out a tarp, which he tied to the top of the truck bed and pulled taut over our bodies as we lay all the way down. I could see Brian and Ali in the blue-tinted light that crept through, and we passed cheeky glances, saying *this is fucking living* with our wide eyes and jumping eyebrows. This was exactly why Ali ditched her friends.

When we got to Ernesto's hometown a few hours later, the end of the line for us, he invited us in to warm up. We were already so grateful for his hospitality and generosity, but he was just getting started. He opened a small safe in what seemed to be his office, full of papers and framed documents, and brought out a nice-looking bottle of whiskey. Pouring us all a drink he drained the bottle with his small, strong, stumpy hands. We sipped, warmed up, and shared laughs and small words that switched back and forth between Spanish and English.

We were very grateful and feeling infinitely better than we were two hours earlier. I already loved Ernesto and thought he couldn't possibly get any better at playing the role of *guy-who-picks-up-random-hitchhikers-on-a-rainy-day*, but then he reached back into the safe. He pulled out an unopened bottle of whiskey from its depths and poured us new drinks, saying, *"Fuerte, FUERTE!"* with a huge infectious smile breaking on his kind, round, leathered face.

iii. Montañita Lisa

We crashed at a strange little hospedaje that night in Ernesto's hometown and took a morning bus the next day to Montañita, a beach town where some come to surf but most just come to party. Within 24 hours of making a snowman, we were shirtless on a beach watching waves roll up on the Ecuadorian coast. We crashed at a place called Hostel Montezuma and should have known by the smell, and maybe the name, that this would be our first taste of genuinely bad luck.

It smelled like sewage throughout the floor we stayed on, the door to our room had a suspect lock, and something about the whole place had a haunted house vibe, like the eyes in the surfer paintings were following you down the hall.

The next morning, after having a big night out, we realized that the shit smell was an omen we should have heeded—our room got robbed and we all had copious, weird bug bites. We had it out with the two uncaring dudes at the front desk and eventually stormed out without even getting a refund for our one night. It was the first time, and one of the only times, I've written a review for a place. This is known as *"the TripAdvisor effect"*—in which only strong opinions are voiced.

We moved slightly off the main drag and back behind the small town to a hostel with the word iguana in its name. Reggae tunes, bamboo, hammocks, and good vibes greeted us immediately.

That night we were all seated on the big, wooden, pillow-covered porch with a bunch of new hostel friends, drinking rum-and-cokes and taking turns doing lines of cheap blow in the bathroom and picking crowd-pleasing tunes for the Bluetooth speaker to pump. It was the quintessential perfect night at a hostel.

Things seemed as good as they could get when—mid-banger, mid-line, mid-sip of rum, mid-sexual dance move—they somehow got better. A threesome turned the corner and joined us on the porch, causing Ali to freak out. It was Lisa, Steph, and Rob, three Australians Ali knew from her trip through the San Blas islands a few months back. They caught up, Brian and I were introduced, and our threesome turned to six in that moment. That same night, we also met a Kiwi named Matt and a Scottish lad named Jamie, and we didn't realize it at the time, but this was the first night with our entire travel family. We would stay together, more or less, for more than three months thereafter.

The bed bugs and thievery weren't ideal, but would I take this deal with Montezuma in exchange for finding my first travel family? *Without question.* Shitty things will always happen, but happy people always manage to find silver linings and weave their best stories out of those.

I probably would have just left out the part about Montezuma if it didn't help illustrate this point, but bad always leads to good if that's how you want your life's narrative to flow. This makes the bad not so bad after all; it's just a push toward something else, something that could be amazing.

————

We partied another night in Montañita then took a bus over the border to a small town in Peru that has both a similar vibe and a similar name: Mancora. We stayed at an incredible hostel that felt more like a weird resort, but for seven dollars a night you got a bunk bed in a painted concrete block. We spent our first day there drinking around the huge central pool and sorting out how to get blow in this new country—over time this slowly became Brain's and my job for the travel family. We were the most unabashed and the two biggest of the group, so I guess it made sense.

The girls booked buses, made plans, and we—well, *we sorted out the drugs.*

The first night out in Mancora we ended up at some strange club outside of the lit streets of town playing beer pong. Eventually Brian and I took a tuk-tuk to some sketchy, unfinished house where we did the ole *"try and buy"* and came out laughing, knowing all along that we both couldn't quite believe what we were doing moment to moment. Brian was an aspiring accountant and I was a grad student just five months ago. We were definitely tempting fate, tiptoeing (or tuk-tuking, as it were) up to trouble and laughing at it. Snorting it up our noses and right into our drunk brains.

Together we were far more fearless than either of us would have been alone. It was the sense of brotherhood, a game of chicken we didn't realize we were playing together, and a loyalty to do right by the rest of our family that kept us going—*and we always succeeded.*

We were up really late on this particular night, having drinks with a bunch of other people from the hostel on the beach, passing little baggies around, feeling invincible. Some make-shift beach bar with loudspeakers held together by tape started playing club bangers and hip-hop classics, and we were all getting loose. *I'm sorry Miss Jackson—Ohhhhh—I am fo' real.* I was in a particular mood that I have often found myself chasing in the years that followed to varying degrees of success.

On the dance floor, I was bouncing around from person to person, face to face, and at some point, I was dancing with Lisa. Dancing with Lisa was especially nice, so we kissed. Shortly after, we were in her bed rolling around. We didn't sleep together that night, but we kissed, frenched, smooched, swapped spit and attempted hickeys for hours while rolling around in a cement block dorm bed.

iv. I'm a Duck

The next day was Halloween. I was smitten. I was also a duck. I bought an inflatable duck inner-tube and just wore it around my waist all day, making quacking noises when the right moment presented itself. I was having an excellent time until I started catching a weird vibe from Lisa. It felt forced and purposeful that she was avoiding me, sitting as far away from me as possible, and generally being cold.

I tried to just get on with things, but my spidey-sense was tingling—and it's normally trustworthy. I carved a watermelon jack-o-lantern and I started drinking, all along feeling more and more sure that Lisa was casting strange vibes in my direction. She seemed to be paying extra attention to some other new Aussie guy at the hostel as well.

Brian and I procured Halloween treats for the fam (read: cocaine, which should be clear at this point), and we started in on another big night—this time in costume. I was trying to snort my angst about Lisa away, but cocaine isn't exactly the best drug for suppressing feelings of suspicion. My night was marked by alternating moments of fun and moments in which I'd catch Lisa laughing and having fun with someone else, moments like we had only a day ago, and I would emotionally crash back down then open my small baggie hoping for a remedy.

At the end of the night (read: early the next morning) I remember the overwhelming feeling that I had to at least do something about this, that I couldn't be a passive character in my own sadness. We sat on a stairwell, and I asked her what was going on—with us, and with that other guy. *"Wasn't last night fun?"* I managed, in the most needy and vulnerable tone. I rubbed my face awake with both hands, trying to keep my tattered emotions from jumping ship.

She said it was. She also said that she was really sure she didn't want to be in any type of relationship because getting out of a bad one was the whole reason she was traveling.

This made me feel a little better until her logic brought her to the conclusion that she could hook up with this other guy if she wanted to—and she said she wanted to.

I was hurt. I woke up emotionally whipped and physically destroyed. Staying up until the sun rose for multiple mornings in a row had taken its toll, along with the drugs, and I had contracted what came to be known as *"man flu."* It's basically a full-body revolt—my throat was closed, I couldn't take full breaths, I had terrible night sweats, and I also felt like I was freezing simultaneously. The temperature gauge of my body was flying back and forth from moment to moment like dials on the nuclear core at Chernobyl.

I spent the next few days confined to my bed, feeling bad about my body and my heart. Everything hurt. Everything sucked. Nothing tasted like anything. Nothing cooled me. Nothing made me feel any better. I was an empty shoe box in the back of the closet, wishing without hope to be used for some type of school project.

———

My birthday is only a few days after Halloween, and I spent the day questioning my life decisions, lying in bed, sweating, and feeling terrible. Many times over the years in which I was backpacking I had the thought, *I have a master's degree... is this what you should do with a master's degree?* Normally I would end up thinking, *Yes, this is definitely what you should do.* On my 29th birthday, I was really unsure. I was in a bad place.

Later that evening, Brian, who is a fucking machine, came up to the room to cheer me up. He was back in party mode and confidently reminded me, "It's your birthday, come on man—just smoke a little bit. *Just a little birthday celebration puff.*" My throat was still raw, but I thought I'd take a drag for him. He was just so certain I should, like a dog wagging his tail at the door, 100% certain it's time for a W-A-L-K.

I stepped onto the balcony and looked around outside for the first time in more than six hours. Brian had the entire hostel gathered by the pool in the middle of the compound, ready to sing an inspired version of happy birthday up to me on our second-floor balcony. Although my heart and body hurt, I still felt that I was where I was supposed to be that night. *This is definitely what you do with a master's degree,* I thought, slowly dragging from the birthday joint. I was free. I was loved and looked after by people who were perfect strangers just weeks ago, and I would get over Lisa.

The next day we tried to leave, but our bus got overbooked and we were bounced. Another recovery day for me, but I just wanted to get out of this place that had started to feel a bit sad. We finally did get on a bus the following day, and I was so thankful to make it to Lima. The six of us checked into Kokopelli, a block from Parque Kennedy, and, with the extra day of recovery, I was back and looking for the next high, the next memory, the next line to tip-toe up to and tell a bad knock-knock joke.

CHAPTER 4: PERU

We went paragliding that very first morning, and I talked to my professional tandem buddy about the Lisa situation as we floated above Lima. I talked to Brian about the Lisa thing as we walked along Miraflores looking for a pull-up bar. I talked to Steph about the Lisa thing as we watched domestic-looking wild cats laze in the grass of Parque Kennedy. I talked to Jamie about the Lisa thing as he tried to talk to me about something else. We found drugs and did a power hour to 90s music at the hostel bar. I was hoping that, if I drank enough, "drunk" would become my dominant feeling and beat out sad, dejected, and a bit ill.

It was a night like many others, a bunch of beers and lines, a bunch of laughs and forgotten conversations—except for one. At some point in the night, Lisa asked me to chat. I figured it was because all my chats with other people had come back to her and that she wanted to give me a quick *"buck up kid, you'll be fine"* speech.

We were on the outside stairwell of Kokopelli that leads up to the rooftop bar. It was covered in graffiti. Music was wafting down from above, and Lisa started with an apology. She told me she knew she was being weird and was sorry, but that it was just a reaction to defend herself because she was worried she was starting to really like me, and she had promised herself this trip was about being single and free.

I really liked her too. I stared at her beautiful face and pink lips as she explained what she was thinking. When she stopped, I kissed her.

I told her, "We could just try not to take it too seriously, but also not lie to ourselves if we're feeling something." We ended up on my top bunk in an eight-bed dorm and had sex for the first of countless times. It was, however, to the best of my knowledge the only time we boned in a bed with someone else in the same bunk. We were caught up in the moment and had no idea, but my downstairs neighbor was there the whole time. *Apologies, bunk buddy, but that was one of my favorite sexual encounters of my life, so I hope you'll understand.*

We were great together. The chemistry of our conversations and of our bodies was perfect. We told ourselves that we were playing it cool, but I was falling fast, and so was she.

Our few days in Lima ended with a beer pong tournament where we decided to celebrate my "30th" birthday (I was actually 29) at a backpacker party hostel called Loki since I slept through my actual birthday with the man flu. We ended up drawing all over ourselves and everyone else in the bar with a red marker. We also won the tournament. If my emotional state, the highs and lows of my life on the road up to this point, were on a graph, it could easily be mistaken for a seismograph print depicting a devastating earthquake.

In many ways, this sense of high highs and low lows is par for the course while traveling. There are challenging, lonely, hungry, and sad times followed by an amazing new connection, an all-time favorite life memory, or the best sex of your life.

Sometimes all three are the same thing.

i. Huaca-fucking-china

The newly-formed travel family headed south to Huacachina, a small desert oasis that made its way onto the backpacker trail as a destination for sandboarding. I love most adventure activities, but I'll just say it— sandboarding is pretty fucking stupid. Huacachina was fun for other reasons, though.

Brian and I did our family duty, with the help of the security guard at our little hospedaje, and our first night there we stayed up until sunrise in a room that all eight of us shared.

We got really high—inappropriately high. We made a fort. We told our life stories multiple times, we made grand plans for our futures, and, at some point, I was pretty sure I could see the future. My brain was visceral, palpable, working at the speed of a hummingbird's wings.

In the morning, as the sun broke the horizon, Brian was saying something about *somebody's* birthday… it seemed important at the time, but really it was just an excuse for a mission. We would hike the massive sand dune that started upward just 20 feet behind the hostel, *because it was this person's birthday and we were going to take an EPIC PHOTO FOR THEM!*

We crawled, laughed, and scrambled our way up the sand dune for the better part of an hour, making it to the top with sand in every single pocket, hole, and crevice of our bodies. We hugged and rolled around in the sand wearing buttoned-down shirts and a crown (we got dressed up for the photoshoot), and we took a few pictures for that person's birthday— *HAPPY BIRTHDAY GUY… or KID… or AUNTIE!* On the way back down, we saw a local Peruvian jogging up the sand dunes, making it look rather easy. We rolled and tripped over each other down the dune about 100 meters away, pupils still dominating our eyeballs.

We made it back down and crashed for the remainder of the morning, just in time to take the afternoon tour of the dunes, when we learned sandboarding is more like boring, hot sledding than snowboarding. The best part was by far the actual dune buggy ride and photo ops that we encouraged our driver to stop for every ten minutes. Sand boards make better photo props than toys.

After one of these many *"babes on buggies"* style photoshoots, we got back into the seven-person off-road buggy and the driver punched it over the next dune. I realized at that moment I forgot to buckle my seat belt as my head smoked the roof of the buggy and my knees came up to tap my shoulders. I was crunched like a slinky, and I knew while still in mid-air that this was bad. My ribs were compressed like an accordion hitting an F(uck) sharp.

Pro tip: Always wear your seatbelt.

For the next two months, I was grateful to be surrounded by funny people, but I was constantly begging them to stop being so funny because it folded me over and took my breath away to laugh.

ii. The Beers We Earned

We left the dunes of Huacachina covered in sand and set out toward Arequipa, one of the less-visited old cities of Peru. The main attraction near Arequipa is the Colca Canyon, or the *"Grand Canyon of the*

South," as it's billed. We checked into the Wild Rover Hostel in Arequipa, the girls booked a tour, and we got ourselves ready for a two-day, one-night trek into the canyon of condors (read: we got fucked up at a hostel bar).

The next morning we set off at 7 a.m. for a full-day hike. It was stunning. We *think* we saw condors. I bought a small wooden slingshot. The trek was exactly what we needed, but we were all incredibly grateful to make it to the oasis at the base of the canyon. Our little hotel had a swimming pool, Lisa and I had our own room, and today, more than most days, the family earned their beers. We had an hour until dinner.

Lisa and I snuck off to test the mattress firmness. I jumped like a starfish onto the bed, Lisa followed, and then the entire bed frame collapsed onto the floor of the room. For about five minutes, it was impossible to say words because our throats were choked with unbridled laughter.

We stared at each other and laughed uncontrollably, the bed shattered in pieces on the ground around us, our faces red, our bodies overly tired from a day of sun and trekking, making it even harder to do anything about the situation but laugh. The smile lines on my face hurt. I thought about how I adored Lisa's face and how laughing with her felt so good. I was very much in love with her, although I had my reasons not to say so out loud.

Our tired and happy posse hiked out of Colca Canyon accompanied by two canyon pups that were the happiest animals in all of South America. At the final lunch before heading back to Arequipa and eventually Cusco, I tried out my new slingshot. Ali volunteered as tribute for the ceremony, and we decided to see if a piece of cake balled up tight enough would hold firm after being slung from a slingshot.

Turns out that it does. Turns out I have pretty good aim with a slingshot too. The cake exploded all over Ali's face to the delight of everyone, even Ali.

iii. Room Z

Cusco is one of my favorite cities in South America. It is also where Lisa and I found Room Z, which certainly contributed to my fondness.

As a crew, it became our nature to check into one of the big party hostels in each of these cities. There was no real question of where to stay outside of the debate of which party hostel—*Loki or Wild Rover?* In Cusco, we went with the Wild Rover, and on the first night we ended up in the large hostel bar pushing the party. At some point we discovered that the lost-and-found was essentially a costume bin, so we got all dressed up in wigs and silly ties, generally causing a ruckus, and occasionally sneaking back to our dorm room to do drugs in private. I always used my grad school college ID to break up lines, thinking to myself, *Don't forget where you came from, buddy!* Sometimes I would wonder what life as a diplomat would have been like while I evened out the lines on the back of my kindle.

As a big and boisterous group, we were essentially a walking, trekking, bus-riding, ferry-taking, breakfast-eating party waiting to happen. You see groups while traveling, especially Australians (I'm just calling it how I see it), who have sort of a *"you think YOU party—no, WE PARTY!"* type of vibe, where there's a one upmanship within the group of who's the loosest (or loosest cu*#, if we're still talking about Australians); the vibe can become overtly competitive with other people in the hostel or bar.

I really loved our crew for always being incredibly open to letting anyone in on the fun. If someone joined our table, flashed us a smile, or wanted in on our good vibes, they were more than welcome. We were always generous with our laughs, party favors, and the inevitable *"I love you, man"* sessions that followed.

We ended up calling all the party friends we made, and especially those headed south whom we kept bumping into, our "extended family"—the cousins of our nuclear travel family.

This night we made some new cousins, and Lisa and I invented a party-hostel tradition that we kept up on every stop together after Cusco. We wandered off at some point, looking for a place to *"be alone."*

The very first time we had sex was the only time we hooked up in a shared dorm with other people present, but shared dorms were still a perfect place to get naked if they were totally empty. We walked down one of the long hallways of this massive hostel, snickering, got to the very end, and tried the doorknob to Room Z. It was miraculously open, and entirely barren. We took it as a gift from on high.

We giggled like little kids who were knowingly breaking the rules as we jumped into a bottom bunk; we had the next hour to be together, to be naked, to be in love and on drugs. Room Z was a little slice of heaven, our personal paradise—not to be disrupted by anyone else.

We decided against making up the bed when we left so the hostel staff would guess they had to clean it. We found it in the same exact state the next night, and the next, and knowing this haven of an open and empty room seemed to exist permanently made it that much harder to leave Cusco for Machu Picchu.

iv. Machu Picchu Adventure Tour

The girls sorted out our plans, and we booked a last-minute "adventure tour" that involved hiking, zip-lining, white-water rafting, hot springs, and cocaine. That last piece we added to the itinerary ourselves, but it was part of the adventure for sure.

The four days of trekking and adventure leading up to the trip were full of laughs and coca leaves—primarily for the altitude, which genuinely works and has for thousands of years; there's a very legitimate and ancient reason why the plant is so widely grown throughout the Andes. Of the four long days of rafts and ziplines, my highlight is actually a passing memory, a mere moment.

One morning in bed with Lisa, in a room we shared with Brian, Steph, and Rob, we were up early with the sun and trying to be quiet. I wanted this beautiful girl, who was as comfortable as a new pair of socks at this point, and she knew it—she could feel it pushed up against her—but we both knew that we couldn't. So, in her perfect Australian accent, she told me in a stern whisper, *"Cross yer arms and stare at Broyane."*

I can't even type that without smiling like an idiot. It will always remind me of two people I love.

We had an active four days leading up to our stay in Aguas Calientes, the town at the base of Machu Picchu. Aguas Calientes is a hodgepodge of restaurants, shops, and accommodations all catering to the worldwide crowds, with an enormous river cutting through its center. Lisa and I got our own room for the night and quickly made up for lost time, but *"Cross your arms and stare at Brian"* became a saying that long outlasted that first morning it quietly left her lips.

There are a few ways to get up to the entrance gates of Machu Picchu from Aguas Calientes. You can book a tour, you can take shuttle buses for a reasonable fee, or you can wake up at 3 a.m. and walk with headlamps up incredibly steep steps for around two hours. Obviously, we wanted the authentic experience of showing up at Machu Picchu feeling like we were going to die, so we set our alarms for very early o'clock.

We followed the river out of town to the first steps and took our tired legs up into the mountains, one step at a time. The steps wind up into the darkness, and you can see only what your flashlight allows. We were hoping to be some of the first people in line when the gates opened at 6 a.m.; our pictures would be pure, *not dotted with families in khakis who took the shuttle to the top like tourists!*

This sense that there was a way to "win" Machu Picchu propelled us up and into the darkness. We seldom took water breaks as we pushed hard for the top. Well after the first hour, legs heavy, the sun started to break the horizon line, and we could catch a dim glimpse of just how majestic our surroundings were. We pushed on harder still.

We found an old wooden sign with the trail carved into it, and based on this we were in the final quarter, so we kept grinding—knees raising and sweat falling. It was 5:30 a.m. and we wanted to be the first in line for tickets, to be the first to the famous picture spot that overlooks the entire ancient city, right at dawn when the light was just right. I remember knowing we were on the last stretch of steps; you could just feel the energy of Machu Picchu drawing you closer. We lifted our heavy legs, used our arms on the handrails, and dragged our bodies up and over the final steps onto a clearing—just in time to see two shuttle buses pull up and offload groups of sleepy tourists. They filled the lines and were the first ones into the park when the gates opened moments later.

Although we weren't the first people to enter the park, it felt like we earned that day more than they ever would. We earned our pictures, our sore legs, and the beers that came later. I imagine this feeling is only magnified 100 times if you finish the Inca Trail and see Machu Picchu for the first time through the Sun Gate.

Ultimately, we did get our pictures—complete with tourists in the background and the same stupid wigs we were wearing a few nights before in Cusco. We didn't pack much for these five days, but the wigs made the shortlist for this exact reason.

Seeing Machu Picchu is on nearly every human's bucket list—and it's as beautiful as it is interesting—but after half a day I was ready to get back to Cusco, and ready to be back in Room Z.

CHAPTER 5: BOLIVIA

After a quick stop back in Cusco to collect our gear, the girls organized a bus down to Lake Titicaca, which straddles Peru and Bolivia and is home to the world's highest inhabited island, Isla Del Sol.

It's a uniquely beautiful place, and as a travel family we were really in our element. Everything was simple (except for the vertical hike up to our accommodations), and we were each authentically ourselves in each other's company at this point. That sense of genuine comfort naturally led to all types of the best moments you could ask for—playing the old neighborhood game "sardines" among ancient ruins, chasing pigs along the beach, and posing for all the weirdest and most creative group photos we could possibly think up. Picture a scene in which we're ceremonially sacrificing Brian, circled around a huge stone slab that he's sprawled out on, while he stares up at the sky wide-eyed, a huge Irishman fighting laughter while trying his best to look scared.

These nights were a nice respite from the never-ending South American party, and we were all actually relatively healthy during our time on Lake Titicaca—mostly due to the constant accidental hiking at high altitude and lack of drugs.

We took the ferryboat further across the beautiful lake, the Andes Mountains shooting up into the clouds in the distance. Everything at altitude seems to have a deeper saturation of color; between the bright white clouds, blue water, the yellow and green hues of the island's contours and the rainbow of colors on our llama sweaters, hats, and gloves, we were living inside of an Instagram filter. We looked good. We were happy. We belonged to each other.

––––––

We had just enough time to cleanse our system before crossing the Bolivian border toward La Paz, where I encountered a slight snafu. United States passport holders have to pay to get in, which I hadn't realized was a possibility due to a lack of research (read: no research). I had Peruvian Soles, but, to get through immigration, to keep on my journey, they demanded four clean twenty-dollar bills. My travel family watched me struggle from the Bolivian side as they all got through customs without a hitch, and, as they realized I didn't have what was needed, Lisa ran over asking in her worst Spanish if she could pay. The guards let me reach across the imaginary—but very real—line to get the money from Lisa, so I could pay and be processed into Bolivia. I am not sure how this would have played out if I were alone, but I'm very thankful that Lisa knew what she was doing, that at least she was prepared.

Once we finally all got through, we carried on in yet another bus towards La Paz and ended up staying at a hostel that was also a brewery. For the first time, we chose to sleep somewhere that wasn't a Loki or Wild Rover. The free beer upon check-in led to a hundred more, and we were eventually covered in neon paint playing beer pong on a Monday night.

This was early December, and way back in September, back in Bogotá, I had bought a cheap flight home out of Lima to spend Christmas back in Wisconsin with my family. We all knew our days as a family were numbered, so we weren't wasting any of them. We also weren't talking about that; we were too busy dancing to LMFAO's Party Rock Anthem, sinking cups, and repeating inside jokes.

i. Fish Foot

We ended up moving across town and checking into the Wild Rover in La Paz mainly out of insistence from Brian, who I think felt very much at home in the Irish-themed décor. We were back into full-on party mode, with beers in the afternoon serving as the only remedy to reconcile the body's struggle upon waking.

Luckily, we had the girls, and they were good at planning. If it were left to Brian, Matt, Jamie, Rob and me, we might have never left La Paz again.

We collectively decided that we would head to the Amazon, to a small town called Rurrenabaque, where you could get lost in the deep jungle looking for anacondas, crocodiles, capybaras, monkeys, and, most intriguingly, where you could swim alongside pink river dolphins.

To get to Rurrenabaque, you could fly, hire a driver, or take the local bus. We were advised by everyone we spoke to not to attempt the local bus, and that it often took well over 24 hours. We also didn't have the funds to buy an extra round-trip flight—we were all definitely on a bus-sized budget. So we opted for the middle option and hired a driver. At this point, we were down to seven people as Matt preferred to stay in La Paz and party, which fit us perfectly into an off-road four-wheeler.

We organized a driver who came to the hostel to pick us up in the morning. As everyone finished packing, Brian and I went out to meet him. He spoke a handful of small words in English, had a huge smile, and strong little fat hands that we shook before rounding everyone up. When the crew met in the lobby and asked us about the driver, upon trying to describe how much I liked him, I said, "He's like… MISTER Bolivia. Like, if the country was a man, *it would be this man.*"

In the years that have followed, I've found that if a certain person I've met represents their country perfectly I can't help but think, *This guy is Mr. Japan* or *This lady is totally Miss Croatia* or even *This guy is Mr. Wisconsin,* a perfect fried-cheese-eating, beer-chugging, Packers-hat-wearing representation of my home state. I realize it's partially based on pretty blunt stereotypes and snapshot interactions, but in my mind I promise it's always very complimentary and charming.

———

The drive was advertised as 16 hours, but that was incredibly optimistic. We took off with all the enthusiasm of a proper road trip, but at some point a few hours in we were just bouncing off of each other in the back of the truck as it was tossed back and forth by the rocky Bolivian country roads. It became pretty apparent within the first few hours that sleep would be wishful.

At some point on the journey, I remember asking Mr. Bolivia if we could stop at the next bathroom. He gestured to pull over, and I somehow communicated to him (I think pointing at my butthole) that it wasn't a pee break I was after. More than thirty minutes later, with my anus fully clenched and sweat gathering at my brow, he finally pulled off near a random intersection and gestured to a cement block. I ran inside and found two long troughs along the walls with several guys aiming their pee anywhere they pleased.

I had no other options at this point, so I just took my shorts off and squatted over one of the troughs. I distinctly remember making eye contact with one of the guys peeing, who shrugged and with his old wrinkled eyes told me, *Meh, don't worry about it.* It was one of the best and worst poops of my life. Luckily, I had my own toilet paper.

Pro tip: Always have your own toilet paper.

After another ten hours of smashing shoulders in the back seat while Brian somehow slept, which we all very openly resented him for, we arrived in the small jungle town just after the sun had come back up, a full twenty-some hours after leaving.

We walked up the main road to a park and slept on the grass in a circle around our bags for a few hours before the tourist agency that we booked with opened. Those two hours of sleep brought us back to life.

Ten minutes after waking, we were sitting in the agency, an hour later we were in a jeep, driving out of the small town, and after an hour in the jeep we loaded into a long skinny boat, sitting single-file in lawn chairs. The guide ripped the single-prop motor, and we were buzzing into the Bolivian Amazon up a narrow, meandering river. Capybaras, the world's largest rodent, stared from the shoreline curiously, and at some point we pulled up close to a tree, and a few monkeys hopped on board to our delight. Jamie yelled, *"OY, HEY, make ye-self at home,"* in his Scottish brogue, legs pointing up at the sky as he made room for the scampering little mammals.

We spent the next few days deep in the Amazon, searching for pink river dolphins in the brown water and for Anacondas in the tall grass. We swung from hammocks at the camp and from a rope swing into the river, and it was all so strangely comfortable to be in a remote part of Bolivia with people I had known for only a few months. Lisa and I took as many opportunities to sneak off into our shared room alone as we were afforded. At this point, we would just let the family know we were going to "Room Z" and we'd be back in 30. Everyone knew to leave the room alone for a while so Lisa and I could touch as much of our skin together as possible while impersonating the jungle—crooning like capybaras, hooting like monkeys, and singing like two poetic, tropical love birds.

———

On the last day in the Amazon, we were going to try to find a group of pink river dolphins, and the plan was to actually swim with them for the first time. We took our skinny boats upriver from our bungalows for fifteen minutes before seeing the strange colored dorsal fins breaking the water. The dolphins looked interesting but definitely not cute or cuddly. They had long, weird pink beaks. They looked nothing like Flipper or any dolphin stuffed animal you've ever seen.

Our guides assured us multiple times before we actually entered the water, *"Dolphins no bite. Dolphins only bite fish. Dolphins very nice."*

When we jumped into the murky brown water, I was feeling relatively assured by our guides. After all, this is one of the main reasons people come out to the Amazon in Bolivia. We certainly weren't the first to swim with these dolphins.

But once in the opaque brown water, I was fucking terrified. You couldn't see the dolphins, but they felt our presence and would rush past without warning, splashing behind you, then in front of you. My heart was in my throat, my dick tried it's best to hide inside of me.

The seven of us were making a cacophony of noises that ranged from giggles to genuine horror movie screams. At some point, I heard Lisa scream in a very real way, and I looked in her direction. Her eyes were huge, and, in an instant, she got yanked down mid-scream, the noise swallowed by the brown water. It was like a scene from *Jaws: Pink River Monster.*

I swam over toward her and made it to her right as she resurfaced, yelling, *"It fuuhking bit mahy!"*

I swam her back to the boat and we loaded her in to find her foot with a perfect, ugly dolphin-beak bite mark, blood slowly trickling out from it. The bite didn't need serious medical treatment, just a bandage, but we were all definitely done swimming.

As a way of apologizing, or explaining what happened, the guide shrugged and said with a wry smile, "You have a fish foot. It looks like fish." Somehow, it genuinely did help. We all laughed as we realized this was a story we would all tell forever. This is why you leave home.

ii. My Trip to Mars

We were back in La Paz a few days later, and I honestly don't remember the ride home. I know Mr. Bolivia drove us like the true professional he was, but I think I blocked it from my memory. Once was enough.

I had about one week left before I had to make it back to Lima to catch my flight home for the holidays. The travel family decided we'd spend our last few days together in the Salt Flats of Bolivia, after which the rest would head farther south into Chile, and I would take a series of buses back north for thirty-some hours to the airport, and in the end, to Wisconsin.

We decided against booking anything and got a night bus into Uyuni, the small gateway town to the Salt Flats. We arrived around 5 a.m., exited the bus into the still-dark and frozen town, and walked to a small café that was open for the early arrivals, wrapped in our full-team llama gear. After a hot cup of coffee that brought me back to life, I realized that I left my point and click camera on the bus when I stumbled off it in a daze making morning fog with my morning breath.

I ran back to the bus depot as the sun was rising and asked around for where I could find the bus that just dropped us off. The lady at the office told me it was in a lot nearby, but that the driver locked the bus and was sleeping.

I asked her to call.

She tried hesitantly.

He slept.

I asked her to try again and asked her if I could just go where he lived and see if he had it. She looked away, feigning misunderstanding. At some point during the exchange, my heart sank, and I realized that it was gone. The camera hurt a bit, but a bunch of pictures from the Amazon and the last few months were lost with it—a loss that hurt deep in my chest cavity. It felt like finding your pet's cage open, and all your precious chameleons gone, never to be recovered.

I rejoined the crew, trying my best to be over it, to at least be present, as we searched for the cheapest three-day tour. We booked something leaving that afternoon and spent the morning in a park with a random group of Australians. After chatting with them for over an hour, we realized they were on the same tour. One of the guys had just recently gotten *"mo money mo problems"* tattooed in huge letters on his thigh. They also had an absurd amount of sleeping pills and fireworks, along with a lone watermelon—an accessory to the fireworks. It was going to be an interesting few days. They were certainly winning the *"loosest c*n# award"* for this trip, no matter whom they were competing with.

———

The Salt Flats themselves ended up being one of the most stunning and memorable places I've ever been in my life, still to this day. I've even been back a second time to take more crazy depth-perception photos, to freeze at night sleeping in strange concrete boxes, and to spend hours cruising through otherworldly landscapes complete with red lakes, purple lakes, incredibly large cacti, flamingos, and bizarre rock formations. There is no other place in the world I've visited that feels less like you're still on this planet.

The jeep drivers chewed coca leaves while we drank whiskey in the back. We shot out into the grand white expanse with absolutely no sign of a road or points of reference for where the driver should be heading. We just drove straight into the salty white abyss.

Our days in the Salt Flats with these loose Australians were spent drinking, driving, doing blow, blowing up fruit, and really soaking up our last few days together without ever mentioning a word of that truth.

Lisa and I also tried our best to stay up late with each other because we knew our hours as a couple were limited, and we were really happy as a couple. Late one night, while in our newest Room Z, Lisa looked at me and said, "You know I love you, right?" All I could say was, "Yeah, I know." She knew my rule, and she knew that I loved her. She wiped a tear from the corner of my eye, teasing her big strong American for being *"sach ah poussy."* We were so present in that moment, so aware that what we had is what some people spend their lives looking for, but that it was all going to end a day later, and there was little we could do about it.

The last day in the Salt Flats we drank beers in a hot spring while looking at the Andes Mountains, and I thought about how I was exactly where I was supposed to be. I wasn't meant to be farming, and I wasn't meant to be a foreign diplomat or an NGO executive. I was meant to have an early-morning beer with these people I loved in a hot spring in the Salt Flats of Bolivia. Everything was as it was meant to be.

———

Later that afternoon, we ended up at a small shack in the middle of nowhere, and this was it. The shack was an immigration station for entering Chile. We all held it together pretty well as we hugged, and as they passed their passports over. I cracked some of my favorite family jokes for the last time that I would ever be able to, and suddenly the driver yelled, *"Vamos."*

I gave the whole crew deep hugs. I gave Brian a tight squeeze and confidently told him I'd see him soon, trying not to let him see me cry because I knew he would give me shit. I gave Lisa a big hug, I kissed her, and I told her that we would stay in touch, that I would write to her later that day. Then, without ever deciding ahead of time, I blurted out, "I love you too, but I'm pretty sure you know that," as tears started to run down my cheeks. Tears started falling from her eyes, and she said, *"Oh, fahk youuhhh, I deedn't whant to croy,"* then she turned around. Those were the last words she spoke to me in person.

They drove off into the Chilean dessert, and I got back in my jeep. We weren't even in third gear before I really started crying—my body laid down in the back seat, shaking rhythmically and wailing quietly, grieving the loss of my first travel family.

That sad jeep ride was followed by an even longer sad bus ride. I took the bus from Uyuni back to La Paz that night, and when I got on the bus I took a few sleeping pills that one of our new Australian friends gifted me, knowing I had some forty hours of travel ahead of me. I had slept a total of around twelve hours over the last three nights, and I desperately needed to be unconscious. I wrapped my backpack around my feet, and everything went black.

I was woken up by the bus driver in La Paz, still very disoriented. When I unwrapped my backpack from my legs and lifted it up I knew something was wrong immediately—it was half of its normal weight. I opened it to find my cheap laptop computer missing. Someone had gone under my seat in the night to take my computer out of my bag. They could have taken my clothes off, and I wouldn't have woken up with the amount of drugs I had in my system, but it was bold nonetheless and I was stunned. I stood in the empty bus staring at the bus driver, hoping he would break into laughter and tell me he was just pulling my leg; he only wrinkled his forehead and nodded to the door

iii. Running through My Blood

My camera was gone. My computer that I saved my photos on was gone. Lisa was gone. The low lows of travel were piling on, and suddenly walking around the massive bus terminal in La Paz alone, public crying felt extremely possible.

I wrote to my travel family that night from La Paz about what happened on the bus, and Rob suggested we set up a Dropbox account so that everyone could add their photos for me. I was so grateful for having made such close friends at that moment. Ultimately, I ended up with more photos of those few months than I took on my own, and way more photos of myself living the best moments of my life than I had captured from behind my own camera.

This was the greatest and most important travel lesson that I learned on that first trip. It's the people—not the places, passport stamps, or photos—that make a trip a cherished memory, something that's hard to convey the depth of to your loved ones who weren't there. The bond that was forged is hard to explain. It was always meant to be finite but powerful, a secret society formed and years' worth of history and secrets created in weeks, just to be dismantled and reduced to memories known only by a few. Maybe that has something to do with why those who don't travel never really know quite what to ask a friend who's recently arrived home from abroad.

Maybe it's why they often ask nothing at all.

I took another twenty-hour bus to Lima the next day, jumped on my flight, and a day later I found myself at Redmond's bar in Wrigleyville, Chicago, with one of my best friends, Patrick, who managed the place. He closed the establishment doors at 2 a.m. and we proceeded to sit on old wooden stools at the bar ripping shots of whiskey and drinking Bud heavies until the sun came up. Wearing a ridiculous alpaca sweater, playing my Bolivian baby guitar with my buddy, we shared stories, and I tried to convey what the last five months had meant to me, how it had changed things. How finally making a choice for me and taking those uncomfortable first few steps until I found my feet—it was all better than I ever could have imagined.

I was capable of more than what the world expected of me. I didn't want to wake up and go to work, repeating sequences and sleepwalking through routines; drinking coffee to survive and clock-watching for my lunch break. I wanted to solve puzzles in foreign languages, order from menus I couldn't read from servers with whom I couldn't speak and get a dish whose ingredients I could only guess at. I wanted to carry 20 kgs for miles following a screenshot of a map, half lost in a town I didn't know. I wanted to speak with more strangers, fall into easy love with more strangers. At home I didn't have the willpower to do more on my own, but travel forced me to, like a CrossFit trainer who pushes your muscles past breaking.

I started my trip through South America as a scared puppy who couldn't get himself water. In the end, despite the lost camera, the stolen computer, two phones gone—one to the ocean, one to thirteen year-olds—and all the pooping in my own pants, I knew I was made for this. I was good at rolling with the punches and looking at the unknown with optimism as opposed to fear; excited about whatever white space there was in my schedule or what the room I'd spend the night in might look like. I was just as good at making friends with people as with street dogs and with locals as with backpackers, and everything about the adventure gave me renewed energy and confidence. Some feel a lack of purpose while traveling, but for me the travel was the purpose. It was enough.

Seeing a new town, tasting a new flavor, making a new connection, or creating a new memory—any one of those things was enough for me to feel like it was a day well-lived. Oftentimes, over the previous five months, all of those things happened in the span of a few hours. It was intoxicating, and it was running through my blood.

In that moment at Redmond's, as the sun came up and the whiskey splashed in my liver, I knew that making it back home to the Midwest for the holidays was not the end. This was the very beginning. The world had cracked open for me, and I was strong, fearless, and ready to see more.

Celebratory photoshoot after the success of my independent study. (Photo by Adam Miszewski)

The best snap from our Trinity Fellows Marquette graduation ceremony.

My first group of hostel friends at Tayrona National Park.

The ceiling above us as we made cocaine on the floor.

Amazed by the physical phenomenon that is the equator.

Adventure day in Baños, Ecuador.

Waiting for a friendly driver to pick us up.

The farthest we made it up Mt. Chimborazo before hitchhiking onward.

Halloween in Mancora, Peru. I'm a duck.

In Lima trying to appear normal, but I'm very sad.

Brian, Ali, and me somewhere in the Colca Canyon.

Being the *backpackerest* backpacker.

Brian and me at Machu Picchu trying our hardest to look normal.

Lisa, Steph, and me exploring the islands of Lake Titicaca.

The travel fam, on the famous Death Rode bike ride in Bolivia.

Searching for anacondas in the tall grass of Rurrenabaque.

The boys... trying to impress the girls.

Being bozos on the salt flats. Yes, it's the same duck from Halloween.

Brian and me, in brotherly love.

My first travel family. (Photo by Matt Macleod)

CONTINENT TWO:
NORTH & CENTRAL AMERICA

CHAPTER 6: MEXICO

After spending the holidays with my family and taking an annual pilgrimage up north to Pickerel, Wisconsin with all my best childhood friends, the excitement of home quickly faded. Since I had set my heart on a trip through South America and told everyone that was the plan, I had earnestly thought I would have some adventures and then start my nonprofit career when I got home. I imagined that, after the holidays, I would check some job boards and get a cool leadership role with a youth organization somewhere in Milwaukee, Chicago, or maybe even back in New Orleans. Before I left for Aruba, I certainly pictured myself stateside in 2013.

Every day of the four months I was gone in South America, the feeling of falling in love with travel and new cultures and people was tinged with a bit of guilt. I had built most of my identity around being someone who helps kids, someone who does sacrificial nonprofit work, someone who in his own small way benefits the greater good. I was wrestling with the idea of feeling selfish, feeling uncertain of my place in the world now that I had temporarily let go of the primary thing that my identity was tethered to—the way family and friends would describe me if they were asked, "What does Travis do?" I repeated the same comforting thoughts to myself every day when the guilt would rise, but my internal monologue was often a dogfight.

So you're just going to leave your job working with disadvantaged youth, leave all those kids behind, and go bopping around country to country for however long you want? You're fucking selfish. Most of those kids have never been to Chicago, and here you go to fucking Machu Pichu!

Yeah, but all of these new experiences and the cultural awakening I'm going through will make me better at my future job with kids when I return to it. My travels are making me more well rounded, more culturally sensitive, and ultimately a better person and youth worker!

Be honest—you just like doing drugs, the whole hostel party scene, and sleeping with new women. Who is going to hire you after you've been out of the workforce for this long anyway?

Well, YEAH I love those things, who wouldn't? And if an organization doesn't want to hire me because I took a long trip to experience new cultures and see new corners of the world, then I wouldn't want to work for them anyway!

All I knew in the pit of my chest is that two weeks back at my parents' house felt like enough. Wisconsin is home, but grey, frigid and all too familiar, and the idea of scrolling through a job board, the thought of settling down and staying put, the cold, dirty-snow daily reality that was home sat heavy around me. That winter, I felt the weight of permanence and the dread that comes with making long-lasting, adult decisions. The guilt was powerful, but so was the desire for more.

If I took a job with my degree, it would be a commitment; it would launch my life on a trajectory toward a career, feeling established, putting down roots, a dog, a neighborhood bar where I was a regular, a trivia night I frequented. It all seemed so clear, so inevitable.

I understand the desire behind the sense of stability that comes with making grounding decisions, and I'm close with many people who chased that—prioritizing commitment and a solid foundation at every crossroad. People who put roots down in the form of three or four kids, a first and a second house, a serious job with benefits and a title that shines at dinner parties. I see the upside in knowing what to expect from life, from the following week, month and years ahead. But, for whatever reason, I've always valued not knowing and the freedom that comes with it more.

If anything, my trip through South America had me convinced that the world was wide open, serendipity was waiting at the end of every flight, new friends were around every corner, and that some of those new friends could even feel like family. The adventures and connections could feel more like ordained fate than just a trip.

I still had a few thousand dollars in my bank account from a combination of work throughout grad school and my grandma money. I opened my ancient MacBook (which thankfully I had left in the sanctity of my parent's basement) and sitting on my parents' couch a few days after New Year's booked a cheap, one-way flight to Cancún, Mexico. *My bonus semester might need to be extended to a proper full degree program,* I thought to myself as I clicked through Expedia's never ending questions about things I didn't want and couldn't afford.

I told my parents and closest friends, one more little trip, a few more travel oats to sow, and then I'll be back and settle down. I'll get back to fighting for social justice, helping one disadvantaged kid at a time break the cycle of poverty and uplift his family and community. That's what I thought, at least, and I like to imagine it would make my grandma laugh.

i. Cancún & Isla Mujeres

Cancún is not my favorite place. I quickly got myself to Isla Mujeres after a few drunken nights in Cancún, one of which I woke up to find that my phone had been stolen from right next to my face as I slept. It was my third phone gone in five months, and this one hurt. This time I thought I was experienced enough to avoid such loss, *but no.* I was just building my anxiety slowly so I could set the single day "pocket check" Guinness World

Record in a few years. I must average over 50 a day.

Isla Mujeres had excellent island vibes from the moment I stepped off the boat. I checked into a party hostel right on the water and started chatting to a couple of beefy, attractive Australian guys, Adam and Daniel. They were brothers, and they were babes.

I didn't know it at the time, but as Adam was attempting to hang by a Cirque Du Soleil-style ribbon from a tree and we chatted about our travels, that was the beginning of my second travel family. The brothers were great, but nobody would ever replace or really even compare to that first travel family and adventure, much like it's hard for future lovers to give that same feeling as first love. Like how candy is still good as an adult, but as a child when you first experience candy it's something wholly different in its significance and nature. You'd spend every dollar you had on it.

My South American travel family was a first, and it will always hold a special memory and energy with it. But these brothers and a special someone who joined us became the second crew that formed my travels and helped me fall deeper in love with this lifestyle. There was a significance in proving that it wasn't a one-time thing. It helped me to believe that the overjoyed, adventurous, wander-the-earth-with-a-huge-smile-and-new-friends-feeling was sustainable. I would decide when to stop. Either me or my bank account.

Adam and Daniel are like most Australian brothers in that they are tall, good-looking dudes who like to have a good time. They are not like most Australian brothers in that one, Daniel, is a doctor with an arm sleeve, and the other, Adam, holds the Australian freediving record of 99 meters on a single breath.

Also, although she wasn't Lisa, a Finnish girl named Anna helped me realize that falling into something sexy and fun with a perfect stranger is often easier than having a decent first date back home in a stagnant life— hoping to strike up a convo with an attractive stranger at a bar or to strike gold on a dating app.

ii. Anna in the White Dress

The Australian brothers and I met Anna in Tulum, before Tulum was *Tulum*. There was an evening salsa dance class happening in the courtyard of our giant hostel, which I was not game for. No one who knows me would describe me as shy, but I'm not the type to willingly do some specific dance I have no idea how to do, like tango or salsa. I love dancing, and I actually reckon I'm a pretty good dancer, but a type of dance that you can do right or wrong has never interested me—I don't want there to be rules to groove. Moreover, I don't want to screw up or be corrected.

On this particular night, I was really happy to just be watching. I was fixated on this stunning girl dancing in a white dress with the perfect blend of confidence and carefree ease of not really knowing the steps. She was worth watching, acting like she was alone in her room. I was smitten, and as I watched her dance from the upstairs railing, Adam walked over and said, *"Get ye tongue ohff the flowr, mayte."* So much for playing it cool.

We all drank around a big table later on that evening, followed by drinks at a bar down the road. I swung on a little wooden swing facing the sidewalk bar, thinking about how I had no chance in hell with this beautiful Finnish girl, trying not to stare.

Throughout Mexico I was still messaging Lisa daily, but no amount of "I miss you's" would lead us to actually consider an attempt at a long-distance relationship. She was busy finishing her trip through South America, celebrating Christmas in a pool somewhere in Argentina with the remaining members of our travel family, along with some new cousins. When I finally made it to Mexico, she was on her way back to Australia. It was too far to consider, both of us too young to try.

I missed Lisa, but I couldn't help track Anna around the room, and I didn't have to feel bad that I desired her. I had friend-zoned myself for the preservation of my heart, so kissing this woman didn't become an all-consuming desire. Anna decided to join the Australian brothers and me over the next few days, and I flirted helplessly with the air of someone who knew it was hopeless and as though making her laugh was enough of a joy. I was certain I had no shot. Thank god for drugs.

———

One night we were all at a club, and I had a little bag of blow on me. She told me she wanted to do some that night, and then I said something stupid to make her laugh.

At some point, we snuck into a bathroom and went into the same stall, and I took out the little bag. We did bumps from the corner of my university ID and then, right as I pushed the little baggy back into the drug pocket of my jeans (that little one that I used to always think had no purpose), Anna pushed me up against the stall door, and we were making out.

I was a bit high on blow and full of tequila, I had a new travel family, and I was now making out with a Finnish smokeshow in a bathroom stall in Mexico. She pulled her head away mid-kiss, smacked me on the shoulder and said, *"Hey, stop smiling,"* in her stupidly cute accent.

I was still worried about my future and the general approval of my loved ones; random verses from my dad's 20-plus-year-long life lecture echoing in my head from moment to moment—*"Do you know the difference between a job and a career?" "You can choose any profession you want to, you just have to pursue it!" "Have you considered the Coast Guard?"* (That one always felt pretty out-of-left-field to me too.) In that bathroom stall, I was sure of one thing—I was glad I didn't stay in Wisconsin.

iii. San Cristobal is Magic

We laughed, drank, beached, jammed, and stuck together all the way down to San Cristobal, a magical city in the state of Chiapas in Mexico. There's a lot of advice exchanged on the road, and at some point I was told by a stranger that I would love San Cristobal. I asked him, "Why do you love it?" This random backpacker on the bus paused, then looked up, like there was an answer above him, and said, *"I dunno, it's just magical."*

Our first night in San Cristobal we were walking through the city center with smiling people, colorful bars, and traditional music wafting out into the charming streets. We eventually made it to the major square in the center of the city, and in the middle there was a circular, elevated platform, a small stage, and a big band playing marimbas and horn music, surrounded by hanging Christmas lights stretching out in every direction from the stage.

All around the band and the raised stage, older couples were slow-dancing under the sparkling lights. As I watched the happy couples dancing, I thought, *That guy was right... this place is magic.*

The city was perfect, but things with Anna had gotten a little strange. In my memory, I was playing things cool, but I know myself, and in reality I was probably a little overzealous. She began a week of extreme hot and cold with her energy towards me. In Chetumal, only days before arriving in San Cristobal, she led me into our little jungle room, ripped my clothes off, and we had incredible sex to the sound of tropical birds cheering us on. Now, in San Cristobal, there were full days that I would settle for a hug or even eye contact.

Some days would be filled by amazing travel-family moments, with her right in the center. We got our family portrait drawn on the street by an aspiring cartoonist, whose work was so amateurish that it made us cackle the entire afternoon. In the evening, we would play music around an outdoor fire pit, everyone glowing in the warm orange light as they sang together. The next day I would find her in a hammock, giving one word answers to friendly questions without eye contact.

I was finally at the point in my life where I felt comfortable with women, which I think was a direct result of feeling comfortable with myself. It took until I was nearly 30 to win this sense of feeling relaxed in my own skin. From a lot of conversations about this feeling—and this time of my life—that I could glean with perfect clarity a few years later, it's fairly common to settle into that self-assured, comfortable feeling somewhere around the 30-year milestone. The travel helped me get there, and it was reflected in my relationships with women most clearly.

My relationships with women were more positive and tranquilo, I stopped asking myself heavy questions like "what am I doing with my life?" and "are we going to get married?" and I just started enjoying it all more. I was way more comfortable with who I had turned out to be, and I was much more present, which I've come to learn is an attractive quality to women, because I was also having much more sex than ever before. *#data*

But I couldn't figure out this hot and cold vibe with Anna. One day, jungle sex and lots of belly laughs, the next day, a van ride where she would give off the icy chill of someone who would rather be anywhere in the world than the backseat of a twelve-person van with me. I didn't get it, and I honestly still don't. I could easily chalk this up to the stereotypical *Women, right?!?,* but I don't think that's fair, and I can't say this happened all that often. I've definitely had experiences where I felt like I couldn't read a partner perfectly, or where my expectations didn't match hers, but never an unexplained on-and-off switch like this.

Anyway, we got naked and rolled around a few more times, and I went to Guatemala by myself. Travel family number two was just a month in Mexico, two Australian brothers and my first experience with a beautiful woman from Finland, whom I still don't quite know how to feel about. It's all rather hot and cold in my memory as well.

CHAPTER 7: GUATEMALA & BELIZE

Leaving for Guatemala, I took a 5 p.m. bus from San Cristobal, which I thought would take me straight to Quetzaltenango (feel free to just pronounce that in your mind however you'd like), but, around 10 p.m., we stopped and were told to get off the bus.

We were at a small border town that I couldn't find on Google if (read: when) I searched for it today. I got out, slightly delirious, and immediately a bit on edge. There were lots of people, feral dogs, noises, dim street lights, and I could feel eyes following me. I grabbed my backpack and realized after talking in my 8-year-old present tense caveman Spanish that I would need to sort out a bed, and quickly. I found a strange little bright-orange room with barely enough floor space for my backpack. It was essentially a door that opened up into a bed. I was grateful, but still felt the strange tingling of my growing backpacker spidey-sense.

I had a loaded-up hard drive with movies from some fellow backpackers I met in Mexico, and that night I watched Hugh Jackman sing his heart out in *Les Miserables*. Throughout the movie, I could hear a constant commotion, an angry-sounding man in the hallway, and, every time I would pop my head out, this very intense and distressed looking man, standing under dim hospital-like fluorescent lights, would be staring down the bright orange hallway directly at me. We'd make momentary eye contact, and I'd close the door, a bit shook, grateful my door had a lock on it.

It felt like he was guarding the passage and there was no way I could leave. He had a predatory look and a dark energy I could still sense through my locked door. I was stuck in this small, orange room that I couldn't even stand on the floor in. It was claustrophobic and unnerving, but I just kept telling myself I would be fine if I just kept the door locked and stayed in my room with Hugh Jackman. *Me and Wolverine, we got this.*

It didn't come easily, but eventually I slept, and I was fine when the sun rose, sprinting to the bathroom to take a fire hose of a morning piss. I never even unpacked, so I simply collected my things and bolted down the hall and back across the street to the bus depot where I got on the first bus I could find for Guatemala. Not that I could locate it if I tried, but that little town was not a place I would want to find myself in again—and is the type of fairly common backpacking experience that doesn't make it on anyone's Instagram. I was so grateful to be back on a bus with my Tom Robbins book—staring out of the window, always moving, a shark who has to keep swimming to stay alive.

————

Quetzaltenango was charming. I walked around the small town square that first day, stopping to watch some street performers in the sunshine at the edge of a small park. I kicked around a soccer ball with some laughing kids. I ate some delicious street food, then finally wandered back home to the hostel and had a few beers with some strangers. It was a beautiful first day in a new country.

I woke very early the next morning for no apparent reason and then, in an instant, I felt the reason grab my stomach. An invisible hand reached inside me and squeezed my intestines, causing me to bolt upright in bed. I scrambled to the bathroom and violently peed from my butthole, writhing on the toilet as stabbing pains shot through all 30 meters of my intestines.

I spent my next two full days in Guatemala traveling from my hostel dorm bed to the bathroom down the hall, where I was spending a good amount of time fake coughing to cover the sound of terror coming from my butt. Every time I reentered the bathroom it smelled like an unsolved murder and I feigned playing the detective to any poor soul I discovered, shrugging my shoulders and looking quizzical, especially to those brushing their teeth.

I was in the midst of my first serious bout of food poisoning on the road, and my anus was rubbed raw by rough Guatemalan toilet paper. It hurt in the exact same way your nose might during a serious sinus infection. The way that wood must feel when made smooth.

I had enough time in bed to consider what caused this projectilepooping situation. It dawned on me as I revisited all the things that went into my mouth. During that first sunny walk, I ate three delicious pupusas on the street. Pupusas are basically stuffed corn tortillas. They were delicious, the way that tortillas, cheese, and meat are delicious in whatever form they come in.

I remembered piling on this sopping wet cabbage that came in a little plastic bag with it. The cabbage, the water—the lightbulb clicked on, I was certain.

Pro tip: Wet salads and veggies have caused many a chaffed butthole while traveling, so consume with caution.

After thirty-six hours of no food, no fun, and only poops (which I doubt even deserve to be called poops with that viscosity), I was finally able to hold down a few bananas and some toast. I was getting my energy and color back, and with it came the urge to explore. I booked a hike up an active volcano to see the sunrise for the next morning.

The trip left at one in the morning, the hike started around two, and the sun finally came up around 5 a.m. It was more common in my travels that I went to sleep after 5 a.m. than having already gone on a hike by that time. On this particular morning at 5:30 a.m., I was cold and sweaty, covered in the nighttime, watching smoke pour from an active volcano from a high clearing, while sipping hot chocolate as the sun gradually brought more and more of the distance into view. These new passing hostel friends and I sat and sipped in silence as the volcano billowed smoke out into the morning haze like a well-stocked chimney.

I was proud of the sweat I spilled that morning and for being awake at 6 a.m. without the assistance of drugs. The early morning adventure was exactly what I needed, and I finally started feeling a normal, solid poop forming in my bowels.

i. Decent Musicians Wanted

I made my way down to Lake Atitlan, where I checked into a hostel on the lake and recognized some guys I'd met at a party in Quetzaltenango. The vibe and the faces were both familiar. Backpacking through Central America started to have this familiar feel. The same Bob Marley song wafting in the background, the same colored hammock swinging lazily between the same two palm trees. The same dread-headed guy with the same sundress-wearing girlfriend. I loved every bit of it.

At this hostel, one thing that was brand new was a leather-craft-making, only-brown-clothes-wearing, saw-playing, vagabond type from the northwest of the States. His name was Nick.

When I say saw-playing, I mean an actual saw that you would use to cut a branch off of a tree. He was traveling with one, as well as a fiddle, both of which he would play with a gnarly bow that was frayed wildly in every direction. Nick's facial hair matched his bow perfectly.

I was traveling this entire stretch through Mexico and Central America with a baby guitar (or guitarito, or guitalele, if you will) that I bought in La Paz at the end of my time in South America. It was six strings and tuned slightly differently than a normal guitar, but all songs and chords played the exact same. I was feeling pretty comfortable on it and had been playing a little with the Australian brothers, but Nick and I started playing regularly and we clicked immediately.

Pro tip: If you're going to travel with a guitar, invest in a travel guitar or guitalele. Most airlines (except punitive-ass RyanAir with their rules) will allow a travel guitar to be stowed in the overhead at no cost as your "extra item" (read: purse, essentially). Almost all airlines will charge well over $50 for a full-sized guitar in a case, which really adds up during extended travel.

My first day in San Juan, a vibrant little backpacker town on the lake, I happened to notice a flyer at a popular Irish-themed bar. The flier read: **"Decent Musicians Wanted**." My first thought was that it was a hilarious flyer, and my second thought was, *We're decent.* I told Nick about it, and we decided to stop in and ask if we could book a gig. The tall guy behind the bar handed me a guitar and said, "Well, let's see." I started playing one of my go-to songs… *"shorty get down good lord, baby got yah moving all over town, strictly bitch we don't play around…"*

He interrupted me thirty seconds in and said, "Right on, can you guys play Thursday night?" Nick and I said, *"Yeah, sure!"* in unison. I followed up our over-enthusiasm by asking, "How does it work?" The tall, dark-skinned man said, "Just show up at 7; we'll have it all set up. You guys get dinner, drinks, and $100 cash, plus you can put out a tip jar if you'd like." He could have said anything, and we would have been excited, but $100 was real money.

———

It was a Monday, so the next few days Nick and I had a real purpose and drive. A lot of days while backpacking, your sole purpose is loosely to spend as little money as possible while hoping to see something cool or do something you might remember. This week for me, it was to try to become a band with one gig and with one all-brown-wearing, beard-having, lumberjack-themed hipster.

Nick was a good musician with incredible range. We would switch off leading on guitar every few songs—he would play and I would drum along, or I would play and he would strum his fiddle or his saw. Both options were fun and sounded pretty polished after a few days.

When Thursday came around, all the guys we got close with at the hostel came out to support us, and we somehow managed to fill the bar. Nick and I opened with a few crowd-pleasers, settled in, and sounded like we belonged up there.

We equaled the $100 the bar paid out in the tip jar as well, so we each walked away with $100 cash that night. That was the first money I made while traveling, and it felt good to go back up a bit after months of seeing my bank account go one way, like Jim Carrey falling down a hill. I just spent it on drugs though, because... *I earned it?*

ii. Old Drug Lady & Madison

Lake Atitlan had one famous drug dealer—an old woman who lived in a nice house. There was also a famous woman who sold bread. The bread lady walked around screaming, *"Pan de coco, pan de chocolate, pan de..."* all day long. She even had her own t-shirts on the lake. The drug lady was just an old woman whose house you could go visit for any drug you could imagine. A few of us from the hostel, including this girl Madison I just met, wanted ecstasy or molly, and we were directed to the old lady in the nice house by every local we asked about drugs.

On the way, we met a guy who told us he could take us. After following him for a bit, he said, "Let me help. I'll go get what you need from her." She had an intimidating reputation, so we were half-disappointed and half-relieved to not have to sit across from her. We waited in the sunshine on some steps, and ten minutes later the guy came back with some ecstasy pills, and we paid him the rest of what we owed. He most certainly got his cut of the profits as well, and we headed back to the hostel giddy that everything worked out.

A few hours later Madison and I were either laughing or making out. It was the most fun I'd ever had taking ecstasy up to that point in my life. I think I was just feeling so good because the drugs felt free after the gig, this girl seemed interested, and I was at my best. Golden nuggets and precious cherubs were falling out of my mouth. Everything I said resulted in laughter. That night, I wanted time to stretch and slow down and for the feeling to be permanent—I had found that feeling I was often chasing. Of course, the night ended, and the world-beating drug and "paid-musician" high quickly reached the end of its pendulum swing.

———

Madison moved out of the hostel for a homestay the day after our ecstasy-soaked giggle-and-make-out fest. I thought nothing of it because I always knew that was her plan, and homestays were common for backpackers hanging around Lake Atitlan as a way to commit to speaking more Spanish. I had the same plan myself. What did throw me off was her vibe whenever I saw her in passing over the next few days. She seemed a little cold, distant, like I was a telescope's view away from her despite being on the other side of the street.

Less than a week after our drug adventure and ensuing hilarity, I ran into her at a party at the one bar everyone ended up on Friday nights—it was that type of town. We were all drinking heavily and I was happy to see her. She introduced me to a guy that was staying at her homestay as well. I still thought nothing of it.

She continued being outwardly weird toward me, so I eventually asked her if we could go somewhere to chat. We walked off from the group, and I asked her, "What's going on? Didn't we have the best night ever together just a few days ago?" She told me, "Yeah, it was fun, but I met someone I'm really into."

It doesn't take a detective to figure out it was this younger, more handsome guy from her homestay. I wasn't in love with this girl, or anywhere even close. For some reason though, it really hurt. I dragged on the conversation in a longer, more painful way than I needed to. I wanted her to know this was *"not cool"* and to say *"what the fuck?"* multiple times.

Like most matters of the heart, it wasn't about Madison, or the short-lived relationship and all its budding potential. It was about me. It was a blow to the ego. It's human nature to want to be liked, and, since my childhood, I think I've fallen pretty far toward the *I-really-like-to-be-liked* side of that spectrum. I've always wanted my parents, teachers, friends, and even perfect strangers to like me. This girl was a perfect stranger, then someone with whom I shared a great night, and it hurt squarely on the ego that she chose to spend her time and swap her spit with some "bro" who seemed boring but was younger and more attractive. I reacted the way most normal guys would; I felt like shit, got aggressively drunk, then made out with someone else in a dark alley that night. One domino slowly tapping the next.

I kept cruising south through Guatemala, through Antigua to the temples of Tikal, and eventually I made it east to Belize. It was a small country and it was just, well, right there. *"Why not stop in?"* The plan was to pop over to Caye Caulker for just a few days; I had heard good things. The good things were spot-on, so I stayed, settled in, and began regularly sporting a lady's sailor-style one-piece swimsuit.

iii. Whatever Comes My Way

I checked into a hostel on Caye Caulker named Bellas; it looked like a house that was slowly expanded until it was big enough for a few bunk beds and could be called a hostel. I was home. The local guy who ran it—let's call him Darin—was a legend, and I knew on the first night that I would be staying longer than I had originally planned.

That first evening, there were about ten of us all drinking around a fire in the backyard that bumped up against the water, moon-light streaking towards the horizon. Someone handed me a guitar, and about five minutes and two average covers later the neighbors yelled over the fence to keep it down. I was about to shout "no worries" when Darin picked up a huge stick and was at the fence yelling back, "This is my fucking house, and my friends can play guitar if they want, so get some fucking earplugs if you don't like it—or just fucking join us! It's fucking Friday!" It was an artful mix of angry and nice, delivered with the energy of someone you weren't about to argue with.

We all confidently danced for hours on the wooden floorboards of the kitchen later that night as we traded off picking songs on an old school iPod. I ended up wearing a traditional-looking sailor-themed female one-piece swimsuit, complete with a sailor's hat. Drinking in that outfit, dancing in that kitchen, new friends all around, *"apple bottom jeans, boots with the fur"* in the air, I was thriving. Only days ago, I was in an ego-bruised, sad state, confused about a girl—but now I was Captain Fiesta in my sailor costume, pushing the party and ready to drink until the sun came up. Ready to yell at someone on the other side of the fence about any objection they might have.

The crew at Bellas became fast friends after several nights that mirrored the first, including more appearances of the sailor swimsuit, once even out on the town to the local reggae bar, complete with stripper pole. Two of the people at the hostel, my English mate Jack whom I'd met in Mexico and seen a few times over the previous month, and a Canadian girl named Jill, had the SAME FUCKING BIRTHDAY THAT WEEK! Jack and Jill. Same birthday. Same age. Randomly at the same hostel in Belize. The universe was conspiring for us to throw an epic party.

We went directly to the source—the small Belikin beer-bottling factory on the Island. We pooled our money and came back on a golf cart overloaded with bottled beers. Back at Bellas, we dragged the canoe from the water behind the hostel into the front yard, filled it with ice, and loaded 200-some beer bottles into the vessel. It looked awesome. It worked. We all felt like party geniuses. We even baked a cake and wrote "Jack and Jill" on it in shitty frosted lettering.

I was so at home at Bellas, so settled into the traveler lifestyle, and I felt important to the overall joyous and fun-as-fuck vibe at the hostel. I was carrying myself with more confidence and swagger than I had at any point previously in my travels or my life. I was the shooter who sees the ball go through and knows he won't miss when the next shot leaves his hand. I was the Mariachi band playing on the streets up to apartment-dwellers, without knowing the mood of or moment for the occupant, assuming blasting a trumpet will be well received and even optimistic that he'll get paid. That mariachi-shooter confidence might have been the reason why I ended up fooling around with multiple girls that week—three to be exact.

I'm not a very aggressive guy with women; I'm more of a "whatever comes my way" than a "baby, baby, baby, *HEY, baby...*" type of guy. I don't think I was particularly forward that week either; maybe it was the one-piece. Honestly, I know it was pure confidence. The idea is as old as time, but it's true. Women are attracted to someone who is "feeling themself"; not in a cocky way, in an authentic way. Most weeks I still have a bit of that, but this entire week it was like I'd eaten a Super Mario mushroom for swag, and it was drawing people toward me—some of whom were women.

I ended up in an all-too-familiar place on Caye Caulker, where I was in love with everything, but I knew, for the sake of my life, to be a human—I needed to leave. Like being deeply in love, travel expanded my spectrum for feeling, and I was living too much at the far ends.

––––––

I ran off with two hilarious and cute Canadian girls I'd met at Bellas a few days earlier to some other island nearby. I honestly don't even remember which. I started sleeping with one of the girls, and the other made me laugh no matter what she said, so we were a pretty perfect threesome (which never actually happened sexually, to be clear).

We cruised from the island to a small beach town, Placencia, in the South of Belize, famous for "the world's longest path." It was... long. *Whatever.* The sex started feeling a bit forced, and I felt anxious for something else. I had grown a reputation in my short time on Caye Caulker that I didn't want to have to live up to anymore. Travel can be a way to escape whatever past you might still have lingering around you, but, in this case, I had created enough of a reputation in a week that I wanted to run away. I didn't want to be in constant party mode, and I didn't know how to stop with these girls.

I don't remember exactly what happened my last few days in Belize, but I do remember buying a white and pink Hawaiian shirt at a thrift shop in Placencia. That exact shirt has since been written all over and, to the best of my knowledge, is still hanging on the wall at Skid Row, arguably the most famous bar in Central America. If you've ever traveled in Central America, you've no doubt seen a Skid Row tank top. The beautiful dive bar is on the island of Utila in Honduras, the place I would head next, the place I hung this shirt and accidentally ended up calling home for the next five months.

CHAPTER 8: UTILA

I knew I would end up on Utila, and I had been patiently waiting to get there to sign up for my open-water dive certification. It was one of the few plans I had in mind when I first flew into Mexico, because Utila is so well known for some of the best and cheapest diving in the world. It's also got a crazy history of how the island developed, involving tales of Captain Morgan, Robinson Crusoe, shipwrecks, lost treasure, and a wild mix of pirates pillaging and indigenous Hondurans. The history, tall tales, and characters of the island have given it a well-earned reputation.

Since the time that Captain Morgan was thought to be frequenting the island, Utila has become a backpackers' and scuba-divers' paradise. The main road that runs the entire bay of the lone populated side of the island is essentially organized like so: dive shop, dive bar, dive shop, dive shop, corner store, reggae bar, dive shop, restaurant, and so on. It's a unique place and home to some very interesting characters, several of whom I'll introduce you to.

My weeklong stop in Utila turned into a five-month stay pretty easily after the dive shop offered me a deal to go from open-water beginner to Divemaster—that was just too good to refuse. It also felt nice to have a tangible purpose in life again and to stay put somewhere. As soon as I made the decision, I was stoked, I felt at home, and I fully unpacked my bag for the first time in over six months of travel.

My five months on Utila was one of the best chapters of my life, but when I finally got on the ferry to leave, I never felt more like I was escaping from somewhere.

When I made it to land I felt like Leo at the end of The Beach when he's at the internet café and everything is so domestic, basic, and normal. Scenes from that previous Utila chapter of my life, flashing in my mind, triangulated between a bad dream, a hedonist fantasy, and actual, real life. I could have stayed. I could still be there. It would have been so fucking easy actually. The hardest part about Utila is leaving.

i. Self-Appointed Social Chair

Before I knew I would stay, Andrew, my roommate from Milwaukee the year before I left for the road, took his spring break from grad school to come and get SCUBA certified with me. We met two beautiful, young German girls—let's call them Greta and Betty, at the dive shop around the same time. There was also a whole motley crew at the dive shop, complete with cute blonde instructors, a goofy skipper, as well as the alpha-male head instructor and his beautiful, blonde girlfriend with huge, perfectly fake boobs. This is also where I met Dave, my lifelong dive buddy.

Dave was Canadian, and you could tell from your first conversation with him. A *"sowwry"* or *"oh yeah"* would slip out in his sandpaper-soaked voice, one perfected by Marlboro Red cigarettes and rum. He had sporadically-placed, incredibly random tattoos and a love for cocaine that I still haven't seen matched. He was the perfect dive partner and an even better island-wrecking partner, and we got along like brothers from the day we met. No expectation to be best friends, just a mutual understanding that we were.

Dave, the German girls and I were getting our Divemaster certifications at the same time. Without even realizing how important this detail was when I first agreed to stay, it led me to having yet another family abroad. They became home. Rebecca, the dive shop owner, hooked Dave and me up with a cheap two-bedroom, ocean-side apartment. I could spit into the ocean when I opened the front door. We had some amazing times at that apartment. There were also weird nights when the ongoing cocaine and alcohol binge felt more depressing than euphoric, but that's basically an analogy for my entire time on Utila.

I fell fast in love with diving and became privy to more underwater magic then I had ever realized existed. Plus, I started learning all the hilarious underwater sign language to point things out: "trumpetfish" (plays fake trumpet), "parrot fish" (covers eye, like a pirate patch), "a dolphin" (makes head fin with one hand then Adolph Hitler mustache with the other). I was diving twice a day most days. One of the perks of signing up was that I could dive as much as I wanted for free until I completed my mandatory 40 dives before starting the Divemaster course—the first level of becoming a professional diver.

I also had to complete the *Advanced Diving* and *Open Water Rescue* courses. Both were fun, and open water rescue was my favorite to later help out with; you basically get to cause chaos on a boat and fake-die in the most creative ways you can imagine while less-experienced divers try to "save you." Dave and I would always take lots of ketchup and random props with us when we helped with these classes.

––––––––

Along with diving twice daily, I became the self-appointed "social chair" of the dive shop. It wasn't a real role, but I just kept saying it, and eventually others did too—there's a useful secret trapped in there somewhere.

Underwater Vision, another dive shop on the island, had the reputation of being the Island's crazy-party dive shop. It was well-earned. I spent a lot of time at their shop and was close friends with a lot of Underwater Vision staff and divers in the end, but I wanted my shop—Bay Islands College of Diving, or BICD, to at least compete, to be in the conversation of *the most fun dive shop on Utila.*

We started throwing weekly "shop parties" in our alley next to BICD. I would charge the equivalent of $5 in the local currency for a plastic cup, and the alley would fill up with people drinking unlimited punch that we mixed with alcohol you could use as mosquito repellant. We'd gamble with dice, blast tunes *("apple bottom jeans… boots with the fur"),* and make a few hundred dollars for the ocean conservation NGO associated with our dive shop. It had the appearance of a greater purpose, but I was really just after the good times and the reputation that came with it. What would my nonprofit, Christmas-past ghost say?

When Easter came around that spring, I had cemented my role as "social chair"—which everyone still knew was a fake title. Either way, I decided to throw the island's first underwater Easter Egg hunt. I first did a home experiment to make sure hard-boiled eggs would sink—THEY DO! Then, on Easter morning, I boiled three dozen eggs, colored them, took a mask and fins, and jumped into the ocean behind the shop, holding my plastic bag of colorful eggs. I planted them all around our boat docks and piers—tucked under coral and rocks, surrounded by schools of fish. We had fifteen-some people turn up for the Easter Egg hunt, and it was competitive. It was awesome. I was earning my fake title.

I spent about a grand in total on the Divemaster certification. I was having a blast on the island but bleeding out financially. I spent money on "nose beers" (read: blow), some on actual beers, and a surprising amount on tequila in fifty-cent increments. Tequila Tuesday was a big deal on the island, and I don't think I missed a single week at Tranquila, a sprawling, ocean-side bar.

iii. Water Cay Wasted

I decided to look for work about six weeks into my time on Utila, and I ended up getting a gig at a bar called "Rehab." I've never entered an establishment with a more ironic name, let alone worked at one. The irony seems a bit on the nose, but the deeper irony was truly known only by those who worked there—who worked for Lee.

I'd never experienced alcoholism in the upfront, day-to-day way as I did working at Rehab. Lee's mood swings would shift dramatically from one hour to the next. He'd shove a $20 bill in my hand and tell me "You're keeping this place together, I'm so glad I've got you on the team." Then, an hour later, he'd see me tallying something in our notebook (very official accounting system) and say in a malicious, dark tone, barely able to open his eyes, "I know you're stealing from me, I'll catch you one of these nights." I'd have to talk him down and remind him that I'm a good guy, that *"I'm helping to hold this place together, remember?"* Ten minutes later, we'd be ripping Sambuca shots with the rest of the staff and he'd say, "You know I was just giving you shit man, you're doing a great job." Then he'd add in all seriousness, *"Just don't fuck with me."* That cycle could repeat for hours some nights, and it did repeat for months.

Two months into being on the island, I was feeling settled. I had local friends, a fun albeit weird job, I was playing on the island's soccer team, the one doctor—Dr. John—and I were tight, and I knew a couple of places to get drugs, including a takeout window at a burger joint. I could walk up and ask, "Puedo tener una hamburguesa de pollo y dos bolsas de cocaína." ("Can I have a chicken burger and two bags of blow?") I really knew I was home when, the day after a soccer game, the cute, older, corner-store lady who I got beers and snacks from said, "Ay, el gringo que puede jugar!" ("Hey, the gringo who can play!")

Also, Greta, one of the cute, young German girls who was also earning her Divemaster with BICD, and I were ending up in bed together most nights. We had a strong sexual connection, even though she was much younger and hotter than me. She looked like a German model, with a severe face, short blond hair, and a taut bikini body. She pursued me the first night, and I remember always feeling surprised that she would pursue me again the next. Then I would just feel pretty fucking happy about it laying in bed after having erotic morning sex.

At some point, we were a couple without ever really putting that label on it. She was always quick to point out, "We can do whatever we want," but that turned out to be each other pretty much every night. One weekend when I was working at Rehab, handling the average traffic with ease, slinging Salva Vidas (the local beer) and mixing basic cocktails, Dave pulled up to the bar to enjoy a dinner of rum-and-cokes-and-cocaine. He liked to hang at the bar when I worked, putting away drinks, burning smokes, and doing bumps in the bathroom every fifteen minutes or so. Together, we would egg drunk people on to do the shot challenge, where you simply had to drink five neon blue shots in ten seconds to get a tank top. "They taste great; *it's EASY,*" we were quick to reassure anyone. On this specific night, Dave was telling me he knew the German girls were out somewhere but that he couldn't get a hold of them. We were going to some late-night beach rave after I closed the bar, and we figured they were probably there; it was a small island. It was harder to avoid someone than to find them.

They were there, but Greta was with some other guy—dancing, making out, ignoring us entirely. I was a bit heated but more confused than anything, and Dave and I left the weird beach rave after twenty minutes. We ended up back at our place doing lines of blow on our little porch overlooking the ocean, Dave giving me a wasted pep talk—*"Fuck it, man. She's young and wasted. She doesn't know what she's doing. She'll apologize tomorrow."*

I ignored her for the next few days and tried to keep it out of mind, but she was indignant enough to be upset with me for ignoring her, claiming "I always said we could do what we wanted." She also told me that she had hooked up with this guy months ago and then he ended up on Utila. I responded with a cold, snarky, *"Cool, that explains it then doesn't it?"*

I carried on for about a week just trying to not end up in the same room as Greta, in a failed attempt to keep her out of mind. The dive shop ended up planning a weekend staff trip out to Water Caye—a small, private island off of Utila that has a single toilet, a couple of picnic tables, and is basically a vision of paradise. You could walk the entire perimeter in about fifteen minutes. It was my third time out to the island, so I knew the deal. Day drinking, day drugs, debauchery—it was fucking wonderful. There were some new people I didn't know on the trip, one of whom was a cute, flirty brunette from Canada who seemed to be hitting it off with Greta.

It was typical of these Caye parties for random people to end up making out, but, when I saw Greta and this brunette kiss, I can't say I wasn't intrigued—Greta had never mentioned any forays into experimenting with women. As the day went on, the drunker we got, Greta took a few steps away from "we can do what we want" towards apologizing. I think she missed me and was trying to say whatever she could to get us talking, to get our relationship back to what it was. She wanted to fuck this guy who visited, then she wanted to go back to fucking me.

After taking the boat back to land, we re-upped on some blow ("una hamburguesa de pollo y dos bolsas de cocaína, por favor"), and Greta had a proposal—a threesome. She said she had asked the frisky brunette, who was keen. I was still upset with Greta, unable to shake the image of her grinding and making out with this random dude only a week earlier, and I saw exactly what she was doing with this tempting offer. So I said, *"NO WAY! NOT AFTER WHAT YOU DID!"*

Just kidding, I had my first legit threesome that night. It was fucking awesome.

———

I spent my months on Utila diving, doing drugs, eating egg-and-cheese baleadas, working at Rehab, and getting to know the locals. There was Lee from Rehab, whom you've met. There was Web, a skinny, tanned, and high-energy older guy who used to be a minor-league pitcher years ago but was now known for the hot sauce he made at home, bottled in empty coke bottles, and sold to every restaurant on the island. He would stand at the main pier when new ferries of divers and travelers unloaded, screaming, "Welcome to HELL!" and laughing in a low, demonic growl. We played a lot of pool together at Skid Row, and he almost always won.

There was also Dr. John who was, in my opinion, by far the most legendary and interesting figure on the island. He was, in fact, a doctor—the only one on the island. He also had a huge bag of cocaine on him at all times, which, once you were friends with him, he would offer you a bump out of from the end of a pair of skinny medical scissors. Then he'd nod to you in his cowboy hat and jump his eyebrows up and down before doing an even bigger bump himself.

One night, Dave and I ended up at the doctor's house, which was tucked back into the jungle, a ten-minute amble from the main drag. It was half-museum, half-house, full of jars of dead things in formaldehyde and taxidermy creatures hanging from the wall. He was a mad man but in the best possible way—unpredictable, gregarious, smart, fun as fuck, and a genuine wild card. He embodied Utila better than any single person I met on the island. There's a famous story of Dr. John doing blow while

91

operating on a bullet wound. The guy who got shot lived. The legend of Dr. John grew.

iii. Halliburton Fame

My legend on Utila pales in comparison to Dr. John's, but I did depart Utila feeling like I left a bit of a legacy. It all started the first time we dove on the Halliburton, the single shipwreck of Utila. It was about three weeks into my time on the island as part of our advanced training, and, upon surfacing, I told Dave "I'm going to poop the Halliburton." He knew exactly what I meant.

The Halliburton, being the only shipwreck, became a significant sight, one where people who spent time on Utila would often leave something behind before leaving. There were bikes, laptops, personal artifacts, and other knickknacks scattered about on the deck of the boat, most heavily saturated in the captain's bay. Someone had also left a perfect white toilet exactly on the bow of the boat, just sitting at the very tip—it was asking for it.

Every time I dove the Halliburton over the next four months I would make the joke, *"I'm going to poop the Halliburton."* I didn't really believe it myself; it was just fun to say. One night, toward the end of our Divemaster training, we organized a staff dive, where the whole crew was going to go on a night dive together. We decided to do a night, shipwreck, deep-dive—*all three things*. As we were gearing up, Dave passed me a scandalous look and said, "Dude, this is your chance. No fucking customers around." I knew exactly what he meant.

My joke, my ludicrous dream, finally had the chance to become reality. As we took a small skiff out, loaded with ten close friends and co-workers, word got out that I was thinking of actually doing it, of pooping the Halliburton. Everyone was in unanimous agreement: This was my time, and I had to do it.

Luckily, I did sort of have to poop.

Upon descending, we were all giggling, and I was already taking off my trunks. I floated majestically down onto the toilet, Dave my eternal dive buddy behind me, supporting, spotting. The rest of the staff formed a semi-circle in front of me—GoPros running.

We chatted on the boat before the dive about what would happen if I did it: Would it float up, would it stay, would it be eaten by fish immediately? As I squeezed out this perfect poop twenty meters below sea level, one of life's great mysteries was answered—my poop sat there in the toilet perfectly. It was beautiful. We all sign-language cheered and then carried on with the dive, getting naked, riding the rusty bike around underwater, and generally just being weird as fuck together, in the way that a close group of friends earns with time and shared experience.

Back on the boat after we resurfaced, it was a full-on celebration. I felt like I had just accomplished something in life that I had always aimed for, like completing a doctorate or publishing my first book. You know how people have their life bucket list but then do something that wasn't on it, decide it should have definitely been on that list all along, then add it after it's done just so they can tick it off. That was this. I added and then ticked pooping twenty meters underwater on a sunken ship to the joy and amazement of my friends.

———

The next afternoon, I was working at Rehab, still glowing from my poop. Two twenty-something Canadian women were talking at the bar right in front of me. One mentioned she did the Halliburton dive that morning.

Go on.... I thought.

"My instructor and I were at the front of the boat and noticed something in the toilet."

Oh did you, go on... I begged her in my mind.

"We couldn't tell what it was. It looked like a sea cucumber, but my Divemaster didn't think it was a sea cucumber."

No fucking way. At this point, I was holding back from bursting with laughter so I just leaned over to them and whispered, "It was me who done it. *It was my poop."*

I told them the story. Others at the dive shop started telling the story as well, and within a few days I had my fifteen minutes of Utila fame. It actually lasted until I left the island, and maybe if I went back they would still remember. Maybe there's a statue—my stocky bronze body bent over on a toilet, air tank on my back, fully naked from the waist down, grimacing fiercely, trying desperately to squeeze out a turd and not to let my friends down.

Anyway, for a bit, after nearly 30 years on earth, I was best known as the guy who pooped on the Halliburton. My parents would be so proud of their sons: Austin, the successful lawyer in New York clerking for a federal judge, and Travis... "Well, *he pooped the Halliburton!"*

iv. Snorkel Test

To complete your Divemaster—the divers out there reading this already know—there is the long-standing and universal tradition of the "snorkel test," which is how you *officially* finish your Divemaster. Different parts of the world and different dive shops do it in their own ways (Underwater Visions' version involves a whole kinky show of rescue scenarios and taking in a beer through the nostrils with a scuba mask on), but most at least encourage (read: force) their new Divemasters to put on a snorkel and mask, then ingest through their mouth whatever is put down the snorkel. It's also just a great excuse for a big ole ragin' party.

We had ours on the roof of the dive shop, and the staff decided that Dave and I would go last. We watched our European buddies go—*it didn't look too fun.* We watched Greta and Betty go—*they hated it,* but they did it. Then it was our turn. We were told many times leading up to our moment at center stage that the staff were saving us for last because they were going to be ruthless.

I strapped on the mask, sat next to Dave on the bar, and slapped him on the thigh, looking into his eyes through the dirty mask, as we could hear all the staff clinking bottles and giggling behind us. The first thing I tasted was whiskey, followed by a cacophony of fucked-up, unplaceable flavors.

There was Rum.

Warm Beer.

More whiskey.

Creamed corn.

Vodka.

Hot sauce.

A raw egg?

Beer.

Baked beans.

Whiskey again.

Hotter hot sauce.

Pineapple Juice.

Rum and *spaghetti sauce?*

It felt like it wouldn't stop. I physically held my snorkel in my mouth and just kept swallowing whatever ended up in there as it rushed down the snorkel towards my throat. It was brutal but lasted all of one minute, and, when it was over, the cheering drowned out the shit taste in my mouth—I was three times as drunk and getting hugged by everyone. I played my trumpet fish, wore my pirate fish eye-patch, did some blow like a blowfish, and let the booze begin to work its dark magic.

An hour later, I ended up behind the bar at Rehab (even though I wasn't meant to be working), shirt off, suspenders and a bow-tie drawn on my chest with a permanent marker, blacked out from booze, wide awake from blow, feeling like a hero. Everyone at the bar was stoked for me. It was the end of months of learning theory, passing technical diving tests, and hard work, and I was officially done—*I was officially a Divemaster.*

I skipped over a lot of the hard-core diving stuff, but I should say BICD takes the theory and technical sides of the diving super seriously, and it wasn't an easy feat. The full underwater equipment exchange with another person and only one oxygen tank is no joke. I earned that certification and partied accordingly.

We were ripping shot after shot of Sambuca at the bar, and I was a Divemaster, I was the guy who pooped on the Halliburton, I was the guy who helped to manage Rehab, and I was back in that Mario Brothers Mushroom mode for the night—overflowing with booze, blow, and confidence.

One of the girls at the bar was feeling me too and was not shy in letting me know. I had lost track of Greta, but she knew I was at Rehab "helping out." I ended up making out with this girl in a very blacked-out state. I could hear Greta echoing, *"We can do whatever we want,"* in my mind, and, at that moment, making out with this girl was what I wanted. Thirty minutes later, fucking her in her bunk bed back at a random dive shop was also apparently what I wanted.

I found out later that Greta had come looking for me at Rehab after I left, and that she found out the story from some other people (Greta had been on Utila a long time as well and had plenty of friends on the island); when the sun rose the next morning, she was not alright with it. I reminded her that about a month prior she'd fucked some other guy and told me I was acting childish for being upset about it, but that didn't seem to matter. I told her that, had she never done that, I never would have done this, which I still think is true. Our relationship wasn't based on celibacy and trust, so I let myself act out of character, guilt-free.

She thought things were different since we had gotten back together. Maybe they were to her, I still don't know. I'd never cheated on any girlfriend in my life, and I still didn't feel like I had, but this was definitely kicking at that line in the sand. Needless to say, Greta hated me. She didn't speak to me my last week on the island, and things just generally felt off. Dave, the two German girls and I were now a foursome. Greta and I had been thick as thieves, best buds who happened to sleep together a lot. She never admitted that she had real feelings for me and still never has; looking back was how I found out, by ruining it I learned her true feelings.

———

Our relationship never recovered, and to this day she won't respond to me on Facebook. It was time to leave the island. Divemaster accomplished, island fever sinking in, and my most important relationship outside of Dave ruined, I needed to rinse off the all-too-easy drug habit, adultery vibes, and hedonist life that I had come to love.

From the summers I worked as a camp counselor to my years running after-school programs for kids, one of my top youth-work mantras was always, *"End everything while it is still fun."*

If you're playing kickball with a group of ten-year-olds and after an hour the kids start saying, "Can we do something else, we've been playing kickball forever…," the next time you toss out the idea of playing kickball their reaction will likely be lukewarm. But if you end kickball thirty minutes into it to unanimous pleas of *"NO, it's a tie game, let us play 10 more minutes!"* imagine the difference in their reaction when they find kickball on the schedule the following week.

I've realized that everything in life is like this, and I've tried pretty hard to make sure I end every chapter knowing that when I look back, my memories will be rose-colored and the sentimental good feelings will far outweigh any other feelings that were real at the time. Utila was the one place in my life I got dangerously close to crossing that threshold.

I still look back at Utila as an amazing adventure, a time when I accomplished something important, when I first got intimate with the underwater world, and when I got lost on a tropical island full of booze, drugs, and fascinating characters. I definitely almost got too lost, but I managed to end it while it was still fun—just in the nick of time.

CHAPTER 9: BRISTOL BAY, ALASKA

I flew back from Honduras to the States and was back under my parents' roof in late-May. It felt weird—like it had never happened. Nothing had seemingly changed; I was back to being a Wisconsin boy watching SportsCenter on his parents' couch. Without blow in my pocket or at the chicken stand down the street (maybe they were slingin' out of Bruegger's Bagels, but I never asked), I didn't even consider it. In fact, cocaine rarely crossed my mind at home, and when it did, only as a relief somewhere in the middle of SportsCenter's Top 10. *Good thing I don't have a serious cocaine problem.* I wouldn't know how to get cocaine in Milwaukee if I wanted to, which is still true to this day. Turns out that with enough whiskey and weed grown by scientists, it didn't matter one bit. When in Rome, when in Utila, when in Indonesia, when in Wisconsin, when in college; all call for different vices. The key is to always count your vices on one hand. If you have to take off your shoes, you're in real murky waters.

I had a rough plan to leave Utila sometime in May and head to Alaska for the summer well before things took a sad turn with Greta and I started to feel like I had to leave for my own sanity. I met a few guys on Utila who did the seasonal pilgrimage up to the 49th state: They would make money fishing and then travel for the rest of the year. The conversations piled up, and I started to draw a mental image of myself in Alaska—my backpack and a cool winter beanie on, tucked between two huge glaciers, moose, elk, and wolves all wearing knockoff Ray Bans scattering the scenery, money falling from my pockets. I'm wearing the knock-off Ray Bans in my mental picture too, shooting finger guns.

If three people recommend the same book to me in a given month, I'll always read it. I had never daydreamed about or really even considered visiting the biggest state in the union, but I didn't have a plan for how to make more money. As the random fishing conversations piled up, it felt like the universe was whispering *check out the Alaska book.*

After getting off the Utila ferry on mainland Honduras, Dave, a few other friends and I took a short trip inland up the Cangrejal River where we spent a few nights and went on an epic whitewater rafting trip. It was nice to be reminded within a day that there were plenty of adventures to be had outside of Utila. Life existed outside of the island. I was like a New Yorker finding it hard to believe things exist beyond Manhattan.

I told my folks the plan I had conjured up to go to Alaska, and at this point in my travels my stepmom Sue was pretty supportive, but my Dad feigned support and not so subtly hinted toward a general concern about my life choices. I'm sure he thought his hints were subtle, but they weren't. My stepmother had helped ease this dynamic from early on in their relationship, even before they got married; joining our two families and giving me new siblings in Charlie and Claire the summer before I started high school.

A year before they married, the summer after my seventh grade year, 10 of my closest friends and I wanted to do bad things and try adult stuff, so we took one cigarette into a circle of trees behind our local Walgreens. After we each took two puffs and coughed three times, four police officers arrived on the scene. They took our information as we all cried. We ran home to our parents and admitted our sins, snot and spit covering our faces. The cops never called, knowing exactly what we would do, knowing the snot-dripping confessions were inevitable. My father, after he finally calmed down, wanted to ground me for two months—the remainder of the summer. Sue, a high school guidance counselor, convinced him that trying and disliking a cigarette was completely normal for a 12 year old, and that two weeks was a punishment that better fit the crime. He was not being a *flow-meister*, but he ultimately deferred to Sue's expertise on the topic. It was not the last time he'd worry about what his two sons' decisions meant about their respective futures.

———

Back under their roof, he would frequently change gears in a conversation about politics in Wisconsin or the Green Bay Packers' wide receiver depth with, "So Trav, what's next for you after all of these travels?" or "Where do you see this all leading?" or "Have you ever thought about being a pharmacist?" (again, one of the more surprising ones) or my personal favorite, "Do you know what the difference is between a job and a career?" When I would jump in and say sarcastically, *"Well yes father, a job is something you do just for money and a career..."* he would start laughing and say, "Well, at least you've been listening to me! Always wear your seat belt, *haha hohoho!"*

Throughout high school and college, "What if you were dead in a ditch?" is a question my Dad would always ask if I hadn't checked in for some time. I would coyly respond with a smirk, "Dad, you'll be the first one they call when I'm found dead in a ditch, don't worry." With my mom's passing, I fully understood his protective nature and his worrywart mentality, but I decided to push back. Growing up under the care of a parent who worries a lot, who looks at the unknown with suspicion and unease as opposed to optimism and positivity, there are two things you can do: follow suit and let the world scare you, or decide that you won't.

Of all the qualities that make someone a "good traveler" in my view, general optimism has to be the top one. On a true trip, the unplanned type with no return flight, there are countless unknowns every day. The way you perceive those unknowns is the number one thing that will not only set your mood, but also play a huge role in dictating how everything turns out, how each story and adventure is ultimately remembered, told and then used to shape your identity over time.

Was it a hectic, unorganized day and you were stressing to figure things out while a sketchy guy tried to rip you off? Or was it an unplanned, serendipitous miracle of a day during which a wonderful stranger sorted you out and things fell into place the way they were always meant to— PERFECT! Embracing the unknown, not worrying if everything will work out, dealing with things that go wrong when they go wrong instead of worrying about them beforehand—that is key. Simply put, in the famous words of J.K. Rowling, *"Worrying just means you suffer twice."*

While we're on the subject, another thing that ranks near the top of my list of qualities that make a happy traveler is simply having the ability to wait well. On any type of adventure, you'll undoubtedly spend hours just waiting for things. I keep a plethora of podcasts downloaded, books on my Kindle, and movies on my hard drive at all times, and not only do I not mind waiting—*I enjoy it.* In line for customs I'm listening to a riveting tale on This American Life, on a bus I'm immersed in a Kurt Vonnegut classic, and waiting for a ferry to arrive I listen to the new Nahko and Medicine for the

People album while doing a ten-minute stretching routine. A few hours before my flight takes off, I sit down to write. I like to make good use of my time, and a lot of it is trapped in travel purgatory on the road, so I might as well let the hosts of Radio Lab occupy my headspace with the newest on CRISPR cloning technology instead of begrudging the thirty people in front of me waiting in line to get through security. I don't love every part of a fifty-hour travel weekend, but I'm generally happy, at peace, and well entertained throughout it.

Pro tip: A.B.C. Always be charging. All of the devices, downloads, apps and maps are only as good as their battery life.

For my first year on the road, I deflected all of my Dad's life questions with my chorus of "one more trip," until that felt almost like a polished comedic routine we had.
"*Alright, you've had some fun but when are you going to get a 'real job,' Trav?*"
"As soon as you take a trip out of the country old man… *heyyyyoooo!*"
"*Ohhhhh, you always were funny!*"
Then my entire family would chime in with *"Don't say jelly donut!"* I guess you have to be in my family to get that part.

————

Even though we were always incredibly close, this comedic dialogue started to carry weight, and, when we weren't joking about it, the real conversation that had gone unsaid hung in the air like a stale elephant-in-the-room fart. Finally, we had it out once on a cruise along Lake Drive, headed from the city back to our family house on the north shore. It was the heaviest and most important conversation we'd had in years, but it mattered.

While driving down the tiger-striped street, the burnt-orange street lights illuminating Lake Drive in an artful pattern, I asked my Dad if he would ever doubt my life choices if I was married with two kids, working a job I didn't love to support a family, and living in a house in the suburbs that I owned. I was describing a lot of the people I grew up with. People I am still close with.

He was taking a rare moment of silence and reflection thinking about the question, so I just kept going. "People who are locked into tons of life commitments like houses and families and serious jobs are probably the people you should be asking if they're okay, Pops. That's all pretty serious. It's pretty heavy. My life is light as a feather, and I feel free. I'm happier than I could have ever imagined, and I'm no longer worried about *figuring it all out.* I'm more concerned with enjoying the ride. I'm not sure how long this travel portion of the ride will be, but even if it's eight years, that's still only 10% of my whole life if I make it to 80."

His prolonged silence and a sense of momentum allowed me to pile it on, "I'm sorry to say, Dad, but I don't really give a shit what you say about me to your neighbors at your next dinner party. Sorry I'm not a sexy conversation-starter or that you're not proud to share what I'm doing with my life like you are with Austin, but I'm happy as fuck. You should be happy for me. You should be proud that you raised a son who can travel the world and make connections and figure it out as he goes and come home with stories and friends from different corners of the world. I need to chase my own definition of success, to find my own purpose, and I'm sorry if it doesn't match yours, or if it doesn't match your whole generation's or society's in general. But I just can't care what you tell the Shuters about me when you're out to dinner with them. That can't be part of how I decide what to do next or which direction my life should go."

Without his saying anything, I could tell by his face that he agreed with me. He knew what I was saying was true. He loved me and supported me no matter what I did, and I think he just needed to know that I was good— that I would be good. I was going to do my own thing, and I needed him to stop worrying even more than I do about what I was doing with my life.

I kept going as he thought about it all, tears welling in his eyes, hands at ten and two, driving the car exactly at the speed limit. "You raised a good man, now please let me do this. Let me live an unconventional life full of foreign people and places—it'll all work out, and you won't lose your suburban friends over it, *I swear*. Also, I'll bring you back cool stuff from other places, so everyone wins, Pops!"

It took this conversation for him to realize that "Go out and make yourself interesting," one of his most constant refrains throughout my childhood, was exactly what I was doing. I was trying my best to take his advice and make him proud, and I was incredibly happy doing it, except for the one missing piece—I needed his support.

Toward the end of the drive, he said something that resembled, "You know I love you more than anything. I just want what's best for you, that's all," as he wiped tears from his cheeks with the puffy beige sleeve of his Lands' End jacket. I gave him a sideways hug as we pulled into the driveway, and I kissed him on the temple before softly teasing him in his ear, "You'll be the first one they call when I'm found dead in a ditch in Thailand, Dad. Don't worry."

i. Girdweed

The week I spent at home, I found myself googling "fishing jobs Alaska" and just casting prayers into the internet through my fingertips. I had zero experience, I didn't particularly like recreational fishing, and I had no connections. I was experienced with "boats" and having the Divemaster and water-rescue certifications felt like something, but I was essentially grasping at internet straws.

I ended up buying a flight to Anchorage with the idea that I would get settled then start asking around and simply will myself into employment. I had this romantic vision of myself "walking the docks" where fishing boats would be waiting for a young, fit, eager worker with zero experience to approach them. This doesn't exist, it turns out, so I'm fortunate I got an email from Bill through AlaskaJobFinder.com just three days before leaving Wisconsin.

I had replied to a post Bill made about needing a crew. I sent a lot of messages in the week I was home, so I had forgotten about this specific one, but it was the first time I actually got a response.

My actual email:

I saw your job posting on Alaska Job Finder and I wanted to email to see if you are still looking for a deckhand. I just returned home to Milwaukee four days ago from Utila, Honduras, and I will be flying into Anchorage this coming Friday. In the posting, I saw you wanted the crew member there by the 21st of the month, which would be no problem for me. I have experience as a deckhand on a diving boat because I just completed my Divemaster course and have been working on a boat for the last couple of months. I have a letter from my captain that can confirm this.

I don't have experience commercial fishing, but I am a very hard worker, I pick things up quickly, I am a positive and friendly co-worker, and I would be more than willing to do any sort of dirty work asked of me. I've done a fair amount of jobs that are physically demanding—from tree planting and gutting houses to biking customers around on a rickshaw—and I am very confident I could handle the rigors of working on a fishing boat. I attached my resumé and a photo so you can get a better idea of who I am and what I have been doing. I hope this email finds you well, and I hope there's a chance we can talk about working together this summer.

Hope this finds you well,
Travis

Bill wrote back:

I still have one opening for my Bristol Bay Gillnetter for the 2013 season. Your resumé looks good. I'm interested in what practical skills or abilities you have as they relate to a commercial fishing vessel, i.e., cooking, boat handling, any water time, EMT training, working in a confined environment. I also need job references I can contact. I'm attaching a job manual for you to look at, which also has a sample employment contract I use. I will have to make a decision before the end of the week since the season is only two weeks away, so please respond ASAP.

Thank you,
Bill B.

I officially got the job through a few more exchanges the day before I got on my flight to Anchorage. I was ecstatic. I was going to Alaska determined to make some money and have an adventure either way, so it was so nice to know the first few steps of my plan.

Make it to Bristol Bay.

Find Bill.

Learn how to be a commercial fisherman.

I arrived in Alaska about ten days before I had to meet Bill in Bristol Bay, so I found a hostel in Anchorage and started my summer as an Alaskan. The thing that was most striking the day I arrived is that the sun just doesn't set. I went out partying with some people I met at the hostel, and going outside at one in the morning drunk on whiskey to a perfectly bright sky is a weird reality. The sky eventually got dark blue, never fully black, and then just started getting brighter again. It was unnerving and a constant reminder of where I physically was on the globe.

After a few days in Anchorage, and a few conversations with folks more knowledgeable than myself, I decided to head south. I had enough time before my fishing gig to explore the Kenai Peninsula, a well-traveled area of Alaska, including two big tourist towns of Seward and Hobart. I first stopped in Girdwood, an hour south of Anchorage, which the locals call "Girdweed" (for good-reason). I remember watching game six of the Heat vs. Spurs NBA finals where Ray Allen drilled the corner three to keep the Heat's season alive. Then I somewhat remember getting extremely high with a dude I met at the bar, who one sentence after our opening exchange asked, *"You smoke weed?"*

I ended up stoned at a random campsite in town, attempting to hang my brand-new camping hammock that had a built-in bug net. I treasured it. I found some random ropes—I had brought my own carabineers—

identified a couple of perfectly spaced trees and proceeded to expertly tie it up.

I lied down to test my handiwork, one of the carabineers immediately gave out, and I crashed down hard to the pine-needle-covered-earth. I laughed at myself, stoned as fuck, rolling around in the pine-scented dark trapped in my hammock for a good while, before finding the zipper and crawling out for a more successful second attempt. I slept sparingly that first night, then spent my second night in a little hostel. After two nights in this 2000-person town, I decided to walk out of Girdwood to the main highway that heads south toward Seward. The plan was to hitchhike. *If I could do it in Ecuador, I could certainly do it in Alaska*, I reassured myself. I was also told by many Alaskans that hitchhiking was part of the culture and practiced by both travelers and locals alike across their huge, sprawling state.

I had a little fold-up Crazy Creek camping chair with me at the time, so I got to the edge of the road right near a little gas station at the entrance to Girdwood, settled in my little camping chair, sipped my gas station coffee, and stuck my thumb out. It almost immediately started raining, like a scene from every Ben Stiller movie where things just go wrong for him. I put on my raincoat and continued with my plan. Someone would stop, I was certain. I spent the next hour getting rained on, thumb out, periodically taking shelter under the gas station covering giving myself pump-up speeches. *Come on Trav, don't wimp out—someone will stop!* After about an hour and a half, I told myself ten more minutes and then I would call it and head back up the road to Girdwood and check back into the same hostel, soaking wet, having nothing to show for my misery or morning.

As I sat in the chair, counting down the minutes to quitting, right around ten minutes, right as I was ready to fold up the chair and kick rocks all the way back to Girdwood, I looked down into the grass to my right and saw a fresh rolled-up dollar bill that had been there the whole time, hiding in the wet green grass. I picked it up.

But it wasn't a dollar bill—it was a ONE HUNDRED DOLLAR BILL! At this point in my travels, with less than $1,000 in my bank account, $100 was a huge deal. I felt like the entire last week of my life was free. I held the wet bill up with two hands howling and laughing as it rained on my head. I would have looked like a fully insane person to someone watching at a distance.

Moments after I found the money, I was still laughing like a lunatic as a truck pulled over near me, and a friendly, fat, bearded man stuck his head out, saying, "I'm headed to Seward if you want a lift." I yelled back, *"I JUST FOUND 100 DOLLARS!"*

I loaded my backpack into his truck, and we peeled off. The rain also stopped shortly after we got moving, and blue skies unfurled ahead—a soaking wet $100 bill was drying on the dash, and I was a happy salmon. Only five minutes before, I was poor, wet, and on the verge of just giving up on my plans for making it anywhere other than my dorm room in Girdwood before finding Bill and starting work.

I told my ride, let's call him Rick, how I appreciated him stopping in the rain as we started driving, and the story about finding the 100 dollar bill. He said, "Well, it's your lucky day." He asked me what I was doing in Alaska, so I told Rick about the email exchange with Bill and how I was going to be a commercial fisherman in about a week, but didn't really have any idea what I was getting into. I told him I didn't even know what a gillnetter fishing boat was. He just laughed and said, "Well, son, it sure is your lucky day. I was a gillnet fishing captain for ten years. I can tell you all about it."

The next two hours, as beautiful mountains and glaciers rolled by outside the windows of Rick's truck, he taught me about commercial fishing, all the gear I would need, how making sure my hands stay healthy is important because for hours at a time you're popping fish out of these long nets by their gills.

"Udder butter is the key to keeping your hands from getting all mangled and cut up, that's the trick, son. You can't put too much udder butter on there."

He schooled me on fishing culture and what it's like to be on the water for a month straight. That gillnetting simply meant you catch the salmon by their gills in the net, then, as deckhands, we pop them free one by one as the net is slowly reeled back onto the boat. That would be most of my work. I was stoked. I now knew what my job was, and for the first time I could picture myself as a commercial fisherman (still in my knockoff Ray Bans shooting finger guns). I was pretty confident I would be an excellent fish-gill-net-popper, as long as I just kept the udder butter on hand.

ii. Kenai Peninsula

Once I got to Seward, I checked into a strange, homey, little hostel, threw my bags on my pink sheets and did some exploring. I ended up walking down one long, beautiful dirt road along Resurrection Bay built into the side of the mountain. I didn't know it at the time, but it was a road and a bay that I would come to know extremely well in the second half of my Alaskan adventure. The road led to Miller's Landing, a fishing, camping, and kayak guiding adventure camp.

I spent the next few days exploring the Kenai Peninsula. I hiked Marathon Mountain and walked on Exit Glacier. I met up with some new friends from the hostel in Anchorage who ended up joining me as we camped out along the way to Hobart.

Hobart is the absolute end of the peninsula and proudly claims to be "a quaint drinking town with a fishing problem." I wanted a feel for the local culture, so I stopped at the famous Salty Dog Saloon and had a Miller High Life with a dollar shot of whiskey. The Salty Dog is the kind of establishment where you can smell the character in the wood of the rafters. It's the kind of place that was the setting for some of the best stories you'll never know. Most of the ceiling and walls of the Salty Dog are covered with dollar bills. I took one out of my wallet, and the bartender tossed me a marker. I wrote "Utila -> Wisconsin -> Alaska" across the bottom of it and the obligatory *"GO PACK GO!"* across the top.

Halibut became my favorite fish to eat that summer, but they look weird as fuck. They are giant flounders that live on the ocean floor. The ocean's oriental rugs. One of their eyes actually migrates around to whichever side of the fish ends up being "the top." The largest Halibut caught in Alaska history weighed 459 pounds to give you a sense of the size of these expensive dinosaur fish. Also, for some reason, their cheeks are delicious; they cost a premium, but they're worth it.

I didn't recreationally fish in Hobart—the main reason people visit this small town at the far end of the peninsula—but I watched the guys who process the fish for a long time. Most of their work was cutting up 100-300 pound halibut, then taking the fleshy white meat off the bone to be sold, shipped and eaten all over the world. One of the guys working a knife started chatting me up, seeing my warranted interest in the ancient, deep-sea fish he was carving.

He told me that he lived in Halibut Cove, pointing across the water to what looked like wild mountains, rather than a town. Halibut Cove, he went on to explain, was a very small town at the base of the mountains across a wide expanse of deep water, a boat ride away from Homer, with a population of less than 100 people. Here I was, thinking I was at the end of the Earth, only to have a further end-point pointed out to me, one so removed it wasn't even connected by roads. I wondered what the people in Halibut Cove would point to, as the further off, smaller, stranger, more authentic Alaskan town. Was there a shanty town of ten bearded old men deep in the mountain who ate off the land? Would they point further on towards an old, leaning cabin, deeper into the folds of the mountain, occupied by one lonely man, beard to the forest floor, eating a raw fish with his bare hands, totally naked? *Was there an end to this?* Alaska, in so many ways, felt like a one-ups-manship of ruggedness, self-sufficiency, and becoming one with the land. I never asked the knife-wielding fisherman what lay beyond Halibut Cove.

———

My week of adventure was up, and after hitching another ride and paying for a bus, I found myself back in Anchorage eating all the cheese I could handle at a pilot-themed pub that was famous for serving unlimited cheese from a gigantic block right on the bar. I consumed a day's worth of calories in twenty minutes.

From Anchorage I flew into Naknek, Alaska, the gateway town to Bristol Bay and the mecca of salmon fishing. My small plane was filled with fishermen exclusively. It was the only reason to fly into Naknek, outside of maybe bear hunting or something else *super* Alaskan.

A lot of things I learned about Alaska are super Alaskan, and they deeply etched their way into my memory. One is that the state is so large that only one-quarter of it is accessible by road; the rest is just wild nature and you need an airplane to see it. Because of that, Alaska has about 15 times more pilots licenses per capita than the contiguous United States. During the first jog I went on in Anchorage, I ended up circling Lake Hood, which is lined with small, two-to-four passenger prop planes that take off from the lake to all corners of Alaska. Hundreds of planes flown by normal, working-class people, so the folks who know the land best can go visit parts still untouched by man.

There is also something that kept happening during my summer there when interacting with folks. Locals, people who had earned their "Alaskan" title, would ask me what I was doing. I would say, "I'm here for the summer, working as a deckhand on a gillnetter," and they would each respond, "So, you've never done a winter up here?" When I would answer no, they would laugh, shake their heads, and say, "Well *then you don't know Alaska, son.*" Winter was coming, *always*, and you could see people preparing for it even in the heart of the summer. Surviving a dark, long, cold winter in Alaska was something wholly different than enjoying its beautiful, never-ending-day summer. I didn't earn my official "Alaskan" title with a summer of work, but maybe it was for the best. I'm pretty competitive, and if I stayed longer than the season, maybe I'd end up as the bearded, naked man eating fish raw, yelling at no one and everyone *"you don't know Alaska!!!"*

iii. Fishing Man

When I arrived in Naknek, I had no idea where to go. I had the name of our boat, and I knew my captain's name was Bill, but that was it. I was directed by some seasoned fishermen toward the boat yards and given some vague idea of where a "new boat" was likely to be. I knew that "sockeye.net" (futuristic name, right?!) was brand-new based on our email exchanges, so I wandered through the yards, looking for shiny, virgin boats, scanning their names. The boats were all propped up on blocks or trailers and looked huge and out of place in the dusty open field—like fish out of water.

I finally stumbled up to a shining, silver boat, about twelve meters long and five meters wide, and I found the name "sockeye.net" freshly printed on the side. I called up, "Hello, Bill... *you there?*" An old man popped his head out of the window with a friendly, "And you must be Travis."

I met the other two deckhands, Cory from Oregon and Ricky from Miami. Cory was in his mid-20s and a low-key, camouflage wearing, ATV riding, "good ol' boy" type of fella. I liked him right away, and I knew we would get on just fine. Ricky was a shirtless, 18-year-old hotshot kid from Miami with an eight pack and gelled hair. He made up for his lack of height by making sure his abs were always flexed, and he also had an answer for every single question that was ever asked—regardless of whether he was the one being asked or if he even knew what the fuck he was talking about. If I asked Cory what Oregon was like, Ricky would start answering.

We had two days to get the boat, nets, and food prepped for four weeks on the water. Cory and I deferred to Bill on everything and just constantly asked what we could do to be helpful. Ricky just did shit, half of which was the opposite of helpful. The day before launch, I was holding a small Swiss-army knife and popping the string ties that held a massive net together, one of our three nets, like a scrunched slinky. I knew how important it was to cut only the ties, not the net, and was therefore moving slow and being very careful.

Ricky thought he had a better way to do this, so he reached down at the net as I was cutting a tie. The knife popped a tie loose, then jumped right into Ricky's hand. He didn't need stitches, but he was bleeding pretty badly while also trying to blame me: "What the fuck, man?!" Before I could decide to apologize or yell at him, both Bill and Cory, who were outside watching the whole thing, jumped in saying, "What the fuck were YOU doing, Ricky? He's holding a knife and he was doing that just fine without your help, man!"

That was the start of my relationship with Ricky—I stabbed him. That was the only time, but I thought about stabbing him many more times after that.

We got the boat stocked with all types of food and gear, tucked away into all the hidden corners of the boat such that not a single square foot was wasted, and finally dropped it in the water. I was officially a fisherman. This strange goal that I put into motion after meeting a few Alaska-lovers while traveling was happening, and I knew it would be hard work, but I wanted it. I wanted my hands to hurt, I wanted to be up at 6 a.m. picking fish out of a net, I wanted to look down into our holds at thousands of pounds of fish, I wanted to scream, *"MONEY ON THE DECK,"* as fish popped their own gills out of our nets and flopped around at our feet, and I wanted to kick at the salt water splashing on the deck while howling at the sea like a mad man. All of that happened a little bit, but mostly, I baked brownies and read on my Kindle.

iv. On the Water

If we had one, I definitely became the "boat mom"—mostly out of boredom. The Alaska Department of Fish and Game is very much on top of regulating fishing based on how many salmon make it back up the river in order to keep the population healthy for future generations. (Fun fact: Salmon always go back to the exact same river they were born in to spawn.) This is something that I 100% agree with in principle, but waking up on a fishing boat, where all you want to do is fish, but you can't fish, is a bit like torture. How many books can you read or episodes of the Deadliest Catch can you watch until you bake everything on board the boat?

We had two days of fishing right when we got the boat on the water, which were filled with mild successes, but primarily they were days of learning and shaking the rust off, mostly for Captain Bill. Bill was a captain in the 90s. After owning a Midas Car Parts company in Wyoming the past ten-plus years, he decided he wanted to get back in the water so bought a new boat with his Midas money. This is all part of why he took a chance on me, which I was keenly aware of.

After those first two days, and a few hundred pounds of salmon, the next day the radio brought bad news. We were all up at 6 a.m. getting into our fishing gear just in time to hear the AM radio crackle with the message: *"Bristol Bay Fisherman, please be advised, the catchment numbers remain too low for salmon fishing. Fisherman, be advised, **there will be no fishing today**. Stand by until tomorrow's announcement."*

Starting that morning, we heard that message around 6 a.m. for ten mornings straight. The salmon run into Bristol Bay is normally so consistent that you could set your watch to it, but due to global warming and the change in weather patterns, this year it came a bit early. The sockeye.net missed the first three really good days of fishing prepping the boat, we squandered two without much to show for it, and then we were put into a coma by the regulators. I read books. Baked salmon. Slept. Baked brownies. Roasted salmon. Slept. Got fat. Did pushups on the deck. Baked some more. Cooked more fresh salmon. Got fatter. Cleaned up around the boat. Slept some more. Time crawls forward when you're stuck on a small boat, especially when you can't even fish.

In the last ten days we were out on the water, we started to make some money back. Before I flew up to Alaska, I called Bill on Skype, and he told me about how the contract for a deckhand would work. He said, "If things go as planned, you'll be looking to make 8, 10, maybe 12 thousand dollars." I was down for the hard work and fisherman lifestyle, but I'd be lying if I didn't say the money was a huge motivating factor for the whole adventure. I had depleted my initial travel purse, so I wanted to make enough money to travel for nine months and was thinking I might just become a seasonal Alaskan fisherman. Fish, travel, fish, and then travel again for years. My master's degree certainly wasn't in fishing, but there was good money in it, *so fuck it!* My Dad would just have to accept that the seaman's life was calling me.

For that dream to be possible, this first summer in Alaska was paramount, and it wasn't off to a hot start. Once we were able to start fishing, we started to fill our holds and would then sell off our fish to the tender boats we worked with. Tenders were much larger boats out in the bay that worked with an enclave of smaller fishing boats to collect the salmon, hand the fish over to the processing plants, and pay out the fishermen by the pound. One of our tenders was "Time Bandit," the famous boat from *Deadliest Catch*. That massive black boat works every season, most famously for crabs (read: reality TV) in the winter.

Along with fishermen, there are a lot of guys working Alaskan summers on the tender boats or in the fish-processing plants, where the risk is minimized and the returns are more certain because you'll average out among all the boats on the water. Fishing on a commercial fishing boat entails much higher risk, just like fishing—sometimes you catch fish, and sometimes you don't. Sometimes you have braggadocious 18-year-olds on board and a rusty 60-something-year-old captain who can't stop fucking up.

In the last ten days of fishing, we caught 10,000-some-pounds of salmon, which isn't nothing—it's 10,000 pounds of fresh fish. But we could have done far better. Bill, in those ten days, made two of the biggest mistakes a captain can make. He ran the boat aground on a sandbar. We were stuck there until the tides changed direction and the water rose enough for us to get off it, costing us nearly three hours of prime fishing. Two days later, he backed up over our own net. The gillnet lays out behind the boat like a mile long volleyball-net-tail, and at some point we backed up over ours and got it wrapped up in the propeller. That put the boat out of commission the rest of the day, which was one of the better days of the entire salmon run.

To Bill's credit, he did get his long arm down next to the motor and cut away at the tangled mess for well over an hour, bringing his bloody hand up every now and then, saying "I think we're getting close," while Cory, Ricky, and I just gave moral support from the deck, half-glad it wasn't our mistake, half-annoyed we weren't on another boat. It was in these moments that I had to remind myself that this was the only boat that would take me—a guy with no references whose only prior experience with salmon was eating it.

It also seemed like we were just getting unlucky. Sometimes Bill would get really excited about what he was seeing on his sonar scanner, so we too would get excited on the deck in our bright-orange overalls, Cory and me chest-bumping, getting ready for a haul. Then, when the net was slowly wound back up, it would fall short of our hopes—a few hundred fish, not a thousand. The season came to an end, and the bay switched over from fishing for Reds to fishing for Silvers. Ultimately, we caught 10,000 pounds of fish. I talked to other deckhands who caught upwards of 40,000 or 50,000 and would make a decent little purse from that—probably about $6,000 to $8,000 depending on the number of years working for their captain. It was a down year for most boats, but we led by shitty example.

My last day on the boat with Bill, as we were getting things organized for our return to land, he asked me "did you ever actually read that contract, Travis?" I told him "No, I was coming no matter what it said, so I just got on the plane and forgot about it." He explained to me how first-year deckhand contracts are typically structured. I would make 7% of the catch, so whatever 7% of 10,000 pounds of salmon is worth, and I would pay for 7% of the groceries and 7% of the gas for the boat. I told him, "That sounds about right to me. So what does that mean, in terms of my pay?"

Bill paused before gently saying, "I haven't run the numbers fully yet, but it doesn't look good, and basically, well, I'm not going to ask you for any money back, which is what the calculation will most likely tell me, so let's just say—*you can keep those boots.*" Bill was a lousy captain but a good man, and I'm forever grateful to him for taking a chance on a guy who doesn't even fish for fun.

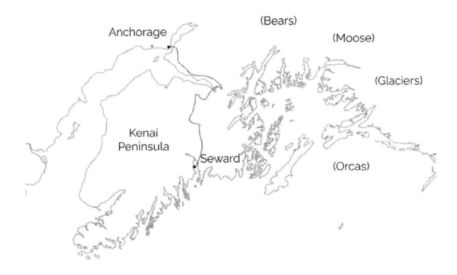

(Trees)

(Bears)

(Moose)

Anchorage

(Glaciers)

Kenai
Peninsula

Seward

(Orcas)

CHAPTER 10: SEWARD, ALASKA

I still remember my first steps back on land after we got the boat back to its spot in the yard. It was the same feeling you get if you jump on a trampoline for an hour then go back on the grass, and the earth feels extra hard. I was standing in my favorite fishing boots, the entirety of my payment for fishing my best and living on a boat for 26 days, swaying back and forth to counteract the fact that the earth wasn't rolling. I still have the boots, and they're excellent.

Cory, Ricky, and I got beers at the local bar near the boatyard and talked about everything that went wrong on the water, how we all hoped to make ten grand and were leaving empty-handed. Ricky and Cory were both talking about their flights home as I stirred in my barstool, looking at the deeply Alaskan decor, locking eyes with a moose bust. During the conversation and after a few Budweisers, I became determined to salvage my summer in Alaska. It was only the start of July now and I figured I still had time to get rich—or at least make enough money to make my next move, to buy the next flight.

I looked back at all the emails I'd sent from my parents' couch in Wisconsin before I had gotten the flash of good luck in the form of Bill's original email. One place I was exchanging emails with was a spot called *Miller's Landing* in Seward, which I remembered walking up to after aimlessly wandering out of town and down a beautiful road that hugged the bay. They had a gift shop, restaurant, and a beautiful rocky beach on the property. The website looked like an Alaskan postcard. I sent them an email back, fishing for something—this time with hopefully better results.

Two days later I was back in Anchorage working a cleaning shift at the hostel I had made my home base, trying to save the $15 my bed that night would cost me by vacuuming a cozy Alaskan hostel. During a break, I noticed that a new email from Miller's Landing had come through and I read it, dustpan still in hand. It said, "One of our Kayak guides didn't work out and just left mid-season, so if you can get to Seward in the next few days we'll see if you have what it takes."

I was a former camp counselor who taught canoeing. I'm an eternal optimist and I believe in my abilities, so while working that equation out on the white board of life, it somehow made sense that I could be an Alaskan kayak guide. Canoes and kayaks are different boats. They have different paddles. I had kayaked maybe *twice* in my life, but yes—let me take these paying tourists in kayaks out to glacial waters surrounded by animals that kill humans.

———

The confidence I had wasn't totally unfounded. I was a genuinely good paddler (in a canoe) and had been recently honing my ability by consistently getting two friends up and down the Milwaukee River after eight beers and three joints throughout my second year of grad school.

Earlier I mentioned the right ACL I blew out in high school, crushing my soccer-star dreams. I did go on, however, to get a full ride for division three St. Norbert College, where I again tore my ACL—this time the left—during the eighth game of my junior season. At the time I was leading the conference in scoring with seven goals, but after that game I never played highly competitive soccer again. Toward the end of my first year in grad school, back home in Milwaukee, I forced myself into a third knee surgery after I tore a bit of my meniscus somewhere deep in the third hour of playing pickup basketball at the indoor university hard courts. This was after I ran five miles that morning. Looking back, it feels like a script to hurt one's already fragile, bitch knees.

Following that third knee surgery at the age of 27, I was so frustrated by those two joints, so done with my legs fucking up my plans, that I did something tangible about it—*I bought a canoe.* I figured, if my lower half was going to let me down, *why not pick up some arm-heavy hobbies?* After several of my mates and I went out to the sticks and got the Craigslist canoe back to my apartment in Milwaukee, and after my friend Brad and I portaged the canoe through the East side of Milwaukee, past day-drinking onlookers, we finally got it into the Milwaukee river right under the Humboldt Avenue bridge. Apparently, *this is fine.* Apparently, you can tie up a canoe to any tree along the river with a chain you bought from Ace Hardware. Apparently, you can leave it there for as long as you want, through all four seasons of Wisconsin weather. Apparently, if you have a life jacket and a flashlight, you can pound beers and smoke doobies while bar hopping the establishments on the river all the way from the East Side, past the Lakefront Brewery, through downtown, to Barnacle Bud's in Bayview. Apparently, Milwaukee is the cool uncle.

Not only was the canoe the most fun adult toy I had ever owned, it gave me the sense that maybe I was a natural—maybe *I was a born paddler.* My knees were balsa wood, my legs were a liability, but my arms, *my arms were employable!*

From the shag carpet in my Anchorage hostel I emailed them back that I would be there, and I finished the cleaning in a blur. I booked the morning train for Seward, and lied in bed that night, thinking, *I have what it takes, right? I mean, I did drunk paddle the shit out of that canoe back in Milwaukee. That's gotta count for something, right?* Once I got to Seward, I found myself walking down that same rocky road that hugged Resurrection Bay that I walked when first visiting the small fishing town. This time, it already felt like I was home; in fact, I was determined to make it home.

————

I got to Miller's Landing in the afternoon, and before I knew it I was in a kayak paddling around with one of the more experienced guides there, a half-man, half-bear creature named Trampus; I couldn't make up a better name for this guy. He was a cross between Duck Dynasty and Sons of Anarchy, and his whole guiding style was to be a bit of a dick—one whose approval you sought desperately. So there I was, out on the water, doing everything I could to win his approval.

We paddled out in fairly rough conditions, and he got his boat moving. He was a big, strong guy, and I was able to keep up with him alright. When we were out in the middle of nowhere, he came over and rocked the back of my boat, then flipped me right out into the glacially cold water.

As I scrambled to grab my paddle he said, "We'll do a proper training on the exact technique to get back into your boat regardless of the conditions, but I wanted to see what you would do right now." I was able to cowboy myself back up and into the kayak, despite the arctic water. He gave me a nod of approval, laughed, and said, "All right, let's go get you dried off." We paddled back to the lodge, and I was shivering more with every stroke. I grabbed a pair of shower tokens, took a two-minute shower, put on my warmest clothes, and then met Trampus and the matriarch of the organization back in the lodge.

Trampus said, "You paddle pretty well, man," and then walked off, and I was left with a small, intimidating woman. It was obvious that she was in charge—of the room, of the conversation, of the entire operation. She gave me a forced smile and said, "Trampus thinks you could work out, so let's see." I gave the most earnest smile I had mustered since coming to Alaska and said, "Thank you so much, I really needed this and can't wait to get started."

i. Faster, Rookie!

The next few days were full of training sessions with other seasoned guides, and I learned the exact technique of using a paddle float then making a T with your paddle across the kayak, allowing one to crawl back into it even in the roughest ocean. I tossed myself into the water and climbed back in a dozen times to prove I had it down. I towed other guides around the Bay to show that I could get someone back who had given up or been injured.

As I paddled, dragging the extra 250 pounds of half-man-half-bear, I looked back to see Trampus with his head resting in his folded hands, his long dark hair blowing in the cool breeze, casually looking around the bay for wildlife. When he noticed I was taking a peek back, he would bark, *"Faster, rookie!"*

The main thing I needed help with wasn't the kayaking. The canoeing experience did translate a bit, years of doing pull ups was finally paying off professionally, and I turned out to be a natural at the physical aspects and rigors of the job. It was the "guiding bit" I was lost on. I didn't know what a single animal, glacier, or plant was called, and there was cool stuff to point out in every direction, fascinating Alaskan lore to entertain guests with on every hike. My biggest worry wasn't the danger of the job but being the guide who would respond to a simple question like, "Oh, that over there? Well, *that's a duck of some sort, I'm pretty sure...*"

I studied the Bay itself, I studied the animal books around the lodge, I searched out fables and tall tales, and I just listened as much as I could to the other guides. I did two tag-along tours after being there for three days, and they started to paint the edges of the job into focus for me. People are curious about Alaska, but they also just want to talk about life and make a connection with someone. I love people, the outdoors, being on the water, and nature, so before I even took my first tour I was certain this was a dream job. The nature piece and animal knowledge would come with time. I was ready to guide. I was ready to make some money.

I didn't care what tour I was put on, or the politics of who got what, I just wanted to work as much as possible. Every trip made some money, and I truly was in my happy place as a guide. I was extremely broke at this point, so the $50 we'd earn for a half-day tour was huge, but what mattered the most were the tips. If I took a group of six or eight people, oftentimes I'd make more in tips then I got paid out by Miller's Landing, with four different couples each dropping $20 or more for a job well done. It was motivating to be as charming as possible and to show a secret waterfall or two.

I eventually learned all the secret waterfalls and as much as most guides about what was what in beautiful Resurrection Bay. I could name all the glaciers, bays, animals, fish, otter species, jellyfish species, moss varieties— pretty much everything alive or on the map. I could even show you the trick where you use a certain type of moss to start a fire. "Old man's beard" was highly flammable and would light up into a little flash fireball in your hand. That trick will earn you a $20 tip.

———

I was making okay money; I was at least back to a point where my week-to-week funds were going up, and the financial stress started to dissipate. All the guides lived in semi-permanent tent structures, sleeping in bunk beds. It was basically a summer camp for drunk, dirty adults. Miller's Landing took something around $80 dollars out of our weekly paycheck for rent, and we happily paid it. We'd drink beers, play guitar, and stare at a fire every night. I've never lived in a place where every single night closed with friends around a campfire. It replaced television and computers. Fire was our Netflix. The guitars were our Spotify.

We would also frequent the few bars in Seward most nights, and eventually, I knew a bartender in every hole. My favorite spot was Tony's Bar and Liquor, where there was an old jukebox, beef jerky for sale, and bags of chips pinned to the wall mixed in with their t-shirts, which featured the bust of an old salty fisherman, looking stoic, giving the middle finger. It was easy to spend half the money you'd make that day on drinks that night, and I noticed "staff wanted" signs at a few restaurants, so, on a day off about two weeks after arriving in Seward, I went into town and dropped off my resumé at a few places. Before I left Alaskan Nelly's Family Diner, they offered me a job, and I was back later that day for my first shift.

Nelly, after whom the diner was named, was one of the first female explorers to ramble around Alaska. She ran a postal route with a dog sled and is a bona fide legend. The vibe was that of a family joint—we didn't even sell beer. I drew a cartoon maze one day of Resurrection Bay that we photocopied and handed out to kids with crayons so we could hang their good work all over the restaurant's walls.

On a four-hour dinner shift, I could leave with $150 in tips for slinging big burgers and halibut. The back of the house had some characters like any good diner, and the lady who ran the joint was kind and large, with long red hair. I became a pretty good waiter working in Alaska. I could easily turn twenty tables in one night, having made a bunch of dads feel cool, a bunch of kids laugh, and walking out with a hot meal and my pockets bulging with tips. If I had a tour that morning, I could earn $300 on a good day. I was coming up. The Alaskan dream was happening.

I honed my skills and developed a good reputation. I even got my first overnight paddle, where I took a group of four 60-year-old women deep into the bear-filled woods for their first proper camping trip in decades. I racked up some great reviews on the Miller's Landing website and collected characters and stories all summer, one of which was the annoying, confident guy who eagerly volunteered to take the solo kayak. Doubles are more stable, but sometimes groups are an odd number, so an "experienced paddler" usually volunteers. Five seconds after launching his boat, he tipped into the glacial water, and we had to get him on the beach, start a fire, and have him change clothes to the backups we kept on hand—standard protocol for a wet guest. I enjoyed watching him paddle in an old, borrowed, brown sweater for the next hour.

There was the curious couple who met at circus college, and, when they asked me to take a picture of them, the woman crawled right up her lover and comfortably stood on his shoulders.

There was the sweet couple who worked for a helicopter-tour company in Denali every summer and were just on vacation exploring Kenai for a week. I had a few beers with them in the lodge after I took them on a paddle, and we exchanged numbers as they invited me up to Denali at the end of the season.

There was the time we saw a huge black bear on the hiking trail.

There was the time we found what must have been over a hundred bald eagles in a single cove.

There was the time a family of sea otters played all around our kayak pod for most of the tour.

There was the angry couple, recently married, who each threw their paddles in the water to protest their partner. There's a reason double kayaks are called *"divorce makers"* internally in the kayak biz.

Finally, there was the blind woman and her sister, which was my favorite tour of the whole summer and one of the best lessons I've ever received.

ii. Sister Paddle

One day, the guides all got an email asking if someone would feel comfortable taking out a blind guest. Without thinking more than five seconds about it, I knew it would be memorable, so I wrote back first. The sisters showed up two hours early to do a practice paddle with me to make sure they would be fine, the blind sister in the front and the older, seeing sister in the back. I gave them the little intro chat and launched them out. It was a bit windy, but they managed to paddle straight out, around a buoy, and straight back, their matching long brunette hair blowing in all directions. It was amazing to see how they worked together and communicated, to see how the blind sister could feel the water with the paddle right away, and, after a few missed strokes, she found the water, and was an excellent partner. She also had the biggest smile on her face once she found her stroke, which made her sister and me smile in return. Back on land, we were all excited and felt ready for the tour.

Unluckily for us, over the next hour the wind continued to pick up.

I told them that we could still go out in these conditions—it would just be a bit difficult, so it was their call. They were still in for the tour, and the other four guests were happy to try it as well. These other four paddlers were two young couples, both seemingly fit. I launched all three boats, and two made it straight out, but one of the couples got turned sideways in the wind and waves and washed up against the shore. I drained the small amount of water from the boat, got them back in, and relaunched them. Same result. I tried a third time, and they just couldn't get past the first small breaking wave. Watching the other two boats drift farther and farther from shore, I told them that we could give them a refund, but if they couldn't make it past the first wave they should stay back—I had to head out to be with the other guests for their safety. They were disappointed but understanding.

We paddled in rough waves for about 45 minutes to the closest stop where we would go on an hour-long hike, then paddle back. The two guest boats made it just fine, and we walked around while I pointed out plants, animal tracks, and lit moss on fire. When we eventually made it back to our boats, we were all very aware that the wind had only continued to worsen. This time, it would be blowing in our faces and would prove challenging for even the most experienced paddlers. We had to make it back, and waiting it out wasn't an option, so I launched the boats, hoping they would dig deep and power through. I told the sisters as I launched them to let me know if it was too difficult because I had my tow rope and could help if needed.

We got all three of our boats out on the angry water and were making very slow progress back. The remaining couple started arguing and had their heads down, looking deeply frustrated, close to breaking. I looked at the sisters, strong winds blowing in their faces, both with huge smiles. The couple's boat, however, kept getting its nose turned sideways, and they were spending all their energy just trying to stay straight. After the couple got turned 90 degrees a fourth time, I could see the tension in their boat rising, so I ended up tying my tow rope to the front of their kayak, keeping them straight all the way back across the Bay.

We all made it. Everyone was relieved and overjoyed back on the grey pebble shore of Miller's Landing. I gave both the sisters big hugs and told them what they already knew—"That tour could have been a really bad situation if you weren't such a good team and both such strong paddlers. It's not possible to tow two boats at the same time."

The boat to which I originally paid extra attention, a bit worried it would be a liability in tough weather, was the only boat that could do the whole tour on its own—the only boat that truly had a great time. I thanked them again, and, as we hugged goodbye, I thanked them in my mind for the incredible story and lesson that I would keep forever. *Don't judge a boat by its cover, or something?*

The sisters, the circus couple, the helicopter couple, they were all great characters of my Alaskan summer, but the biggest character of all was Sunny. I fell in love with Sunny my first week in Seward, although I never said it—this time for more than just my own reasons.

iii. Remote Cabin Sex

Sunny was another guide at Miller's Landing; a crunchy-granola hippie type with long wavy brown hair and an infectious positivity. I've never met anyone whose name matches their personality as well as Sunny's. I've also never met a kayak guide who loved kayaking as much as Sunny. It was her passion, her hobby, her job, her happy place. She's the only guide I've ever met or heard of that paddles on nearly every one of her days off.

Sunny had a long-distance boyfriend when we were in Alaska, so we became fast friends, but just friends—drinking buddies, co-workers, and confidants. But, at some point, I think we both knew she was emotionally cheating on some level, because we did *everything* together. We obviously really liked each other, and we told each other that in every possible way, except for with those exact words or by swapping spit and getting naked.

There was one Greek restaurant in Seward that we frequented. We would order big plates of shawarma and I would shake parmesan straight out of the shaker from a great height into her mouth and all over her face and shirt until we laughed so hard that we cried. We had that thing that made the other people in the restaurant envious that they weren't as in love as we so obviously were. If they only knew we'd never even kissed.

The first six weeks in Seward, I didn't have a single romantic thing happen to me. I had a little crush on a cute waitress in town, but nothing came of it. Also, if I was being honest with myself, I just wanted Sunny. I remember seeing her dance at a live show one night and wanting to dance with her [twangy bluegrass music plays in the background]. When I was dancing with the waitress, I remember her checking in on us with the occasional side-eye, wondering if we were going to kiss—waiting to feel jealousy.

It never happened with the waitress. Nothing sexual happened in Alaska at all until a bunch of Miller's Landing guides rented out a remote cabin for a fellow guide's birthday.

———

We packed all the booze, food, and weed we could find into the holds of a few kayaks and eight of us paddled out to a remote, publicly-owned cabin. Alaska has a bunch of these that anyone can rent out for free. Alaska is magical. It's the end of the earth and the rainbow.

We drank, ate, smoked, drank some more, took blurry photos, and played silly games (one involving toilet paper, a rubber band, a coin, and a lighter, which I learned at Bellas on Caye Caulker) until it was very late. Sunny and I ended up on the front porch. Then we ended up alone on the front porch, everyone else had gone to bed. She was about a foot in front of me, talking about something unimportant. We made eye contact, and I made a face asking her, *What do you want to do?*

She leaned in, and we had our first kiss. Ten minutes later, we were both naked, having long-awaited sex on the wooden deck of this cabin. At one point I had her bent over and pushed up against the large front windows, all six of our other friends sleeping inside, while we got to do what had circled in our minds for over a month. We christened the porch a couple of times that night and then slept in different beds. Sunny had to figure out what to do.

The next day she called her boyfriend and told him it was over, and we were immediately a couple without ever having to say it. We still snuck around because Sunny didn't want anyone to think she cheated on her boyfriend or that everyone was right in their assumption that we were into each other. I didn't mean to play homewrecker, but I just couldn't continue to fight such a strong feeling, and neither could she. It was the last month of the season, it rained every day, and Sunny and I had sex everywhere, still in secret—in the boathouse, on the beach, in my bunk, in her bunk, on a park bench. We were a match physically, and we rarely let twelve hours pass without stoking the carnal fire we had burning.

iv. Denali Borealis

We made a plan at the end of the summer to take a road trip up north to Denali. At this point, everyone assumed that we were a couple, but Sunny never had to announce it, which is I think all she really wanted in that regard. I made plans to move to Hawaii after the summer, in large part because there were super cheap flights from Anchorage to Honolulu, but also because Christmas was only five months away and Hawaii was closer to home than Australia, which I had my sights set on. Christmas with my family and the trip to Pickerel with my boys for the few nights before New Years Eve were the two non-negotiables in my life at this point. The two main things that grounded me as a version of myself that resembled previous versions. They were the pegs that held the kite tight to the grass.

Hawaii also made sense because it seemed like an adventure, and I could legally work. My Alaskan money could get me started somewhere, but I would have to keep working. I knew I'd want to come home for the holidays in December. So Hawaii, Christmas, and then Australia was my rough plan. Sunny decided to join the plan; the question was simply for how long.

We drove our rental car up north to Denali and stopped in quaint small towns along the way. We had sex in all of their parks—on all of their park benches. We checked out waterfalls and had sex behind all of them as well. I almost crashed the rental car for reasons you can probably guess.

On the drive north we messaged the Denali helicopter couple and, to my surprise, over a month later they remembered us and the generous offer they made: to get us in a helicopter on the cheap. After a few messages back and forth, we were booked on a helicopter tour a few days later—we just had to cover the cost of gas and tip our pilot.

We were in Denali the first week of September and there couldn't have been a better seven-day window to take a helicopter over the park to a glacier. Fall lasts for about ten days in Alaska: the leaves turn colors and then fall in hyper-speed compared to the slow autumn of Wisconsin.

Up in the helicopter, we floated above Alaska, watching packs of caribou and elk run across the plains—the trees and bushes like wildfire all around them. Every shade of yellow, orange, and red spotted the sprawling landscape.

Our pilot buzzed in through our headphones to point out the summit of Denali—the tallest mountain in North America—peeking out of the clouds straight ahead. When he wasn't pointing out mountains or animals, our pilot was pumping the soundtrack from "Into the Wild" into our headphones, and Eddie Vedder's growling voice set the perfect tone, *"There's a big, a big hard sun, beating on the big people, in the big hard world,"* as the caribou below matched the tempo.

We landed on a glacier and walked around for a bit, with crampons strapped to our boots. I smiled like an idiot the entire time. Sunny and I got into a snowball fight. I tackled her and kissed her, pushing her head deeper into the wet glacial snow. Looking back, I think that this was the moment of strongest love, on the day of strongest love, between us. It's a shame we never know when that moment is happening in real time.

Back in Denali, we were drinking hoppy IPAs at a famous pizza-and-beer joint and looked up the price of the tour on my phone. It normally cost over $250 per person. We just had the time of our lives, on the best possible day, for practically free. We were in love, full of hoppy beer and pepperoni, and overflowing with optimism.

———

On our last night in Denali and one of our last nights in Alaska, I saw the Northern Lights for my first and only time. For years, I told myself, I think I've seen the Northern Lights. I sort of just felt like, I must have, *the sky looks crazy sometimes. Sometimes it's a bit green, you know?* But, I can tell you from experience, if you see the Northern Lights *for real*, you'll fucking know.

Our friend, whose couch we were crashing on to save some money, yelled for us to come outside after taking his dog out to pee. As soon as we stepped on his front stoop, there were huge neon-green stripes waving through the sky. We smoked from a one-hitter and stared up for twenty minutes, just like babies do at strangers—wide-eyed and seeking universal truths.

CHAPTER 11: HAWAII

Sunny and I flew, holding hands, from Anchorage to Honolulu, and met up with my Milwaukee mate, Chris, who had moved out to Oahu full-time right around the same time I left home for Aruba. We smoked, surfed, drank, and hiked for a few days—settling into the aloha vibe. Our girlfriends got on well, and Sunny and I were cheating the system, paying for practically nothing and living in Chris's spare room. I knew it couldn't last, so Sunny and I made a plan to fly to Maui and figure out our own setup. I didn't want to just implant myself in Chris's version of a stable island paradise.

Luckily I had gone to four of Hawaii's islands on a geology field trip my senior year at St. Norbert College, where I was a sociology major, but both a leadership studies and geology minor. I remembered really loving Lahaina, a small, charming tourist-stop town on the northwest coast of Maui. I could still picture this park that had a huge banyan tree with a massive root system that connected underground and shot out from the earth to form natural benches. On weekends, there's an art and craft fair within the massive, connected tree's expanse, the ocean just 100 feet away. I decided I wanted to move there, and Sunny was happy to go anywhere. We were in Hawaii, *how could we go wrong?*

Looking back, that geology trip during winter break my senior year of college was seismic, *tectonic* even. I had traveled to national parks as a kid and have a vague, interesting memory of seeing a mime on the streets of Quebec on a family vacation—but travel was not in my blood until my first trip to Hawaii. I had never been enchanted by a new place before, never been able to picture myself staying there—expanding my world and all the futures it might hold.

Those first two weeks I spent in Hawaii at age 22, I followed my Geology professor, Tim Flood, around to four islands, drawing pictures of outcrops and evidence of volcanoes in a little, yellow field book. We camped, woke up early, and sucked Hawaii's marrow which, in case you're wondering, tastes like passion fruit.

––––––

One morning we went on a snorkel cruise, and I felt alive in the way that only being on a boat in a new place at sunrise can make one feel. Talking to the guide working on the boat, shining like the tropical fish I just swam with while drying off in the hard morning sun, I said, "Pretty cool job, man—how long have you been doing this?" He told me his story: that he'd been in Hawaii for about five years and working on this boat for just over a year.

When I told him, "Man, what a dream job," his response changed the course of my life. He casually replied, "Dude, if you moved out here you could get a job on a boat *easily*, but you have to be up at 6 a.m. Everyone thinks they want a job like this until they've had a few weeks of partying and their alarm going off that early. Paradise makes people lazy." But I wasn't lazy; I was waking up early to draw pictures of rocks for college credit, so I could definitely get up early to get paid for snorkeling. All of my future travels and conversations about what I might do with my life were shaded with the contours of that morning chat with a tattooed, 40-year-old hippie on the deck of a small snorkel boat. That conversation might have been the most important one I had in four years of undergrad at St. Norbert. Thankfully I didn't leave with $80,000 in debt (read: I can't believe most people did).

We can never know where our words will end up or the steely weight they may hold, so be generous and kind with them. They may even cause a butterfly to flap its wings with joy.

Everyone who has fallen for travel, new places, and foreign adventures has had a moment like this—one in which a stranger invites you to imagine your entire life differently, *and it feels possible*. It's intoxicating, and you can imagine the new potential life paths shooting out in front of you, like branches of a tree. Life doesn't have to be pre-set, laid out by a different generation's priorities, guided by the decorum or modesty of a different era. *I could be a snorkel guide in Hawaii* played in my mind as white noise—always there—filling me with bravery and optimism.

i. Somebody Will Pay It

When Sunny and I left Chris's spare bedroom, leaving his real radio station job and real money far behind, Hawaii became financially stressful fast. We were planning on doing what any couple would do when moving somewhere new—find jobs, find an apartment, and pick a local bar to be regulars at. We were taken around one afternoon during our first week there by a real estate agent who was going to show us four apartments. I gave up at the third one, an unfinished studio with no windows, which he told us would be $950 a month. When I pointed out that there wasn't a single window and the floor wasn't finished, he just shrugged and said, *"Somebody will pay it."*

So, like any rational couple, we moved into a shed on the property of what we quickly came to realize was a halfway house. A random guy at a bar, who found out we were new to town and looking, showed us the house and adjacent shed. We were told we could stay in the shed, with a tin roof, chain-link fence walls, and a wooden-fence-like front door, for $50 a week.

We took it. We felt like we could be happy anywhere as long as we were waking up together. We tested this belief to its limit.

After a few days, and realizing just how many people lived at this house and struggled with addiction issues of some sort, we knew our shed wasn't tenable. We were happy to have a mattress and a door that locked, but we needed to leave. We were telling one of our favorite bartenders at Spanky's, a great sports bar that proudly claimed to be "the southernmost Packers bar in the United States," when a guy at the bar overheard us and introduced himself.

His name was Mark, and I liked him right away. He told us he was WWOOFing at this dragon fruit farm nearby and that, as long as you put in twenty hours of farm work each week, food and housing were free. Housing was a tent, but it was a free tent. As he painted the farm into our minds, I realized *my South American farming dreams might finally come true, in the least likely of countries—my own.*

Sunny and I loved the idea. We were both still unemployed, so to have work, a roof, and cool people like Mark around was a dream. We went to visit Mark the following day at the farm. We met Larry and Crystal, the two owners, and we were smitten with the whole thing. We moved in later that afternoon, throwing our backpacks onto an old mattress in a vacant red tent covered with a bright blue rain tarp.

Our new home was, in fact, the world's largest organic dragon fruit farm, and I was about to learn everything there is to know about dragon fruit. Instead of waking up and looking at my Colombian coffee fields, I was waking up and looking down on dragon fruit fields—the Pacific Ocean out ahead of us and dramatic green mountains behind us. We had found our place in Hawaii, and I was finally going to be a farmer. The dominos had been positioned in a loop-de-loop, one I couldn't see so close up to the action.

ii. Homemade Zipline

I will try my best not to let the next ten pages be exclusively about dragon fruit, but they certainly could be. Dragon fruit is incredibly interesting. It grows on a flowering cactus, and the flowers bloom with the moon cycle. On the night of a full moon, the beautiful white flowers grow larger than your face, larger than a personal pan pizza. After this stage, they wilt and recede back into themselves, and the center of that flower becomes a delicious dragon fruit, one whose inner color and flavor you can't fully know until you cut it open once it reaches maturity. Okay, *I'll stop*.

We had lots of different farming jobs, but my favorite was going out at night, once a month, under the moonlight, with a headlamp and paintbrush to pollinate the flowers. We would take pollen from one pizza-sized flower with the brush, and then stuff it in another flower. We were forcing flower sex so there would be future dragon fruit babies. In certain parts of the world, like Asia, there are bats and lizards and other animals that naturally pollinate the cactus's flowers, but in Hawaii, young WWOOFers did this sexy job—along with everything else necessary to run a farm that bore enough fruit to bring to market.

The young WWOOFing volunteers at the farm were 18- and 19-year-old kids who wanted to take an American-style gap year and not just jump right into higher education. They were cool, but Mark, Sunny, and I were the obvious seniors of the crew and, as such, became de facto leaders of the farm. Mark ran the farm-tour operation which included a zip-line that Larry built, *by himself*, from Internet instructions. I don't think I need to say much more about Larry, but based on that zip-line anecdote alone you can presume he's a legend, the type of older guy you meet and immediately aspire to be like—complete with a beard and cool straw hat.

There was also an "aqua ball," which was essentially a human-sized hamster ball we'd put tourists in, fill with buckets of water, and then push down a track as they flopped around like salmon on the deck of a boat, screaming gleefully and getting soaked. We also taught our guests about all the fruits we were growing on the farm. We mainly grew dragon fruit, but we also had papayas, pineapples, avocados, taro, bananas, and other tropical stuff growing in the rich volcanic soil. I learned enough about all of these different fruits to give a riveting two-hour farm tour. Guess how long it takes a pineapple to reach maturity? It's interesting, and you should Google it.

————

After about a month on the farm, Mark left, and I filled his role as the unelected leader of the volunteers. Larry had me make the roster for who would run tours with me. I was equitable, but he made it clear he wanted me on as many as possible so that there would be a slight air of legitimacy when a family of four showed up, not just two stoned 18-year-olds putting you in a climbing harness and pushing you off a home-made zip-line tower. (It definitely was just that when I think back on it.)

We made $20 an hour running the tours, so everyone wanted as many as possible. We were probably getting about five or so a week and it was a great little side hustle, but even with the tours, the general cost of living in paradise meant I was basically breaking even. After about a month, Sunny and I both knew we needed to get real jobs in town. She landed a sweet gig at the Hard Rock Cafe as a waitress. Me, well I got the coolest job I've ever had in my life: I ended up scooping gelato at a little mom-and-pop gelato shop. If you're surprised, just know that I was too… and to be clear, it definitely was not the coolest job I'd ever had. My Dad always credited his biceps, which he was rather proud of, to one of his earliest jobs: scooping ice cream on the south side of Chicago. I figured I was carrying on the family tradition, and the accidental arm exercise was a bonus.

Hawaii Gelato was run by an adorable older woman named Suze who went to Italy for three months to learn the art of gelato making and returned to Maui with the gift. She was good. When I was dropping off resumés, I almost passed the gelateria. I laughed to myself at the idea of scooping gelato but then thought, *It's a funny story*, and turned 90 degrees into the shop. Before I left, I was promised the job. Later I found out that the five older women working there, all in their 40s and 50s, were keen to get a young buck working there. The full gelato pans are very dense, and they wanted someone to help with all the heavy lifting.

From the first day I got to work, these old women loved me. I could move the pans to and fro, up and down, scoop the scoops, wipe the drips, all with vigor and a smile. It was a fun gig, one that wasn't pushing me or growing my skill set in any real way, but I did find that I liked it. It's nice to be wanted. It's also nice to not have to think at work sometimes.

As my biceps got their workout I learned the key differences between ice cream and gelato and can still give a pro-gelato explanation in detail. Even if I live long enough to go senile someday and I forget most of my memories, I'm sure I'll still be able to explain how gelato is folded to get the air out, like taffy, while ice cream is whipped.

iii. The Good Vibe Tribe

Back on the farm, the younger guys, Marta, Sunny, and I were all vibing. So much so that we started calling ourselves "The Good Vibe Tribe." It was written in Sharpie on the shared fridge by previous volunteers, and we adopted it. This came out of a rough stretch at the farm in which Larry and Crystal ended up firing the one local Hawaiian guy who was the only paid worker there. I had told them what he had been doing, realized we were all in a bit of danger, and that he was royally fucking up the—well, *vibe*. Without giving this piece of the story more words than it deserves, I'll just say that he was crazy aggressive and would describe, to our faces, graphic things that he wanted to do to Sunny on multiple occasions. It took all of my effort to keep my no-fight-in-my-whole-life record alive.

The Good Vibe Tribe, true to its name, had really strong vibes and a really chill life. We walked around the fields at night making dragon fruit cacti have sex. We played on the zip-line after smoking bad weed. We weed-whacked the relentlessly growing actual weeds in all the cactus fields. We fixed the weed whacker. We hiked up the mountains behind the farm. We blended impressive amounts of dragon fruit into smoothies using our NutriBullet. We pet all 30 of the farm cats. We fixed the weed whacker some more. We drank in our little communal hangout shack in the middle of all of our tents. We drove around the whole coast in the "Maui Dragon Fruit Farm" van, which had a huge, bright-green, three-dimensional clay cactus wrapping around the beat-up white van. One of the previous volunteers created and completed this art project as part of their *"volunteer hours."* As I said, things on the farm were pretty chill. Also, I started developing a crush on Marta, the only other female on the farm, which wasn't a good sign for Sunny's and my relationship.

———

Our favorite family farm trip was to go to the Little Beach Sunday bonfire. Little Beach was about an hour's drive south down the west coast of Maui from Lahaina, just south of a small town called Kihei. The Little

Beach bonfire happened every Sunday night, and we probably made it every other weekend. It was a chance to get naked, to freak out on some hand drums, and to sample the locally grown produce—magic mushrooms.

If you do ever end up on Maui on a Sunday, make your way to Little Beach before sunset. You have to hike up and over some sharp volcanic rocks to get to the spot, but once you're at the scene *it's obvious*. You'll find a circle of drummers around a fire, half-naked people dancing on the sand, and couples making out in the break of the ocean as the sun begins to turn down it's brightness setting.

There's a ceremonial vibe in the air, and the best part of the evening comes when the little orange sun hits the horizon line, sizzling to a cool like an ice cube thrown into a frying pan. As soon as it touches, all of the commotion stops, the dancers freeze, the drummers rest, and everyone just watches the sun setting in unified appreciation for how beautiful mother earth is, how special this sacred beach is, and how lovely this gift of life is. Several quiet minutes later, when the final sliver of the glowing, little orange slice disappears below the horizon line, when it slips just under the ocean, when the ice cube is fully evaporated, right at that moment—**the beach erupts.** The drummers unleash on their hand drums, the dancers start spinning, and everyone in attendance starts screaming and howling like the wild animals they all are.

Little Beach nights, surf mornings, afternoons spent pushing tourists in a huge wet ball down a hill, days building a giant rock labyrinth on the farm (another fun feature for the farm adventure tour!), everything was golden, you could say. Everything besides my relationship with Sunny. We still got along well, but all of the lust had left the relationship and our love for each other started feeling more like that of a best friends'. Well, at least to me.

I knew it was bad when I started to imagine sex scenes with Marta while Sunny and I were in bed together. I knew it was really bad when imagining Marta in Sunny's place was the only way I could finish when Sunny and I would get intimate. That little mental trick worked pretty well every time, so I could hide my lack of appetite for Sunny, but I knew things were broken. I knew that whatever came next had to be on my own. I knew I was going to break Sunny's golden heart, but it all sort of felt out of my control.

The secret-love-affair-bright-burning-flames of Alaska had dimmed to coals in the Hawaiian breeze. I didn't want to stop being in love with Sunny, but things just slowly shifted after we changed climates—sometime after we traded raincoats and fish for swimsuits and dragon fruit.

iv. Road *Trip*

To the casual observer, Sunny and I still appeared perfectly happy as a couple. We hardly ever fought, we slept side by side in a tent together every night, and we worked in the dragon fruit fields together most days. After a few months at the farm, we even took a couple's adventure together to keep things interesting.

We rented a small car for a long-weekend getaway and set out to drive the perimeter of Maui. We visited Larry and Crystal's other, less-cool farm, a lettuce farm in Paia on the north coast. We woke up at 4 a.m. to see the sunrise at Haleakala, an absolutely massive crater in the center of the island; it's the central figure of the island's origin story. We drove the famous Hana highway down the east coast, making all 620 curves, crossing all 59 bridges, and stopping at several of the hundreds of waterfalls. On the final day of our island road trip we left from Hana to visit the seven pools, the pools at 'Ohe'o, and decided that this was the time to take the mushrooms we'd been toting all over the ancient volcano.

We brought along a decent amount of mushrooms left over from a Little Beach party but never had a ripe opportunity, and I wanted our afternoon at these seven, naturally-formed pools, waterfalls cascading between them, to be a laugh-all-day-memory we would cherish. The first few hours after making the decision were joyful, but panged by moments of the thought, These are strong—*what if it doesn't wear off?* At 5 p.m. we were directed out of the pools and escorted out of the park along with everyone else, who I couldn't help but notice all had much smaller pupils. After chatting in the parking lot about what we should do and a pump-up speech from Sunny, I decided I could drive the small rental car—I would just go *really* slow.

As the sunset gave way to night, the moon tripled its normal size in my front window, knocking on the glass, and I could hear each wave breaking on shore in rhythmic laps as if they were coming through the car's surround-sound stereo system. I just tried my best to drive normally. In my state of paranoia, mixed with trying to reassure Sunny, I doubted whether my concern about one of our tires was warranted, but after listening to it for ten minutes I asked Sunny, "Do you hear something weird? I hear a *click-click-click-click.*" Sunny confirmed I wasn't crazy and, after pulling off to inspect the car in pitch black night, we were able to easily find a large nail lodged in our back-right tire. Looking around in the dark middle of nowhere, we decided I should just drive *even slower* now.

Somehow, I managed to drive for another two hours like this, hallucinating on powerful mushrooms with a rusty nail sticking out of our back tire. We were so relieved when we finally made it back to the farm. We both knew it was reckless, that we were lucky, and that we'd remember this trip forever. Despite the thrill, the dynamic with Sunny remained closer to best buds than partners in love, and successful sex still relied on my own mental manipulation of imagining Marta on top of me.

————

Toward the end of November, I met a dude with long blond hair at the bar who worked at a dive shop. In our first exchange, I told him I got my Divemaster earlier that year, and he told me they were hiring at the shop. That next weekend, I came on two trial dives to get a job at the shop as a Divemaster—it was a dream. I was a bit rusty in the water but personable enough that the shop still offered me a job. It's still probably the coolest job I've ever turned down, but they told me if I took it that I absolutely had to work the holiday season, meaning all the days around Christmas and New Year's.

The entire reason I came to Hawaii before Australia was so that I could make it home for Christmas, to see my family, my summer camp buddies, and my best friends from growing up. So after thinking about it for a few days, imagining life on Maui as a diver for as long as I wanted, I ended up turning it down. Now it lives in my mind as another alternative reality I could have lived, one that I'm certain I would have loved. But I never miss a Christmas.

v. 55 Hour Train

Without having to say too much, I think Sunny started picking up the signs that our relationship was almost over. I did mention that I really wanted to do this next chapter on my own and that I always had pictured moving to Australia solo before we'd ever even met. I was trying to be gentle about it, and I thought saying, "I want to do this on my own," was a nicer way of saying, "I don't want to do this with you."

When I got on my flight back to Chicago, I was excited to get home and a little relieved that Sunny wasn't with me. I felt like I was trying to be honest and to be a good guy about what I was feeling with Sunny, but it's hard to give people news you know they don't want to hear. Maybe I wasn't as clear as I thought.

Sunny had been messaging me during the flight and said something about how she was looking into getting a work visa for Australia too, so maybe we could find a place together. I read the messages, standing in Hall B of Union Station in Chicago, waiting for my train from Chicago to Milwaukee to pull into the Amtrak station.

I cared deeply about Sunny and didn't want to hurt her feelings, so I kept trying to think about what I should do, about what I would want if things were reversed. Finally, I did the one thing I wanted to do least in the world at that moment—*I called her.* I told her exactly how I'd felt, what was going on in my mind (obviously leaving out the Marta detail), and convinced her not to try and come to Australia. She cried. I cried. The train whistle sounded and the woman in the funny hat yelled *"all aboard"* like I was in some type of old-timey Western movie.

I felt terrible but took an honest, deep breath for the first time in over a month as I walked towards my train car. I knew I had to be true to myself—that I had to do Australia on my own. I knew our relationship was over, and I thought that while standing in Union Station I had said what I needed to in order to convince her of that.

———

I spent two weeks back home, buying and wrapping Christmas gifts, catching up with the family, drinking an irresponsible amount of whiskey with my extended family in Chicago, getting my Australian work visa, and drinking even more around the poker table in northern Wisconsin with a dozen of my best guy friends from childhood. It's the best few days of the year, every year.

The conversations up north are a barley and bourbon flavored mix of Camp Minikani glory stories, the best moments and characters of previous trips up north (shoutout to Shrek, Storch and Scary Gary), the Green Bay Packers, and what the other 362 days of the year looked like for everyone. I caught them up on places and people from my trip, and they taught me about raising children, new cars and toys, blockchain technology, and how the underground whiskey and watch markets of Chicago work. We talked about my travels, but I never quite explained what it really meant for me, the same way I'm not sure I made enough space to really know what being a new father felt like. I wanted to know, but it wasn't even close to my reality, making the lenses blurry as I tried to see from their worldview. As they tried to peer out from my perspective, my lenses were covered in cocaine, weird tropical fruit, and salmon juice, so I knew it was hard to relate, potentially impossible. It's not that I didn't want to understand them and what a grounded parental life felt like, or that they didn't care about my year and my growth, it was just hard and blurry—so we drank bottles and bottles of whiskey and talked about Aaron Rodgers.

———

I also booked a flight to Melbourne out of L.A. so decided to book a one-way Amtrak train from Chicago to L.A. I found a flight to L.A. that was the same price as the train, but I wanted to experience taking a 55-hour train ride across the country. I wanted to meet the characters on the train, take in the scenery of middle America, read books, write, and not be distracted by thoughts of what should I be doing. On a long train ride, there's nothing you should be doing.

I read three books, wrote a bit, listened to podcasts, watched all three original Star Wars movies for the first time, and chilled—hard. It seemed, in my car, that the other passengers' favorite use of time was looking out of the window. This felt like a strange use of 55 hours on a moving train, but I guess some people are extremely content to do nothing at all. I'm the type of person who loves doing my laundry because while it's in there I'll go for a run or read something and I'll feel like I'm doing two things at once, like I'm being the most efficient human possible.

I got to Los Angeles and spent the next three nights with a high-school buddy, Nick Lane. He had his normal life and was therefore pretty busy, so I spent my days exploring Venice Beach, a couple of museums, and cruising around L.A., mostly solo. I didn't expect to like L.A., but I found myself enjoying it, the same way I always enjoy walking down a new street in a new city for the first time.

I was, however, quite ready for Australia when the day of my flight came around. I was excited to hit the ground running in Melbourne and was thinking of doing some more farm work after settling in for a week. Farm work is common for young travelers showing up in Australia (pronounced "stralya" or "Oz," if Australian) with a work visa.

I even got a message from an old friend, Meg, someone I used to have a pretty big crush on. She was living in Melbourne and saw from a Facebook post that I was headed that way.

I have the wonderful curse of eternal optimism and just figured I'd get there and find a job. In fact, I thought, I'll find a great job and stack that Australian paper. I had about $1,700 left over from my work in Hawaii, and I was confident it would last me long enough to figure out a new way to make money. I was also sure I'd meet up with Meg and we'd hit it off just like we had eight years earlier, except this time she'd be single and maybe I'd make a move.

One of those two things would happen when I arrived in Melbourne.

The gentlemen of Pickerel. The mates I'm stuck with for the rest of my life.

Terrible family caricature. Pure Gold.

San Cristobal with the Mexico travel family and some hostel friends.

The night Nick and I made $100 each playing average covers.

Jack and Jill's birthday party at Bellas on Caye Caulker.

Post "I pooped the Halliburton" staff dive.

Dave and the good Doctor, two of my best mates on Utila.

Dave and me killing our snorkel test. Beans. Beer. Vodka. Hot Sauce.

Two hours later. 20 minutes before the blacked-out make out started.

Hostel friends in Seward during my first visit there.

100 dollars, just waiting to be picked up.

Boat mom. I put on about 15 pounds during our time at sea.

The boys, when we still thought we were all going to make 6-10k.

One of the only photos I have of myself in a kayak in Alaska.

Loading the boat for a paddle across the bay.

Sunny and me in Denali on our best day as a couple.

Trying my best to become Hawaiian with Chris.

The

Good Vibe Tribe in the Dragon Wagon.

Sunny and me on our little adventure around Maui.

I love these guys, but you can see why Larry put me in charge of the tours.

CONTINENT THREE:
AUSTRALIA

———

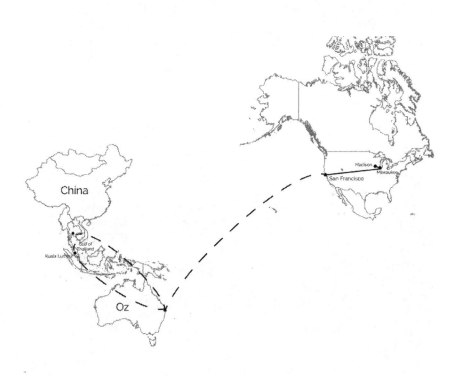

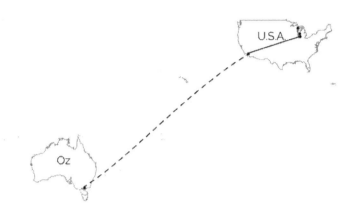

CHAPTER 12: AUSTRALIA, THE BEGINNING

Straight off the plane, I headed for the heart of the city to find a place to stay. I was immediately caught off guard by one thing—*the price tag on everything*. Finding a hostel for less than $30 was a challenge, using the internet was another $10, one beer was $8. My hard-earned gelato money was just vanishing from my bank account fully out of my control, and it was hard to keep out of mind.

I made around $10 an hour at the gelato shop on Maui, probably scooping 50 cups or cones in an average hour. I couldn't stop my brain from doing the math and constantly thinking, *So, I scooped 30 cups of gelato to be able to afford this one scoop of fancy $6 Australian ice cream. So, I guess...no eating ice cream in Australia! Cool-cool-cool!*

I found the cheapest hostel I could and booked into a 12-person dorm room. It was a mega-hostel in the middle of Melbourne, badly lacking soul or character, but Australia had quickly become a bank-balance survival game for me, and this place was cheap—plus, it had free breakfast.

Regardless of what happened the night before, I would always wake up before 10 a.m. for free breakfast. After two days at the hostel, I started taking an entire loaf of bread and turning it into eight peanut butter and jelly sandwiches. Feeding myself three meals of normally priced Australian food was out of the question. Even just eggs on toast would end up being around $20 with coffee and a tip, so I did what any smart person would do: I lived on PB&Js and whatever was left in the free-food section of the hostel for a few weeks.

i. Meg & Goon

My very first night in Melbourne, Meg and I made plans to meet up. This girl I had a huge crush on in my early twenties because of an AmeriCorps volunteer-awareness program just happened to be in Melbourne. She might happen to be single as well. I'd never been as grateful for Facebook.

We planned to meet at a bar for a drink, and I was trying to calm the back of my overly-excited mind which was yelling, in all caps, WHAT ARE THE FUCKING ODDS THIS GIRL YOU HAVE A CRUSH ON, WHO IS FROM WISCONSIN, IS IN MELBOURNE? PLUS SHE'S SUPER HOT AND COOL AND WANTS TO MEET UP—*DON'T BLOW THIS YOU FRIGGIN' IDIOT.*

As she walked into the hostel bar, I tried to tell the front of my mind calmly, *Worst case is that we just get a beer and catch up. It'll be chill.*

She had shoulder-length blond hair, she was curvy in all the places I like, and she had charmingly crooked teeth behind a reserved smile. The ALL CAPS back of my mind started winning my internal dialogue immediately. I knew I wanted to kiss her ten seconds after she walked in. The mental chorus of *DON'T BLOW IT, BOZO* played on repeat as I tried to converse like a normal person, to chew food like a normal person.

Thankfully, she was still great company. She was funny and the conversation flowed without any effort or awkward intermissions. We caught up on my travels and how she ended up in Australia. There was something about an Australian boy from the summer camp she worked at that didn't work out a few months after she arrived in Oz, and I just heard, "I'm single now."

We left the bar, ended up in a park and found a full bag of goon, which all Aussies and youngsters who have backpacked there will know well. It's the famous bagged wine whose fine print on the box says: "may contain fish eggs." Nobody knows exactly what's in it, but it gets you drunk and is super cheap, so it has become a backpacker staple. We were already three beers drunk, so we took turns taking pulls from the silver bag of wine that magically showed up on this park bench. As we looked out over the river and the lights of the city, my mind kept chanting *DON'T BLOW IT,*

BOZO—DON'T YOU BLOW IT!

We ended up walking back toward the city, and I suggested we pop into one more bar—a hip place with flowerpots and cool lamps fixed with old-fashioned incandescent bulbs. We each had a nice heady beer, and at this point I just wanted to kiss her. I was feeling equally optimistic from the serendipity of it all as I was drunk on goon.

After settling the bill we walked out onto the sidewalk, the back of my mind yelling *KISS HER*, to which the front of my mind responded, You know, I think he might actually be right this time.

I turned and kissed her almost immediately. Meg was certainly surprised by the timing of the move but seemed happy that I made it. We ended up getting her a bed in my hostel that night because her place in the suburbs was 30 minutes away by train—and we had unfinished business.

Hostel sex isn't something I can fully endorse, but in some cases *it's just happening*. We dropped a sheet over the side of the bunk and covered each other's mouths. I was just glad nobody was sleeping above us.

———

The next few weeks in Melbourne were filled with PB&Js, fruitless online job searches, conversations with other struggling backpackers, and lots of time with Meg. Thankfully, she had a job at a jewelry store where she was paid handsomely to sit and look at her phone, occasionally talking about rare gems, something I learned Meg had a real passion for. She lived a 30-minute train ride away in the suburbs near the jewelry store with a host family she'd met. This put us in the situation of trying to figure out where we could get naked. The answer was normally somewhere dark but very public.

I've had sex in about eight different public parks in Australia. We'd find a protected corner somewhere, lay down my tapestry, and giggle as we took each other's pants off. We were in the early stages of young love, and it didn't matter that we didn't have a bed—it might have even made it better.

My favorite memories from my first month in Australia are all naked, with Meg, somewhere in the dark in a park with our senses perked to 1000%, alert to every movement and noise—ready to jump up and run, getting close to an orgasm, or, more often than not, both sensations happening simultaneously.

ii. Solo Karaoke

Victoria, Oz

(Kangaroos and shit)

Melbourne

St. Kilda

Wilsons Prom

L ife was becoming untenable. Could a man even survive on PB&Js accounting for 90% of his diet? I also realized I had no place or purpose in downtown Melbourne. I was either waiting for Meg to get off work or hanging out with Meg. I needed to get something going for myself, so I decided to leave the city center and head for the beach.

St. Kilda is the famous seaside neighborhood of Melbourne, complete with a boardwalk, amusement park, penguins (for real!), and more cafés and restaurants than you could visit in a year. There were also plenty of hostels in the area, so my first goal was to get a free-accommodation gig at a hostel, then figure out an actual job from there. I moved into a random hostel that had a bar on the first floor, and I made it very clear that I would do anything to save on the $30-a-night dorm bed. I would do whatever. I would wash the walls. *I didn't care.*

A few days later, I was busy washing the walls of the stairwell with a rag, really wondering to myself if Australia was a good call. It was different, it was sort of interesting—there were kangaroos and shit, and it was still traveling in a sense, but I felt like nobody told me about this part. How you could easily end up holding a dirty rag as a wall-washing-30-year-old who eats only PB&Js. The part where buying four beers on a night out will make you feel like such an irresponsible idiot the next morning because you'll be down $40, where feeding and housing yourself at all is a financial struggle, and how thousands of other backpackers with working visas are in the same boat, so it's not that simple to catch a break or even possible to just "*try harder.*" You have to get lucky.

I was still hanging out with Meg most days of the week when she had the time off and was down to train south to St. Kilda, but I was starting to question Australia in general. I desperately needed a win, when I saw a flyer in the bar of my hostel that made me double-take and think, *Maybe it's a sign…*

The flyer announced a **"Karaoke Competition – Thursday – Winner gets a $100 bar tab."** I didn't think about the logistics of the competition or anything, and I decided on sight I would go sing my broke-ass little heart out and hope for the best.

The next afternoon, I came down to the bar alone and got a beer. *You have to spend money to make money, right?* I quickly realized as the competition was starting that it certainly wasn't going to be judged by a panel of karaoke experts—it was going to be judged by the drunk crowd.

One girl sang an Amy Winehouse tune, and her friends lost their minds. Another guy did "Lose Yourself" by Eminem, and his wolf pack started howling for him. I was feeling a bit sunk, but I was there, and I had drunk three beers for a reason, *right?* So I put my name in, and shortly after I was called up to the stage. As I took the stage, it was painfully obvious to everyone at the bar that I was alone.

Every previous singer walked onto the stage with their friends cheering them on. I walked up to the normal sounds of a working bar in the background.

"Hey guys, I'm Travis… I'm from the States, and I'm here tonight… ah, *alone* if you couldn't tell."

[Glasses clinking in the background, sporadic sad claps from the crowd]

The song came on.

"I hope you guys like 90s hip hop"

[A few more claps from the crowd]

"This is how we dooooooooo itttt…."

I had a few drinks in me and was totally alone in that bar, so I just let it rip. I love Montell Jordan, and I think that came across in my sincere passion. I had nothing to lose, I didn't care what anyone thought, and I knew only one person on this whole continent, so I let myself fall into the pocket and I got caught up in this classic 90s banger.

I nailed the final verse rap and dropped into the lowest voice I can muster: *"You and OG are gonna make some cash—sell a million records and we're hitting the dash!"*

When the track finished, I came back to. I was genuinely shocked at the crowd's reaction. The sympathy play, the song choice, the unbridled passion, some sort of combination of those things had won the crowd over, and I sang my way into the popularity competition. They liked me.

After a few more singers, the host called me and the girl who sang Amy Winehouse back on stage as the two finalists and said it was too close to call—the room had to vote again. He moved his hand from floating just above her head to just above my head. The bar was loud.

He moved his hand back to her, and back to me, and I think at some point it was her group of girlfriends against the rest of the people in the bar. The rest of the bar was clapping for everyone who'd ever gone and sung their hearts out all alone at karaoke.

I won.

It was the first real financial win I had in almost three weeks in Australia, the first uptick since my last gelato paycheck, and I felt like I just won the fucking lottery. A $100 bar tab could easily be gone with five friends in twenty minutes in Australia, but in that moment I felt fucking rich, Richie Rich type rich. The momentum was changing. Meg came and met up after the competition ended and it felt so good to buy her a drink, stress-free.

The tide was turning; a small win is something to build on. Little did I know, that coming weekend I would have an actual win, the kind that would change the course of my time in Oz. (Pronounced *Australia* if not Australian and also not attempting to assimilate.)

iii. Leroy Loves Espresso

I was spending a couple of hours a day at the hostel cleaning out the fridges, washing the walls, doing anything I could to save the $30 nightly charge for sleeping in a cramped dorm room. The set-up was not enjoyable or sustainable, so I started hitting the pavement in St. Kilda as frequently as I could. I whipped up a service-industry version of my resumé, complete with my experience from Alaska Nelly's in Seward, Rehab on Utila, and the minimal bar work I had done back in the States during college and grad school, primarily as a bar-back and bouncer. I was just hoping to convince someone to give me a chance.

I bought a bright orange folder, and I put 30 freshly-printed resumés in it. Then I just started walking into restaurants, cafés, nightclubs, and anywhere it looked like humans could work. I smiled, most people were friendly, and the most common response was some version of, "I'll put it in the stack with the others, *but don't get your hopes up!*"

The streets were full of locals enjoying their Saturday, tourists exploring the streets and cafés of St. Kilda, and backpackers looking for a job. I bumped into numerous people who were also walking around with a different colored folder full of resumés. The competition was high, and the struggle was *real-as, mate.*

The basic principles of supply and demand felt so out of whack with the backpacker workforce in Australia. I came to realize that many just failed and returned to where they came from, having lived a few stressful months in Australia and handing over $5,000 or so to its economy one $8 beer at a time.

It was cutthroat, and my experience was minimal, but I was a bit older than most backpackers, and I was determined. I turned onto Acland Street, the most iconic strip in St. Kilda, famous for its over-the-top dessert shops and cafés. Right as I got to the entrance of Leroy Espresso, a server dropped two armfuls of plastic ashtrays that she was carrying back inside. Fifteen ashtrays bounced and rolled all over the sidewalk in different directions.

I helped her scramble to pick them all up, trying to avoid a bigger scene, and, as I handed her the five that I grabbed, she said, "Thanks, that was embarrassing…" I replied, "No problem! Are you guys hiring? I really need a job."

Let's call her Amy. She introduced me to Sara, the manager, who just happened to be there at the time. Amy told Sara how I just helped her out, adding, "I know we get a lot of applications, but this guy seems nice." I mouthed *thank you* to Amy and then looked at Sara and tried to communicate with my eyes just how badly I needed this.

Sara said, "Alright, well, why don't you fill out an application and leave us a resumé." I sat there and filled out the application on the spot, and noticed Sara looking at my resumé ignoring the busy restaurant. She happened to be from the U.K. and had a fondness for Alaska. She said, "You worked in Alaska. That's awesome. I've always wanted to go there." She looked over at my application, which surprisingly asked as it's final question, "What's your favorite smell?" As she finished reviewing the application, she lifted her head up smiling and sang, *"Freshly baked bread is my favorite smell too!"*

I left twenty minutes after I picked up the ashtrays on the sidewalk, but Sara had told me to come back that evening for an unpaid trial shift to see if I would work out. I left smiling like Meg and I had just finished copulating in a pitch-black corner of a public park.

———

Meg met me down in St. Kilda in the afternoon, and I told her of my fortuitous street crossing, the ashtrays, freshly baked bread, and how I had a really good feeling about this place. We were buzzing, walking these new sunny streets, falling in love more with every day, soaked in youthful optimism that this was all exactly how this was supposed to go. *Of course I would get this job. Of course Meg and I would meet again eight years later and fall in love in Melbourne!*

Our connection carried us through the streets, a force field of good vibes circling us. We passed a busy bar with a huge outside terrace, full of proper Australian lads enjoying the beautiful summer day. A very drunk redheaded man leaned out over the railing of the outdoor patio and yelled, "Oyyy mate, I feeking lohve that sharttt," as his short, thick arm steadied him against the rail.

He was googly-eyed and frothing, pointing directly at me with his other hand, and as I looked down I noticed I was wearing an old tank top from Rehab, the bar I worked at in Utila. The shirt was a knock-off of the classic "**I <3 NYC**" shirt: "**I <3 Rehab.**" It's a pretty controversial shirt in hindsight, probably misinterpreted and offensive to some, but on this day, this drunken ginger man just loved it.

I greeted him at the fence, we got to talking, and about three minutes into the conversation he blurted out, "I like you; do you want a job?" I laughed it off based on his state and the nature of the encounter, but then he carried on saying, "I help run one of the largest summer camps in Australia and you seem like you could do that job." This man I met three drunken minutes ago didn't even know that I'd spent the majority of my 20s working with kids, that I had run a group home in New Orleans, and that "camp counselor" described my professional expertise more than any other two words. I immediately told him, "Yeah, that would be amazing. I've actually worked with kids for over ten years, so it's right up my alley!" He didn't seem to care about that part. He trusted his blacked-out instincts.

We exchanged Facebook info, and after the initial excitement wore off Meg and I laughed on our way back to my place, chatting about the odds of him even remembering that interaction the next morning. He was probably working on his eleventh beer.

That night, I went into Leroy's and crushed my trial. Basically, I didn't screw up anything major, and I worked as hard as I possibly could. Sara gave me a paid shift for the following day. I gave Amy a huge hug. I was ecstatic. I was on the roster. I was officially employed in Australia!

Two days later, I got a Facebook message from Tim, the drunk redhead, asking me if I was serious about working at the summer camp. He said he'd looked over the resumé I sent him and scrolled my Facebook, which was mostly pictures of me being a goof with cute kids. I told him I was keen and that I was so glad he remembered me. He'd send more information in the coming weeks, but the gig was mine if I wanted it.

The following day, I got a message from Sunny.

"Hi Travis. I'm in Melbourne. Can we talk?"

iv. Surprise Visit

I read the message again and again. She's *IN* Melbourne. *Not thinking of coming to Melbourne. She's IN Melbourne.* She's the farthest place away possible from her two homes, Tennessee or Alaska. That flight is well over $1,000. You don't just decide to pop over to Australia for a bit, but Sunny was *IN* Australia, according to this message.

I showed Meg the message. After my first month in Australia, Meg and I quickly felt like a couple without needing to have the "what are we" conversation. We had talked about exes and our past love lives quite a bit. She knew about Sunny. She knew how it ended, that it was my call, that I cared a lot about Sunny, and that I felt bad about being the reason she was ever sad.

Meg encouraged me to go meet her, and in turn I fell a little more in love with Meg. Sunny never really had a chance of winning me back at this point, but I had to assume that chance was part of why she came halfway around the world to Melbourne. I also knew the effort was at least worth $1000 to her.

We made plans to meet the next day at a hipster bar in the heart of Melbourne close to where she was staying. Sunny and I had woken up in the same bed for nearly four months, so I had a lot of nerves about seeing her while riding the train north. I didn't know what she was going to say, what she expected me to say, if she was going to cry, if there would be a scene, if she would try to kiss me...

We sat around on wooden crates stacked up artistically, surrounded by graffiti, holding $8 beers in small plastic cups. Sunny didn't seem upset. She seemed just as nervous as I was.

She was wearing a cute tank top, her long brown curls spilling onto her shoulders, and I wanted to just give her a hug and a kiss on the cheek and yell at her, YOU'LL BE ALRIGHT, SUNNY. *YOU'RE WONDERFUL!* I also realized, just before I shouted that to her, that maybe it's not the place of the person who just broke someone's heart to try to mend it as well. That's not how that should work.

For a heart to heal properly, time and new people have to mend it. That's how that works.

We caught up about the past month, and I debated telling her about Meg. She talked about the idea of staying in Australia, that she could probably find some waitressing work with her experience. *Should I tell Sunny about Meg?* We sipped our beers and laughed about old memories, about shaking parmesan all over each other in public. *Should I tell her?*

Eventually, the contours of the conversation turned a bit sexual, and I could tell that this visit to Australia was indeed about getting back together, that she was certainly hoping we would at least end up naked together. At some point, after realizing the new vibe to the conversation, I blurted out,

"I started seeing someone, Sunny. It feels sort of serious already. I didn't expect that to happen. I'm sorry, I don't know what to say."

I don't quite remember the details after that point in our conversation, but Sunny was back in the States about a week later, and I remember feeling relieved. I wanted Sunny to be happy, I just couldn't be the person who made her happy anymore.

I was too busy trying to make Meg either laugh or cum.

v. This is Totally Fine, Totally Normal

I never realized how lucky I truly was on the day I scrambled to pick up those ashtrays until weeks later when I was working full-time and finally felt settled. I found myself in the reverse role of taking a resumé off a smiling backpacker, saying, "I'll put it with the others, but keep looking, because I don't think we're hiring." In one four-hour shift on the weekend, it would be common to receive five or ten resumés from twenty-something-year-old backpackers looking for any type of work. You could sense the concealed desperation from most of them—you could smell the peanut butter and jelly.

I moved constantly on the floor at Leroy's, always trying to prove that I deserved to be there. I enjoyed serving, and at this point I was good at it. I could carry four plates full of eggs benedict out to a table, hot sauce for the American guy at the next table tucked into my apron, my pad and pen ready to take the couple's order who just sat down. I always used a pen and paper along with my own chicken scratch and abbreviation system that would mean absolutely nothing to any other living soul on the planet. It still bothers me when servers don't write things down. If you get something wrong once a month, that's too much. Plus, you're making people anxious.

After a month in which Meg and I covered hundreds of kilometers on the local train to see each other, we realized something had to give. Meg would come into Leroy's a lot as I was finishing my shift, and the rest of the team there adored her. They knew our young love and our struggle with the distance. At some point, while five gin-and-tonics deep after a morning brunch shift on a Sunday, Sara, the manager at Leroy's, offered to let myself and Meg move in with her temporarily—*rent-free*.

Australia is the land of boom and bust financially. One week I'm paying $30 a night to listen to drunk 19-year-old English kids snore, another week I'm staying in a beautiful apartment near the beach with my girlfriend for free. Life was good. I had work, I had a free place to stay, I was in love, and I finally felt like Australia was a place I could call home. I wanted to run to the end of the St. Kilda pier and hug a fucking penguin.

Meg and I lived with Sara for almost a month, and eventually we got Meg a job at Leroy's as well. She didn't have much serving experience, but it already felt like she was part of the team, and Sara—who hired everyone—was our guardian angel, so Meg was hired.

———

We eventually moved into a new place in the neighborhood that wasn't quite as nice as Sara's, but it was ours, and it was perfect. We had a big backyard, a small blue kitchen, and a bed in which we could be as loud as we wanted. We had upstairs neighbors that we didn't see or speak to once in the many months we lived there. Not a single conversation.

We fell into a routine in that house in Melbourne: working at Leroy's and slinging flat whites to pretentious coffee drinkers, getting stoned at night and watching old movies we rented from the library, arguing about who gave a longer ten-minute back scratch while lying in bed super high. On the weekends, or at happy hour, we'd go out with the crew from Leroy's.

A young Welsh backpacker with a bright smile you could still see through his bushy beard became my best friend at Leroy's. His name was Jay, and he was hired about two weeks after I started. He wore a winter hat while waiting tables in the sun and rolled fat joints that impressed even non-weed smokers.

Meg and I did take a couple of longer trips that broke the routine, one to Tasmania and one to Sydney. We worked together at this two-week summer camp for Australian kids and had a great time while getting paid handsomely. We got big paychecks to go swimming, watch movies, take kids on zip-lines or bowling, every day for two weeks straight. It was as cushy as the ball pits we were jumping in.

Then, suddenly, Meg was leaving Australia.

———

Her year-long work visa was running out, and she was going back to work at the summer camp she loved. Our time together was fleeting, like an Alaskan summer. It seemingly came out of nowhere and was disturbing the routine and peace that I had worked so hard to earn in this new country. Things weren't always easy with Meg, but she was home for me in Melbourne. She was the sun in my St. Kilda solar system.

She had a lot of doubt and anxiety. She warned me about it from the first day we hung out, but all I saw was her cute face and crooked smile. When she would get stoned, she would say things like, "I just want to be out of my head—I want to forget I'm here" and I would laugh it off.

Sometimes we were that perfectly comfortable couple, laughing uncontrollably, causing the rest of the people in the room to disappear. Meg was like a speck of microscopic dust that lands on your eyeball that you can't help but focus on. The world becomes secondary, just a backdrop to observe this cute little microscopic dust with crooked teeth dancing on the surface of your actual eyeball.

We were either together and deeply in love, or she was frigid and aloof—impossible to make smile, and I was somehow more alone than before we first kissed.

That combination should have been enough of a red flag for me to just let it go when we parted ways, but I believed in myself and in us. I'm an eternal optimist and I love feeling tangled in destiny. I believed with my whole being that we reconnected for a reason, and that I had the power to do something to make it right, to change things so that we were always happy in love and not on this emotional forty foot teeter-totter.

I believed I could make it so that she would never push me away but always pull me closer.

That was another lesson in love for me. Some people just aren't naturally happy, and, no matter how much you want them to be, it's not in your power to change their chemical makeup.

For me, I need to be able to make my partner happy—it's what gives me the most joy in a relationship. I need to be pulled not pushed, reassured not toyed with. I know this now because *true learning is experiential*, but at the time, I thought it was in my power to control it, to make her more happy than sad, and I committed to a long-distance relationship with Meg. We told ourselves that we would make it work. When we kissed goodbye as she left for the airport, we told ourselves that we would see each other soon. We told ourselves that everything about this fraught love was totally fine, totally normal.

CHAPTER 13: AUSTRALIA, THE MIDDLE

Once Meg left for home, St. Kilda was a half-empty house following a painful divorce. I didn't want to be there. Everything reminded me of her, life had grown a bit stale, and Australia is a huge fucking island.

I put in my two weeks' notice at Leroy's, told my landlord I wouldn't be staying the following month, and made plans to hit the road. I decided I would go west to Adelaide, then up through the middle of the country. There was a huge and famous rock there that I wanted to see. There were wide-open spaces I wanted to feel. Mainly, all the young backpackers of Australia cruise up and down the east coast, and I wanted to do something different.

I stopped at the Twelve Apostles (of which only eight remain after salt water and time have collapsed four of the jarring rock structures), I saw some koala bears, and I got back in the groove of moving, just me and my two backpacks.

I made it to Adelaide and checked in for a couple of nights at a party hostel. I made some fast friends, and we checked out the city's museums, hiked up Mount Lofty, and had a few great days and nights out together. It was fun to not be slinging flat whites and pretentious pancakes. It was fun to be making new friends. It was fun to be exploring again. But it was impossible to not think about how expensive everything was.

Most travelers in Australia are "having the best time of their lives" for two key reasons. First, they're 19 years old and it's their first time traveling, so Australia is the most exotic place they've ever been; there are fucking kangaroos and koalas and shit.

Second, they're 19 years old and mostly spending their parents' money. Australia has this reputation of being *a safe place to travel*, which it is (as are most places if you're relatively smart), so it's become the big-trip travel destination for thousands of English, European, Canadian, and American first-time backpackers.

I found that this reality made it very hard for me to not get frustrated during a large number of hostel conversations. When a 19-year-old English lad would say something like, "Isn't 'Strayla the fuhgin' best, mate?!" in my mind I would think, *Sure, I suppose it's awesome if you've never been anywhere else and you're blowing your parents' money. I ate peanut butter and jelly sandwiches for two weeks straight just to stay alive because I'm 30 and nobody is fucking helping me! This beer we're drinking is eight fucking dollars, and it's not even good. Part of me fucking hates this place!*

In reality, I would just smile and agree, "Yeah, it's great, mate."

When I started this first backpacking jaunt around Australia, I had around $2,000 that I had saved up working hard for over four months at Leroy's Espresso, taking every shift I could. Again, I couldn't stop my brain from going to the dark place where it would calculate the number of cappuccinos I had made in exchange for the bag of crisps and chocolate milk I just bought at a gas station for $13. I worked hard for every dollar I had in my Australian bank account, and as soon as I left the St. Kilda bubble my bank account was fucked, flying down a double black diamond on a rickety old toboggan.

Days backpacking in Australia were a mental exercise in deciding how to spend time, have fun, see things, fuel my body, and not go broke in a week. $2,000 could last me two months easily in South America without even trying (and with doing all the drugs). I was hoping it would last me a month in Australia, and that was quickly proving a challenge.

i. Underground Town

I cruised north from Adelaide up to a small town that was famous for primarily existing "underground." Coober Pedy was an old-school mining community that became a tourist draw for having the majority of it's accommodations and restaurants underground, where old opal mines had been dug.

Coober Pedy was one of the first places in the world where opals were found and mined, which caused Australians to flock in hopes of finding their fortune in these majestic, precious gems. It's still operational as a mining community, but it's also now a one-of-a-kind stop in the middle of nowhere for travelers trying to see what's in the barren middle of this continent. Once you get off the coast in Australia, the truth is—there's not a whole lot.

Coober Pedy was 36 hours of dust, sleeping underground, mining museums, and sunset beers, and then I was off north again, this time toward Alice Springs, the home of Ayers Rock, otherwise known by its first indigenous name, *Uluru*.

————

Alice Springs is only the 51st-most populated city in Australia (it would be number one if coastal cities didn't count), but, after looking out of the bus window and driving through what strikingly resembled the surface of Mars for twenty hours, it seemed like a huge city. There was a mall, restaurants, bars, and a cool little hostel tucked away from the city center with backpackers from all over the world drinking beers around a fire pit. I listened to a few campfire songs on guitar, played a few songs myself, and thought, *I like it here. I could stay here.*

On the way out to Alice Springs, I had internally debated looking for employment and staying near Uluru doing some type of tour-guiding or hospitality work. I knew I couldn't *just travel* for that long, and I had good friends in Melbourne who had worked here for a year, made good money, and told good stories about their time in the desert (like the one about loud EDM parties in the middle of absolutely nowhere that they would help throw). I started looking at everything through the lens of *what if I just stayed here?* The big, affable guy who ran the hostel with his fiancé seemed so happy, and I thought, *Yeah, I could work here, just chill around the fire and be happy like that guy.*

I had made it all the way to the middle of the continent, so I covered my eyes while scanning my Australian debit card and booking the three-day, two-night "Rock Tour," which was sort of *the backpacker special.* It's cheap compared to the other options out there and still a solid introduction to the outback, including a visit to one of Australia's greatest landmarks—*Uluru*, the rock itself.

ii. Witchetty-Figgity-Grub

A crew of twelve people from the hostel loaded up two beige jeeps early in the morning, and we were off toward the nothingness. I'm sure there was an itinerary for the three days, but I didn't really care what we did or even know which direction we were driving, I just knew I would get to see Uluru and that this might be the last fun, big thing I got to do with my St. Kilda money.

Like a good long book, I don't remember all the details, stories and stops we made over the three days, but I remember the feeling of it. I remember the earth-red color of everything, the ancient mineral smell, lots of walking on and around interesting rocks I wished I could sketch in a little yellow field book, and there never being a single thing above you to protect you from the sun—no clouds, no trees, nothing. I also remember the flies.

They sell these silly bucket hats in Australia with 360 degrees of beads dangling off the rim to essentially bop around and swat the flies for you. Even after picturing this stupid hat and understanding why it was created, you're still not picturing the fly situation to the correct degree of insanity. It's like a horror movie in certain places. You could be looking at the most beautiful thing you've ever seen, but all you'd want to do is get back in the fucking jeep and away from the living, buzzing clouds.

At one point one of our guides, a casual, funny, bearded dude who made me think, *Yeah, I could have fun doing this job,* was showing us some of the more interesting stuff he knew about the flora and fauna of the outback. We touched and tasted a couple of naturally growing things, but he was saving his grand finale for last. He told us about this insect, a worm-like thing, which had more protein per pound than beef. These insects alone were a huge reason the aboriginal communities who populated the center of Australia were able to thrive in such harsh conditions for hundreds of years.

He found a bush and said, *"Ye see how these heya braynches are awl dowyin,"* and told us that's how you find these protein-packed guys, the elusive witchetty grub. They are wood-eating larvae that grow into giant moths, if they're able to live that long. He dug in the ground around the side of the bush that was "dowyin" (read: dying) and started pulling up certain roots and excitedly said, *"Oy, there ye are ye liddle bugger!"*

He peeled a thick, white, caterpillar-shaped grub from the root, leaving behind a wet spot. It was about the size of my ring finger. Surveying the crowd, he asked, *"All-wroyte, who's guna eat this liddle fellah?"* Everyone stared at their shoes or off into the distance like something was happening over yonder. Someone tossed out the suggestion "Travis?" and immediately it was mob mentality. I was nominated as tribute.

To this day I can remember what that grub felt like in my mouth when I bit down into it. It was nature's *Gushers* fruit snack, except grub guts instead of artificial strawberry flavoring. It was and will always be the grossest thing I've ever eaten (including the still beating cobra heart that I swallowed in a cup of vodka outside of Hanoi on my 34th birthday).

I'm a relatively adventurous eater, but being thrown into this Hakuna-Matata-Timon-and-Pumbaa scene, chewing up a huge bug pulled straight from the ground, was another level even for me. This off-white, puss-filled, worm-shaped grub was not something I would put in my mouth again, but as the saying goes, *"Never try, never know."* I'm glad I know.

On the final day of the tour, we got to see Uluru in all of its glory, and it was glorious. It's essentially a giant rock that juts out from the earth for seemingly no reason, with absolutely no other geographic landmarks, or anything breaking the horizon line at all, for as far as the eye can see. It's epic, and in a few hours you can walk the entire perimeter of it. We circled the famous rock, decided against climbing it (there's a path up, but the aboriginal communities native to the area discourage this tourist practice, so it was a pretty easy choice), and then we drove off to get a sunset view of the whole thing from a different vantage point. We drank cold beers, and I took a depth-perception-altering picture in which it looked like I was holding a baby Uluru in my hand.

The middle of Australia was something else entirely, it came with its own earthy, sensory experience, and I was a fan. I did get that minor in geology as an undergrad, so *maybe I just have a thing for rocks?*

iii. Get to the Coast

Back at the hostel in Alice Springs, I video-chatted with Meg, stressed about my bank account, and ultimately decided that I knew I wouldn't be that happy in the middle of Australia. I loved the ocean, and I figured, with all the various ocean-related tourism jobs, maybe I could find work on the ocean. *I was a kayak guide in Alaska, after all!*

My bank account was down to around $500 at this point, so I had to get creative. I'd heard about finding ride shares on the website Gumtree, and I figured splitting gas with someone was going to be cheaper than the $100+ bus ride back to the east coast. There was also no bus directly where I wanted to go. I was hoping to get to Airlie Beach, famous for the Whitsundays, another massively popular destination for backpackers. I was interested enough as a backpacker to check it out, but now my main goal was to get a job. I needed a job in the next two weeks, or I would be living off credit cards and going into debt *quick* as a hiccup.

I figured I would be persistent as hell until I got a job on a Whitsundays party boat. I had some guiding experience, I was a Divemaster, I was hardworking, and I fucking needed it. I would will this future in Airlie Beach into existence. I would lean on it like an overdue slot machine until it cracked open and money poured out.

First, though, I needed to get there, and I needed to be clever about that part. I got on Gumtree, the rideshare platform, and I ended up connecting with a beautiful lesbian couple in an old RV. I met, let's call them Gwen and Mel, in downtown Alice Springs outside of the main mall, and, after chatting over a coffee for a minute (I think they were making sure I wasn't a crazy person), we loaded my stuff into their sweet, old, yellow RV and hit the road. They were an adorable younger couple in their mid-20s, one Australian and one Dutch, on a mission to explore Australia and fall even deeper in love. They told me that first part, and I surmised the second. I thought about Meg's crooked smile and the love we shared.

The middle of Australia is boring. If you could zoom out the camera angle on our little RV ripping through the barren landscape it would look like a single yellow grain of sand in a huge empty sandbox. When you arrive at one of the sparse filling stations along these desolate roads, you have to fill up. Missing one means you're likely to run yourself out of gas and end up stranded in the middle of nowhere. There are more than a few stories of tourists dying from a breakdown or barely surviving running out of gas in the middle of Oz.

While the girls hung out upfront and drove, I ripped through the first season of *Breaking Bad* on my laptop in the back, hooked up to their solar panel to power my computer, chiming in on their convo now and then, genuinely enjoying my first RV trip. It would take us two and a half days to reach Townsville, and from there I would hitch a bus south to Airlie Beach. The trip was all laughs, road trip snacks, being nervous as hell for Walt, and good times—*except for one night.*

———

Gwen and Mel slept in the RV together, and I had a sleeping bag with a rustic outdoor covering and mat that I could use, so I slept outside twenty feet or so from the RV, like a good dog.

The first night I slept beautifully, and although the girls felt a bit bad that I was sleeping outside, I genuinely loved it. That is, until the second night. Somewhere in the middle of Australia, halfway between Townsville and Alice Springs, I set up my little sleeping bag and tucked myself in to sleep until the sun rose and we would hit the road for our last full day of driving. I fell asleep rather easily and was awoken with a fright.

Fast, strong hands were pushing on my sleeping bag, and as I opened my eyes I saw the silhouette of several bodies hunched over right above me, an arm's length from my head.

As I tried to shake the sleep from my brain, I was lying on my back, arms tucked inside my zipped up sleeping bag, in about the most helpless position you can be. My vision sharpened, and I focused in on a silhouette with a slurred voice demanding, "Let me see *yer phown.*" I quickly realized as my senses gathered that these were drunken men who somehow found our RV pulled off the road while wandering about in the middle of the night. All I could think to say was, "No, I don't have a phone," but they were persistent, grabbing around at my bag. I remember my first response of "no" coming out in a passive, kind tone and thinking, *If I was ever going to be upset or angry toward strangers, this is the time.*

I pulled my arms out of my sleeping bag, sat up on my hands and yelled, "GET THE FUCK AWAY FROM ME. I DON'T HAVE A FUCKING PHONE. LEAVE ME THE FUCK ALONE. *WHAT THE FUCK ARE YOU DOING?!*" Like a lone dog, getting harassed by a group of dogs, I poured on the aggression and anger until they thought, *It's not worth it;* let's not fuck with this crazy guy. It worked. They drunkenly stumbled away, and I watched as they slowed down to consider knocking on the RV door just five meters from me. They paused in front of the door, and I yelled one last time, *"LEAVE US THE FUCK ALONE!"*

They finally did, wandering back toward the main road and into the darkness. I didn't fall back asleep until just before the sun came up. The girls woke me up shortly thereafter, and as we started driving they asked me why I looked so tired and frazzled. I told them the story and was surprised it was all new to them—they didn't wake up from my shouting. I was just so grateful for the sunlight, the RV, and to be headed toward the coast. Sharks have to keep swimming.

iv. New Horizons

After arriving in Townsville, we checked into the same cheap hostel and hung out for one last night before I would take the first bus down to Airlie Beach to land my dream job the following morning.

I wanted a tour-boat job, so I decided to go on one of these tours. I figured I could watch the tour guides at work, become their friends, and convince them to give me a chance. You know, *introduce me to the boss,* or whatever needed to happen. I spent two straight mornings walking from booking agent to booking agent for the Whitsundays overnight party trips, asking if they had any last-minute cancellations.

I knew that you could end up with a sweet deal if a spot on one of the boats happened to open up, and I was determined to be the guy who got it.

On my second morning, I got lucky. A spot on New Horizon had opened up, and I could pay just 125 Aussie dollars for the two-day, all-inclusive trip, originally priced at close to 400 Aussie bucks. *You have to spend money to make money,* I reminded myself, so I scanned my Australian debit card, convinced that I would charm and hustle my way into a job. I would be like the tattooed snorkel guide in Hawaii all those years ago, willing to wake up at 6am, willing to work harder than everyone else.

The New Horizon is the smaller version of the Clipper, the largest and most famous party cruise boat of the Whitsundays. The Clipper has a huge inflatable slide and holds more than 50 people, and things typically get a bit messy. The New Horizon is a 30-person, slightly tamer version. From the moment I stepped on deck, I told myself to just enjoy it and reassured myself that incurring massive credit card debt wouldn't be that bad. I did my part in keeping my lips sealed about what I had paid after being sworn to secrecy by the booking agent. It was a lovely feeling to know that, although I was going broke, I was doing it more wisely than the other 30 people on the boat.

The Whitsundays are still the most beautiful expanse of beaches I've ever seen in my life. It's as if god finger painted bright white sand mixed with shallow neon blue water into beautiful patterns right off the coast of Australia. The sand is so fine that it squeaks when you walk on it, and there is nothing but natural elements that shine bright blue, bright green, some combination of those two colors, or bright white. The contrast filter was dialed all the way up. I found myself constantly lifting up my sunglasses to take a look without the lenses, shaking my head, and dropping them back down with wide-eyes, a smile and a puff of air from my nose.

These two days were spent checking out the various beaches, playing drinking games with the other backpackers on the boat, and going on a single dive at the Great Barrier Reef. The Whitsundays are right at the southernmost end of the world's largest reef system, and, since I wasn't planning on going up to Cairns, this was my chance. It was massively disappointing. The visibility was terrible, and what I could see was bleached and dead. Everything was huge and ancient—but dead.

I also spent the two days flirting with cute backpacker girls I knew I couldn't hook up with since I was committed to long-distance with Meg. It was getting harder by the week, but I held onto my optimism that I could make things right in the long run. She would apologize for being so hot and cold, and then we would just stay hot. It would be worth it. What are the odds that a beautiful girl from my past—who's from Wisconsin and loves the Green Bay Packers—would come back into my life at age 30 when we both happened to be in the same city in Australia? *Wasn't this the universe intervening?*

I was a flirt, but I was good. I made it back to the docks after a few days and had some info from the boat crew, with whom I got on well. One of the guys said he'd be happy to vouch for me and that he thought I would be great for the job if I could get an interview. I was able to find the owner of the company at a café, and I approached him, resumé in hand, desperation dripping from every word of my pitch.

He was a nice enough guy, and, after looking at my resumé, he told me I had all the stuff they look for, but that there just wasn't an opening. I told him, "If you think I have a chance of being the next guy up, I'll hang around Airlie for a bit and try my luck—*this is a dream job.*"

That's when he frowned and said, "Lysten kid, you seem loyk a noice enough bloak and I reckon ye'd do good out there, but we heven't hed a new gouy come on in almost a yea now. This is a daymn good job and fellers don't leave if ye get what I'm saying."

I'll always remember that conversation. It was heartbreaking. I had made up my mind that I would manifest this job, that I would succeed in Airlie Beach no matter the odds. Turns out, that's not how these things always work. Somebody needs to leave their job for there to be an opening, and this type of job—getting paid well to party and show backpackers a good time on a two-day trip to some of the world's most pristine and beautiful beaches—well, people don't leave those jobs very often.

———

I had bet the last of my money on this overly optimistic idea. I was now down to my final $150 dollars, which wouldn't get me very far in Oz, Maui, Wisconsin, or anywhere really. Back at the hostel, where I stayed the night before I left for the cruise, I set up a hammock deep into the woods behind the farthest bungalows on the property, and I left my backpack in the van of some guys I had befriended the previous day while watching rugby. I didn't want to do this. I needed to do this to avoid asking my dad to help his 30-year-old son, proving that he was right—I was a vagabond making terrible choices.

I was poorer and more worried about what was coming next in Airlie Beach than at any previous point in my travels. Not getting this job was another lesson from the road: Sometimes when you want something so bad, and it doesn't happen, maybe the universe is still listening. Maybe what I missed out on wasn't what I should have been seeking in the first place. Maybe knowing that I could endure getting that much closer to fully broke, to hitting bottom, would make me more resilient in the long run. There has to be a silver lining in the hurt and stress somewhere, *right?*

In the present moment, fate can be one of two things: Either the future working out just the way you imagined it would, or things taking a drastic left turn, maybe even running head first into a wall. Sometimes that crash or left turn leads to the best opportunities and greatest moments of your life; it's only in hindsight that we can see how so many failures or misadventures are ultimately redeemed.

v. Downs and Ups

I didn't sleep very well in my little hammock in the woods. I was cold as fuck, worried about being caught, and nervous about all the wild animals and spiders in Australia that, as everyone is made to be aware, can kill you. Australians love talking about all of their scary-as-fuck, lethal animals.

The next day, while sitting at a small café, I sent out emails in every direction to different tour agencies, guiding jobs, restaurant jobs, and anything else I could find online. I said a little prayer with every email I sent, hoping I was wrong about God and that he would jump in now. I also walked around Airlie Beach looking for work, and just when I had almost given up, I was offered a trial shift at a fancy Italian restaurant from a scary manager, an older, intimidating woman with the energy of a scarecrow, who told me to wear all black when I came back that evening.

Although I was slightly more desperate for work at this point, I didn't have the same fuck yes feeling about this place as I had back in Melbourne with my first gig. I was going to take the trial, but something felt off. I showed up ten minutes early, looking sharp in a black V-neck t-shirt, black jeans, and my black Samba kicks. When I found the scary manager to thank her again and let her know I was here, she eye-fucked me and then coldly said, arms crossed, "You can't wear those shoes..." As I looked down thinking, Really, *because of the three white stripes?*, she fired again: "...or those ugly bracelets if you want to work here. Fix that and come back tomorrow night at the same time, then maybe we'll see if you can do this job."

As I walked back to the hostel, to sneak back to my hammock in the woods, to wonder what the fuck I was doing with my life and to worry about spiders, I stared at the white stripes on my shoes. I loved these fucking shoes, and I decided before I made it home that I wouldn't be going to that second trial. I didn't want to work for that talking scarecrow, I didn't want to buy new shoes with my last $100 dollars, and I wasn't taking off all my bracelets. I love my bracelets and the stories—the people and places they effortlessly bring to mind.

I grabbed my computer and started milking down my last $100 by grabbing an apple cider tallboy from the corner store, and then I walked back to the café I was at that morning to mooch some WiFi from the sidewalk out front. When I opened my Gmail, I froze. I stared at the subject line of the newest email in my inbox, afraid to open it.

The email was from Kurt, the owner and manager of "Go Sea Kayak Byron Bay."

Hi Travis,

How are you? Thanks for your email. Shoot me your resumé, we may have a staff member leaving to new work opportunities.

Regards,
Kurt

———

I read the email four times in a row, and I just knew—*this was it*. I was going to get this job and be the hardest-working and best fucking employee this guy Kurt had ever hired. *Is God real? Nahhh*, I wondered alone in the dark.

I immediately wrote Kurt back the following email, with an overwhelming number of attachments.

Hey Kurt,

Thanks for getting back to me. I've attached my guiding resumé, my professional resumé from the States (I've worked with youth most of my life before traveling full-time), a compilation of a few reviews I received from clients last summer, and a few photos of myself in action.

I would be really excited if I was able to come down and be a guide for you guys, so you would be bringing on board a really happy and hard-working guide. I'll be looking forward to hearing back from you.

Thanks!
Travis

He responded early the next morning:

Hi Travis,

You have a great resumé and clearly put top effort into your work. If you would like, perhaps come and join us for a tour; let me know if you'd be keen for this and we could work out a day for you.

Regards,
Kurt

We exchanged a couple more emails, and I made a few more stops through Brisbane and Surfers Paradise, finishing what was left of my St. Kilda money. Eventually, I got another email from Kurt that said, "Good news, one other staff member has just notified me he has a job in the Mentawais starting July 2nd. I think we can work you into our roster given this if you are still planning to head down this way at all."

At this point, I was certain. I was moving to Byron Bay. I was a good paddler and guide, I had a great feeling about this guy Kurt, and I was going to work as hard as possible to earn my place in this new company. I had my sights set on the slots when I should have been playing kayak-black-jack all along.

Once I got to Byron, I checked into a hostel where my good bearded friend Jay from Leroy Espresso had worked and lived for months prior to moving south to Melbourne. It was a large, two-story hostel called Aquarius, with a huge bar and an upscale café. I paid for a full week on a credit card with money I didn't have, and it felt right.

I knew I was going to stay in Byron and that I would come back up on my luck; I just had to nail my trial the following morning and things would be on the up and up. What I didn't know is that my trial the next day would be the most challenging paddle of my career as a kayak guide.

CHAPTER 14: AUSTRALIA, THE END

The next morning I showed up to the kayak trailer at 7:45 a.m., fifteen minutes early, eager and ready to learn. This is when I first met Dougie. Doug eventually became a mentor and role model for me, and not only on the water—when it comes to life in general—but I didn't know any of that on my first morning. I just wanted this older guy with long, blond hair and a tan, ocean-weathered face to like me.

I kept asking, "How can I help?" and taking all the jobs that seemed like the worst ones: lifting kayaks off the top row of the trailer, helping customers into wetsuits, and helping folks drag their kayaks down the skinny sand path that led to the beautiful, wide-open beach. There was a brief conversation I heard between Kurt and Dougie over the phone about the conditions, but it seemed like everything was a go. Dougie ended it by saying "we'll be up on tha raydios. Talk thayr mayte!"

On this first paddle with customers and these senior guides I was doing everything I could to impress and to learn, but my main mission was to appear to be a competent paddler. Not being able to kayak well is pretty much a non-starter when it comes to working as a guide, and I hadn't really paddled much since leaving Alaska; I was a bit worried about signs of rust. I was also a bit worried about the two-to-three meter wave that was barreling out in front of the beach.

Dougie and Ben led the intro and safety speech for the tour, trading off sentences with the trust and timing of a ventriloquist and his dummy. The 24 people who were joining us learned how to paddle, how to flip their boat back over if it capsized, and how they were supposed to get over the intimidating barrel of a wave that was crashing loudly, interrupting Dougie as he talked about it, just in front of us. There are three main things to keep in mind when attempting to get your kayak out past the break: 1. Keep your kayak straight, 2. Get your speed up, and 3. Read the wave and time it so you crest the swell just before it breaks. The first two parts I knew I could do, and the third was a guessing game to some degree.

I was told to help launch boats and get myself out once the customers were all on the water with Ben, guide number two for this tour. I helped chubby couples, kids with their parents, and friends on vacation approach the wave, and I gave the biggest push I could as my feet left the sand, praying they would make it over the swell before it crashed and enveloped their boat. One of my boats got turned and came back to shore, something I learned eventually was rather common. I helped them flip their kayak, get back in, and then fist-pumped at them as they looked back after a second, more-successful attempt. There were no more customers left on the beach.

It was my turn.

I pushed my double kayak out, and jumped into the back seat. I watched the sets of waves coming in, as Dougie did the same thing 30 feet down the beach. I essentially knew I'd be fine after the break, but we didn't have surfable waves in Alaska, and this part of sea kayaking was very new to me. This part could cost me my dream job. I paddled with long, steady strokes out toward the waves, and, as a large three-meter wave broke just 20 feet in front of me, I picked my moment and started paddling as hard as I could, pulling as much water as my paddle could scoop behind my kayak—swift, strong, long strokes that got the kayak moving fast. The second wave of the same set was approaching fast and rising, I put my head down and dug into the ocean with my black paddle, I looked up to see the white wave breaking right at the tip of my kayak. I stuck my paddle into the bursting frothy wave and pulled one last time.

The wave rolled under my boat, and the front half of the kayak dropped six feet all at once, crashing down with a massive *"THWACK"* as I focused on trying to stay in the boat. I looked over at Dougie, who just nodded confidently like this was all child's play, just another day at the office, which it certainly was for him. It did get easier, but I came to learn that getting tossed on Byron Bay's curling, surfable waves on the way out is something that happened to every guide now and then.

Once all the guides and guests were past the breaking waves, everyone gathered again one last time to finish the welcome chat and test their new whips. The senior guides explained where we were, where we were going, what to be looking for, and some aboriginal history and lore of the area. After all of this, we're finally ready to venture out farther into the Bay, to look for dolphins, turtles, and whales, to have a *mother-fucking adventure*, but first, each intro speech by Dougie had one final piece.

Once all the essential information and our favorite tales were told, Dougie would look around at all the guests bobbing softly up and down on their kayaks and change his tone, now slightly serious and somber, to say, "But always remember, the *MOST* important thing while kayaking..." He would scan the guests, letting a long, pregnant pause linger. Then, reverting to his cheerful tone, he would lift his eyebrows under his baseball cap and sing his motto, *"TRA LALA LALA,"* then quickly turn his kayak 180 degrees and begin paddling farther out to sea. All the other kayaks would eagerly follow behind like baby ducks trying to keep up with their all-knowing mother.

It was magical. I saw Dougie do this more than 100 times while working with him, and it never got old or became cliché for me. It set the perfect tone for an adventure, and I came to take it as life advice that applies to nearly everything, but especially the most serious or stressful things—while traveling in a new country, starting a new job, going on a first date, losing your virginity, trying to write a book, "Always remember... the *MOST* important thing... *TRA LALA LALA."*

We all followed Dougie out to sea under a slightly overcast sky, out around "the pass" (a famous surf break), and toward Wategos Beach, the primary home of the dolphin colony that lived in Byron. An off-shore wind began picking up as we paddled out, but it was still manageable, and everyone was smiling, paddling, and feeling the dolphin vibes. Dougie caught a glimpse of the pod swimming together in deeper water, about 200 meters from Cape Byron, out in the dark sea, a sea that sloshed and flowed halfway around the world, all the way to Chile.

With the wind really starting to blow, it was a judgment call. After he yelled, "Stay close together and follow me," we all turned our boats toward the dorsal fins and deep ocean. I stayed toward the back of the pack to help encourage slower paddlers. As we got a bit farther out to sea, the wind picked up again—another two to three notches this time—and even with the dolphins less than fifty meters away, Dougie called an audible and started directing all the boats back toward Wategos, a slightly protected bay.

Things can change quickly in nature, and, by the time the boats were all getting themselves pointed the right direction, the wind had picked up yet again, and dark clouds started rolling in above. I could see the nervous looks on Dougie's and Ben's faces. They were both incredibly experienced guides, and I could read in their body language alone—*this was a very bad situation.*

The previously closely-assembled group of all twelve customer boats started getting pulled apart in the violent gusts of wind as rain started falling in fat, almond-sized drops. From above we were a meandering strand of Christmas lights with 12 bulbs, some beginning to flicker.

Dougie and Ben could just point and repeat the instructions: "Everyone get ye-selves to Wategos beach. *Paddle hard!*" I noticed Dougie attaching his tow rope to a boat so he could help one of the slower teams, and I followed suit. Towing was something I did a lot in Alaska with the heavy winds there, so I tied my tow to the boat of two very light teenage girls who I had been chatting with and keeping an eye on as things worsened.

The girls, trying their best to help me, and I made slow and steady progress into the headwind and eventually felt a break as the protection of Wategos Bay cut the wind speed in half. At this point, Dougie and Ben were calling for all boats to land themselves at Wategos—an entirely separate bay from where we started. This was the only option. We needed to get the boats off the water immediately.

I got the girls within 20 meters of shore, disconnected my tow, and watched them paddle in, falling out of their kayak and tumbling in the waves as they arrived onshore. I turned around and went back out to help a married couple who were still 50 meters or so from the protection of Wategos, looking miserable and making terribly slow progress. They were really grateful when I pulled up and tied myself to them. I put my head down and paddled as hard as I could back into the wind. Once I got them into the Bay's protection, I noticed Ben was on the beach with nine boats, but Dougie was tied to another kayak, paddling hard, slow and smooth. He gave me the same look that he gave me earlier, his eyes under the brim of his black cap saying, *The ocean, ay?!*

Once Dougie and I pushed our guests' kayaks ashore, we paddled ourselves in and double-checked our count. Everyone was on land and off the angry ocean. We had a lighthearted laugh and chatted with the customers as we radioed our manager and fellow guide, Em, who came around to Wategos with the company van.

"*That was pretty crazy, huh?!* Did anyone see those dolphins out there though?"

"*Well, you won't be forgetting today any time soon!*"

Twenty minutes later the second group of customers rolled with Em back to the kayak trailer, grabbed their belongings, and I'm sure a warm cup of coffee and a nice lunch somewhere in town. Dougie, Ben, and I cleaned up the gear and got it organized for transport back to the trailer. As Dougie and I carried a kayak up from the sand he said "Well, I know that was meant to be just a trial for ye, but I don't know if we could have pulled that off without ye, mate! I'll be sure to tell Kurt you were a champ out there."

I told him thanks and sheepishly said, "Yeah, that was pretty wild. Just glad I could help, man!"

Back at the trailer about an hour later, I finally met Kurt, the tall, bald, upside-down-triangle-shaped owner, who was all shoulders and torso from a career as a competitive surf-ski racer. He approached me and told me, "Dougie caught me up on the tour and that ye really helped the boys out on the wadda. I think it's fair to say ye earned ye-self a spot heya. I'll get ye on the roster for as meny paddles as I cayn next week." I tried to hide it, but I'm pretty sure I was unmistakably, visibly overjoyed by this news. I was again employed, and it wasn't just the first job I could find—it was a dream job.

Before I turned and skipped my jolly ass back to Aquarius, Kurt laughed and yelled out, "Oye, and I should hav sayd, I know that was meant to be a troyall, but you'll surely be getting paiyd for that paddle, mate! You can pick up yer pay every Sundahy at the trailer!"

Thank the heavens and the demons, the dolphins and the hardwood court, for that third knee surgery and Milwaukee's cool-uncle attitude.

i. Cheer Up, Slow Down, Chill Out

It's often said that Byron Bay either welcomes you into the family or spits you out, and, from my first full day in the Bay, I was certainly tested, but I knew I was being welcomed by this place with open arms. It felt good to be home.

I was able to earn tours pretty quickly and was averaging about five or six paid paddles a week among the stable of more senior guides.

Dougie was guide one, and not just on the morning I trialed, but in general at Go Sea Kayak. He was the most senior guide, having worked for Kurt since he started the company, and he must have been close to 1000 tours. He also lived in a van that was parked just in front of the beach where our kayak trailer lived. His van was tricked out with a bed and covered in pictures of dolphins, and Doug was the happiest and most active fifty-something-year-old person I'd ever met. He was also kind, hard-working, fair, and—most importantly—he knew how to live. He found the thing that made him happiest, which just happened to be dolphins, and he built a life around it.

The roster for the kayak company, which I'm sure is similar to most outfits, is that the guides are ranked on every tour from guide one through guide four, and a guide is added for every eighth guest who signs up for the tour. We capped our tours at 30 people, so guide four only got work after the 25th person is added to a trip. It probably goes without saying, but the guide rankings aren't random; they're based on some equation of seniority and equity that was pretty unclear. I figured working my way up to get some guide-one tours would be practically impossible, but I was going to earn a solid spot as guide two on as many paddles as I possibly could.

I loved the work and could make 160 Aussie dollars a day, which often involved the experience of seeing a customer cry and say some version of, "This is the best day of my life." It was hard work, but I loved the exercise, I loved being outdoors, I loved dolphins, and I loved making people happy. It was a match made in work-visa heaven.

———

There is something profoundly strong about the energy in Byron that's impossible to ignore. Anyone who's stayed there for longer than a weekend—the kids spending their parents' money backpacking, or the crunchy, circus, surfer, musician, hippie crowd—will all tell you the same thing about the town's gravitational pull. Byron Bay's unofficial slogan, which is written on swaying wooden boards right under the government-funded "Welcome to Byron Bay" sign says, "Cheer up, Slow down, Chill out," with a few colorful peace signs for good measure. I embraced the mantra and felt the hakuna matata vibes from day one.

Beyond life on the water in a kayak, my life in Byron Bay started to take a beautiful shape. I found my people at the hostel I moved into, based on Jay's recommendation, and eventually Jay himself returned. Jay, my closest friend in Melbourne, came back a few short months after I arrived in Byron and happened to move right into my room. I guess it was his room first.

The staff dorm room at Aquarius was a motley crew of twelve young people who were all working for peanuts (read: a free bed) in exchange for living the dream. We had a little patio in the back of the room behind a sliding door, and anytime I came home after sunset I could find a crew out there smoking rollies, grinding up weed, and drinking cheap bottles of white wine while somebody played acoustic guitar. It was a little plot of paradise. If I could have a door in my house that opened up to any one place in the world forever, I would choose this patio.

The characters on the patio were named Leticia, Lev, Ryan, Benny, Marcus, Julia, Jay, Vinny, Dominic, Carl, and Jess. They were all different lengths, different shades and colors, different sounding voices, different gifts. They were from France, Canada, Germany, Sweden, Wales, and the U.S. We knew that the mingling of our paths was one in a million, that we were lucky for it, and we appreciated it to the fullest—staying up too late, waking up too early, taking too many drugs, and playing music a bit too loud. We reveled in our good fortune to be together, happily doing chores for a free bunk bed.

I moved into the staff dorm three weeks after getting to Byron because I convinced one of the managers at the hostel to let me take over running the evening entertainment in the bar. Every night, Aquarius put something on for their guests—a ping-pong competition, karaoke, a quiz night, jelly wrestling—there was always something. I would hand out flyers along the beach during the day then grab a few free drinks and the microphone at night, welcome everyone to Aquarius and explain how whatever was about to happen was going to work. I basically got drunk and talked shit into a microphone—*a second dream job.*

Ping pong night was a big deal, and well over 30 people signed up every Thursday to compete for the crown (read: a $50 bar tab). Karaoke was always fun. I took jelly wrestling as my night off and let some other bro-dude host the event because the whole thing gave me the heebie-jeebies.

My favorite night of them all was an open mic night that I started about a month into the job. Byron Bay was saturated with talented musicians, and on Sundays they started coming to Aquarius to play a few songs. I encouraged everyone to get up and play. I would cheerfully plea, "Even if you only know one song that you normally play to yourself sitting on your bed, get up here and share. *I promise we'll cheer like crazy no matter what you do!"*

Many people performed in public for their first time at my open mic, and nothing made me happier. I would also make the crowd play random bar games between acts to win free beers, and the whole vibe of the evening was open, silly, and supportive. I still specifically remember the feeling I would have after open mic night ended, beaming with positivity and gratitude. Head over heels in love with the music and the vulnerability that had just been shared, and swimming in the idea that making music happen and helping people express themselves was my job. The fact that only two months prior I was sleeping in a hammock in the deadly-animal-filled-woods made it that much sweeter. Eventually, they started paying me $25 an hour for the big party nights because the bar was doing so well since I took over host duties.

———

Before I fully took over hosting responsibilities at Aquarius, I felt like I wanted more work than I was guaranteed to get at Go Sea Kayak. A bad week of weather could have all the guides on hold, so I dropped resumés at a bunch of cafés near Aquarius. I ended up getting lucky with a trial at a place called Mokha: I met a guy who worked there who told me he was on the schedule two nights a week but was leaving. My pitch to the owner was that I would be entirely happy working only those same two nights, and I promised I'd crush it—*it worked.*

I nailed my trial, got the gig, and not too long after that the ownership at Mokha changed, which was the best thing that could have happened for me there. A micromanaging, intense, gel-haired man whom I never felt at peace around was replaced by a South Korean couple whom I absolutely loved and who came to love me back. After they took over, I felt entirely myself there, shooting the shit with customers, pounding free coffees, and stuffing my face with unfinished food in the back of the house while goofing with the chefs. "Travis' corner" in the back of the house has been a feature at most of the restaurants where I've worked. I'm not going to let half a chicken burger go to waste, and if I would hypothetically drunkenly kiss you, I'll even eat the rest of your fucking soup.

I also ended up working a lot more than just two shifts. After Moses bought the place, I was able to work as much as I wanted. When I wasn't on the kayak schedule in the morning, I'd help open up the café, and on nights I didn't have to host anything at Aquarius, I would close the place. It would have been a great job anyway, but Mokha also hosted the very best local musicians on their front patio every evening, and I could drink as much free coffee as I wanted.

So when I wasn't getting paid to drink and talk into a mic, most nights I was buzzing from caffeine, dancing to incredible live music, flirting with tables of cute customers, shoveling leftover fries in my face, and beaming like I had just won a karaoke competition. I found myself most Friday and Saturday nights working while watching Ziggy Alberts and Kyle Lionhart perform brand new songs that shot Byron's magical frequency into the ether, spilling invisible rainbows into the street and creating a hive of swaying, smiling, on-lookers—eyes closed, heads back. Every night I would inevitably think, *"How do you get famous if these guys aren't famous,"* while listening to songs like Days in the Sun, Simple Things, and Sleep By Rivers.

I would hear a Ziggy Alberts' song several years later playing as background music at a grocery store in Lisbon, Portugal. I had a good friend add a Kyle Lionhart song to a shared playlist as his "favorite song of the year." An Australian girl I met years after I left Byron told me "stuff like Ziggy Alberts" when I asked her what type of music she liked. It was a magical time to serve on the front patio of Mokha. Although I didn't need their commercial success to confirm that for me—seeing their careers eventually take off helped me make a bit more sense of the world.

I was pretty good at being a waiter from Alaska Nellies, and I knew you could make good money serving from Leroy's Espresso, but I never imagined I could love serving this much until Mokha, until I was getting paid to watch as the next generation's best singer-songwriters carved out their own unique space in music.

I worked as much as I could in Byron because I loved all three of my jobs and taking an extra shift meant an extra hundred dollars, but I still had some downtime. In my off hours you could find me working out at the pull-up bars near Wategos Bay, reading a book from the library under the shade of my favorite tree, or playing Spike Ball on the beach. I got Spike Ball to send me a free kit after a convincing email to them: "I am the social coordinator for one of Byron Bay's largest party hostels, and I want to spread the joy of Spike Ball!" It worked, and at first I said it to get a free toy, but I surely did spread a generous amount of Spike Ball love across Byron Bay's famous beach.

Along with my pile of books, one afternoon I decided to check out Jumanji and Dead Poets Society from the library. News had come from overseas that Robin Williams was dead. That he killed himself with a belt because he was depressed. I couldn't make sense of how Mrs. Doubtfire, Patch Adams, or the genie from Aladdin could be anything but ecstatic. "I'm Mickey Mouse, they don't know who's inside the suit," a Keanu Reeves quote that I framed and hung on the wall of my brain played on repeat as I processed it, failing to glean any meaning from it other than *living must be so hard for some people. I should always try to lead with grace.* My dad loved Robin Williams, and their energies as short, excitable, middle-aged men felt related, so I was sad to know Robin Williams was gone and sad because I knew my Dad was sad in Wisconsin.

———

This honeymoon period and the deep love I felt for Byron was also aided by my first real foray into LSD. I had dabbled at a festival years before, walking around in the dark holding my shoes, as feeling my soles on the earth was the only thing that made me feel normal, while Skrillex mixed a robot porn soundtrack in the background. He filled the dark air around me with more darkness. After that evening, after sleep never came, in the morning as I lay wide awake in my dirty tent, I thought to myself "maybe acid isn't for me." How wrong I was.

I felt a deep spiritual connection to the energy of Byron, and it steadied my reservations. The land itself, the dolphins, sturdied my constitution. Although MDMA was the more common party drug in Byron, I found myself one evening at a beach rave, holding a bottle of white wine, ingesting a half-dose of acid that I paid for and then placed on my tongue all while spinning in circles on the sand dance floor several feet in front of the DJ booth.

The acid mixed with the white wine in my stomach, and I felt the precious grains of sand beneath my feet. I thanked them each in my mind, wondering where their journey that ended underneath my feet had begun, considering each grain's unique age, staring out at the water a stone's throw away. I took another half dose of acid about two hours later, wanting to double down on the euphoria released in my mind.

I danced with friends, drank more white wine from a bottle, fell in love with a twenty-five-year old French girl from my hostel with long brown hair and *mise en abyme* eyes that went backwards into infinity, and then let her go again, having decided that's how love should work and also that I should always love everyone and every living thing. Every precious living thing. At one point the sun began to rise, and the stars remained. I could still somehow see the solar system as it had been twenty minutes earlier, now shining in the soft pink light of the first sun.

As the sun predictably defeated the night, I walked the eight minutes back up the beach to the path towards Aquarius, towards my eleven roommates on their camp-style bunk beds. Before committing to sleep, I sat in an "L" at the edge of the water, so the soft waves would lap up past my waist, high-fiving my belly button. I saw ancient patterns in the surface of the water, and how there was twice as much hydrogen as oxygen in the magic potion. The fractaling surface put me in a trance and I didn't realize when it started, but as I connected back to my breath, I found I was breathing with the ocean. Each time it lapped past my toes and up to my waist I took in a deep full breath, and let it out again as the water rushed back past my knees in its gentle, ancient way. I was more aware of myself and the connections between all living things than I had ever been allowed to feel.

The next morning as I walked to work, I waved at the trees, and I promise you—*I promise*—they waved back.

ii. Slap-Dap Daisy Chain

Although I keenly remember what it felt like living in Byron Bay and becoming so ingrained in the community, I have always struggled to explain to anyone why I loved my time in Byron so deeply. Three genuinely fun jobs that paid well were part of it, but it was so much more than that. Since then, the best explanation of why I loved it is that, after about two weeks of living there, when I would walk the three blocks from Aquarius to the grocery store, barefooted, to re-up on some vegemite, bananas and ramen noodles, I'd end up saying "hi" to twelve different people, giving out a few slap-daps (the universal surf town greeting, a quick high five followed by a quick fist bump) along the way. It was my beach paradise home, and I was a contributor to it. We were all atomically connected in a never-ending slap-dap daisy chain of well wishes and positive energy.

Between paddles, shifts at the restaurant, and drunk nights at Aquarius, Meg and I kept in touch, and I kept my record of being a faithful boyfriend alive against all odds. It was especially hard in Byron at times, with the undeserved status of being "cool" simply because I had lived there for a while. In the eyes of a beautiful new girl who had just showed up for a few nights, I was apparently the coolest. I was the guy with a microphone and weird haircut who seemed to know everyone.

Even with the undeserved attention from women, I was good. Meg and I had a plan to meet in October and travel Vietnam together for a month, so I held that in my mind. I pictured that long-awaited hotel sex daily. It didn't really make sense for me in hindsight. I only had a year to work in Australia, and the whole point was to make money, so spending a bunch of it to leave town and make no money was—well, *it was for love.*

After four months of coming up in paradise, I packed my stuff and left my three great jobs and wonderful friends to head to Vietnam. I didn't have to leave all of my friends too abruptly, because a group decided to drive with me a few hours to the airport in Brisbane. It was a good excuse to drive the coast, to get out of the Byron bubble.

———

Driving north on the Pacific Motorway, passing a joint around, sun shining down on us, a heavy white smoke began billowing out of the front of Marie's truck. She had just merged onto a new highway and had to drive slowly with this plume of smoke obscuring her view and freaking us out for a while. We threw the joint out the window and got off at the next exit, catching glimpses of cars and the road through puffs of heavy smoke. Luckily enough there was a repair shop not too far from the highway. What was rather unfortunate, for Marie especially, was that the repairs would cost more than she spent on the car, which she had just bought several days before. This was her first real drive with it, and it basically exploded. Even the old bearded mechanic seemed to have genuine grief for Marie having learned more of the details.

We consoled Marie and tried to think of a backup plan. We called our Canadian mates, Ryan and Lev, who had a big sleeper van, and convinced them, "Come be heroes."

Being the neighborly Canucks they are, it wasn't long before they showed up at our exit, and we all loaded in feeling like everything was still golden. I was going to make my flight, Marie was already laughing about her bad luck, and everything was groovy.

We raced ahead toward the airport with plenty of time to spare. Up through the Gold Coast, past its airport, to the big city of Brisbane. We pulled into the departures lane at Brisbane International, and I pulled my phone out of my pocket to check my airline and the flight info. At that exact moment, squinting at my little phone screen, I read that my flight was leaving from the Gold Coast airport—not the Brisbane airport.

My friends couldn't believe it. I couldn't believe it. After living inside of a $100 margin of error, buying this flight was a huge purchase, and I still don't know how my brain confidently remembered the airport so incorrectly that I never even thought to check, not the day before, not the morning of, not even when broken down off the highway worried how I'd make my flight—I never once thought to check. *I knew it was Brisbane.*

Pro tip: Always double check your flight info. Some cities have two airports and some relationships won't survive that.

My friends were nice enough to stop at the Gold Coast airport since it was on the way home. When we pulled into a parking spot in the large empty lot, we saw a single plane rise up into the night sky. It was the exact time of my flight. We watched my plane in silence, slowly disappearing into the night sky toward Asia, Meg, temples and phở.

That night I wrote Meg and apologized. I knew she wouldn't be excited at the prospect of being in a pretty intimidating foreign country without me. Australia was about as exotic as Meg's previous travels had gotten. I promised to buy the very next flight out that I could. I dropped another thousand-plus dollars on a flight and waited one more full day and night to leave. That extra night, I had one of the best acid trips of my life with five close friends huddled into a circle on a beach laughing at everything anyone said, deepening my connection to nature and the drug itself. Maybe it was all meant to be. I'll never forget that night, and I must have made the $1,000 back by now.

———

The day of my second flight, my friend Benny, who also recently bought a van, had told me he was happy to drive me to the airport, as long as I knew which one I was going to. (*HAHAHAHAHA!!!*...Germans and their sense of humor!) I triple-checked and found Benny three hours before the flight so we wouldn't be in any rush. We went to grab his van and found it had been parked in by some cars whose owners we oddly didn't know. We proceeded to run around the hostel asking everyone if they knew whose cars these were. We finally found the keys to one, then the other, and got the two cars moved. Benny jumped in his new van, and we still felt like we were alright with time. Cutting it close, but we'd be fine.

Then his van wouldn't start.

This is how it all actually happened, and it's not the only story I've heard like this about people trying to leave Byron Bay. There are multiple other reasons and stories that account for why I came to strongly believe in the power of this geographical location, why in certain ways I became way more open to some pretty hippie truths in Byron Bay. But this story was the first that I lived through. It was way past coincidence, and I deeply felt like the town didn't want me to leave. Like it had a gravitational pull on me, invisible hooks in my soul letting me go only as far as a kite can fly. "Byron Bay either welcomes you in or spits you out," might not be strong enough of an expression. For me, it was, *Byron Bay either spits you out right away or tries to keep you forever.*

There are also ancient aboriginal truths that speak to this same cosmic power. The original name for Byron Bay was Cavvanbah, which in the native language meant "meeting place." The site of the now well-visited lighthouse up on top of the cape, the easternmost point of Australia, was originally a meeting place for aboriginal tribes from all over the east coast to gather at certain significant times during the year. They'd hold ceremonies, convene, and eventually begin the long walks back to their permanent homes.

Byron Bay, or Cavvanbah, was only a meeting place; no tribes actually lived there full-time despite its intense beauty and the lush surroundings, because even a thousand years ago they knew there was something inexplicably powerful about the location, and they worried if you stayed too long you could lose your mind.

If you know this story, while walking in the streets of Byron Bay it becomes quite easy to think to yourself, *That guy playing that drum and singing the same song for five hours straight might have stayed here just a wee bit too long.* Then one block later, *That girl pretending to hold a ball that's clearly not there, dancing in a circle and talking to nobody, she should maybe move on to the next stop.*

———

Eventually, with a crew of friends helping, we got Benny's van started and he rushed me to the airport. I arrived just 45 minutes before my flight, so they let me board, but I couldn't check anything. I watched as the tip of my fishing spear and travel knife got tossed into a garbage can. I boarded the plane shortly after, thinking, *Whoa, I'll be back in a month, Byron Bay, SHEESH!*

iii. November in 'Nam

I landed in Hanoi and found my long-lost love in a narrow alley filled with hotels and hostels. We had some amazing and long-awaited sex, and then, almost immediately after, things started going downhill.

I love Vietnam deeply, but my first trip there was a great example of how the company one keeps makes so much more of an impact on any trip than the actual sites, colors, and flavors of a country. Vietnam was beautiful and hot, but things with Meg were ugly and frigid, and I was generally miserable in Vietnam. Writing letters to her in my head and feeling genuinely bewildered, switching back and forth between *what the fuck* and I know *I can fix it*.

We couldn't agree on what time to wake up or where to eat, but we also couldn't even agree on the thing we'd always been best at: This was the first time in my life I'd ever argued about sex. I felt like Meg was getting off on the power she held over me sexually, and I was just a sad, sexually frustrated guy who waited five months for a girl who would just say she didn't feel like it most nights while I fell asleep next to her with a rock-hard, five-month-old boner. If you've ever been in bed with another human but felt more alone then you ever have in your life—that was my month in

Vietnam. It was a lot of phở, temples, and delicious coffee, but the whole experience was clouded by relentless, pummeling, emotional torture.

After the trip, I did what any logical person would do—I decided that Meg and I would find a way to work it out. I just experienced one of the most emotionally stressful months of my life, and I was basically like, "Sign me up for more emotional torture and the agreement to not have sex or any interest in anyone else."

I had a strong belief in myself, I suppose. I was sure that, when I got back to Wisconsin in just a few months for the holidays, I'd figure out a way to make it right, to recreate that magical feeling we had just a few months ago in Melbourne, when full rooms of people would disappear around us, made invisible by our love. I could do that! *Believe in yourself, Travis!*

———

I worked every shift I could for the next six weeks, then flew home. I celebrated Christmas with my family then went on my annual pilgrimage to Lake Pickerel in the middle of Northern Wisconsin to walk across its frozen water and sit at Jerry Shuh's Sportsman's Lodge, slugging 75-cent High Life pulls surrounded by my 10 best guy friends.

On December 30, just before New Year's, I moved in with Meg in Madison, Wisconsin. After debating numerous options for where we could celebrate throughout the afternoon, we ended up lying in bed and Googling "world's largest dog" as the ball dropped that New Year's Eve. Our sex that night was warm and primitive, as Wisconsin's bitter winter winds rattled our windows and the candle light licked the walls, but something still felt off.

iv. Drink Wisconsinbly

The first few days back in Madison, Wisconsin, were generally fine, normal at least. We were both still doing an excellent job at not making eye contact with the giant, ugly-as-fuck elephant in the room. There was a very real truth that we were broken, but we were good at ignoring it. Most couples never have to deal with a month like that, even if we could blame it on the newness of Vietnam and Meg's discomfort in Asia in general. I thought being together in Wisconsin might change everything dramatically, but the truth still hung in the air like a rancid elephant fart. I can only write about the emotional torture from my perspective, but it didn't seem like Meg was having a very good time either.

The thing that makes me happiest on this planet is to know I am the source of happiness for someone else. I'm not trying to sound like Mother Teresa or anything—I think I've already revealed enough to rule that out— but it's something I've come to understand over time. It's one of my three life truths, and it's not necessarily an unmitigated good—most qualities are like that, I suppose.

It's the reason I like to be the person who organizes the camping trip we're all taking together or picks this certain, small side street to walk down. What if there's an amazing antique shop down the street and you buy something that you love in there that will always make you think, *I'm glad I was with Travis that day!*

I fully understand that this is not how most people's brains work, but it's how mine does and I can't really help it. I won't even necessarily say, "let's go down this street"; I'll just subtly curve us down it, hope there's an antique shop, that you'll buy something, and that later you'll do the mental gymnastics to thank your lucky stars for me, your pal or lover, *Travis!* Rationally, I know you will never think like that, but what if you did now and then? What if you attributed your favorite day of the trip to my plan, or your favorite souvenir to my trusty navigation, or your new favorite song to my DJing skills? That's why I want to pick the song, because if it becomes your new favorite song ever, then I'll have made you happy—and I'll be happier.

At times in my past I'm sure this has exhausted people—including all of my former girlfriends, or given a bad first impression as someone who loves attention. I think saying someone loves attention can be a one-sided way of saying *someone likes being the reason something was fun*. I often find myself actively choosing not to talk in conversations because I realize my mic-dominance tendencies. *(I have thoughts; would you like to hear?)*

So, in my efforts to become more self-aware now that I'm a full-blown thirty-something-year-old, I've tried to listen more and interject less. To let some percentage of insightful or witty thoughts I have just die in the gloomy graveyard of my mind. Those who know me well might be thinking, "What? That guy doesn't shut up!" but I promise I'm offering less chatter than I could manage. When I do open my mouth, it's because I think I have something to say that can make the person across from me (or the entire room) happy, or a flavor of it—curious, amused, flattered, etc.—so at least my intentions are pure. If anything, my confidence might be too high that I'm succeeding.

———

Back in Madison, you can probably guess what happens next. I tried my hardest and failed even harder. I just couldn't make Meg happy. I was desperately tending to a dying plant, and no amount of water, sunlight, pruning or tiny prayers could reverse the slow, inevitable wilting process.

I could succeed for a few fleeting moments, and making her laugh brought me a deep well of pure joy, but before long I would be in the same room as her with the frosty sense that she would prefer me to be back in Byron or anywhere else in the world. I relished the good moments and stuffed the bad moments into a Santa-style red sack labeled **DENIAL**, and carried on for another week like this, toting my big red bag around Madison, Wisconsin thinking of dolphins jumping in the sunshine.

The straw that finally broke our back as a couple was Wisconsin's own beloved Green Bay Packers. As in most seasons, the Packers were one of the best football teams in the league and in the playoffs with a chance to go to the Super Bowl. Meg was a Wisconsin girl, and she liked drinking beers and the Green Bay Packers as much as the next Wisconsinite. We tend to go pretty hard and have plenty of excuses to black out, the Packers being the biggest excuse of all. In my home state, Bloody Mary's come with a free "beer back" in practically every establishment, and we openly shake dice on the bar every twenty minutes to find out who is buying the next round of whiskey in hopes that it might be the bartender. *"Drink Wisconsinbly"* is our unofficial state slogan, and this was our day to do just that.

Our alarm went off at 11 a.m. on this Packers Playoff Sunday morning. I woke up like an overly excited kid on Christmas morning. I was just tucking my Packers scarf into my Packers jersey when Meg rolled over in bed and told me in a slow sleepy voice, "I don't think I'm going to watch the game, but go have fun without me."

I paused, incredulous, and started to reason, "But, it's a Packers playoff…" then bit my lip and solemnly stuck my Packers socks into my boots and started heading toward the door. I said 1,000 words by just biting my tongue, shaking my head, and leaving. Meg knew exactly how I felt. I got a shot and a beer at a classic Wisconsin dive bar just down the street from our place and found my stool in front of a TV surrounded by green and gold Packers fans. Everyone in Wisconsin, the entire state, was getting drunk together before the noon kickoff. I shook dice with the bartender and wide-bodied strangers to either side of me. An old man with a neon-orange hunting hat lost and had to buy the round, raising his whiskey with a conspiratorial grin as our offensive line was getting introduced on T.V.

I waited, still optimistic that Meg would come for the start of the game. *She couldn't not like being around me SO MUCH that she would miss her favorite team's playoff game? It could be the last game of the season. It's the Packers!*

I pulled out a fortune cookie that I had received at dinner the previous night when Meg and I were getting along well enough. It read, "The real power is the ability to choose." I read it over in my mind several times, slower with each repetition. I took a sip of my Miller High Life, then I pulled my phone out of my pocket and looked up buses back to Milwaukee. I booked one for that afternoon that would leave after the game ended, and I texted my Dad to let him know. He liked Meg, but he also knew to some degree the strain the relationship had put on me. He didn't seem too shocked, he just wanted to know what time my bus would get in so he could pick me up downtown.

Meg did show up at the bar at halftime, wearing a Packers jersey, trying to not make eye contact with the huge fucking proverbial elephant in the corner—who was also wearing a Packers jersey—trying to act like things were totally normal, like having sex that morning was something we did instead of having a weird unspoken argument about the Packers and our relationship. I told her that I had bought a bus ticket home. She didn't seem too surprised either. She was sad, but she understood we were broken as well.

———

That evening, I was back in the northern suburbs of Milwaukee at my parents' place, and I sent emails to all three of my bosses in Australia, wondering if they would be willing to pay me cash-in-hand if I made it back to Byron on a tourist visa. Before I went to sleep that night, I got three emails, all more or less saying, "Just get back here, mate. We'll work everything out." *They seemed happy!*

That same night my Dad came to chat as I watched the Milwaukee

Bucks game on his couch, sympathetically hoping to help his son see well past a broken heart into the bright and exciting future he had. My Dad's future involved me staying in the States, pursuing a *"real job"* and re-finding my predetermined path as a homeowner with a career, right alongside the other suburbs-raised-30-year-olds.

My Dad is one of the most caring and passionate people I know, and our chat started with the genuine urge to make sure his son felt supported, loved, and positive about his future, but there was no way for him to get through this conversation without his fatherly colors showing—his deep desire for me to course-correct toward anything resembling what my brother or closest friends were doing.

My Dad was a retired special-education professor, the first in his family to pursue higher education, let alone receive a doctorate. I was working on being the first in the family to get a master's degree but not use it—in favor of being a flip-flop-wearing vagabond. He loved me, and he wanted the very best for me, but he couldn't make choices for me, and my Dad has always had an issue with control. If you go somewhere with him, he's driving. If you're watching TV with him, he's holding the remote. If there's a commercial on the TV, *you bet your sweet little ass that it's muted because he's not trying to be influenced by these corporate trolls!*

After that conversation with my Dad, imagining the process of picking up the pieces of my nonprofit career along with my heart, I booked a $1,000 flight back to Australia out of San Francisco before falling asleep.

I had the power to choose, and I wanted to be happy again. More importantly, I wanted to be able to make others happy again. My Dad would have to hold onto his middle-class lifestyle and orthodox career dreams for me for at least one more trip. He was disappointed, but finally seemed resigned to just let me go. Part of him knew that I wouldn't be happy if I stayed in Wisconsin.

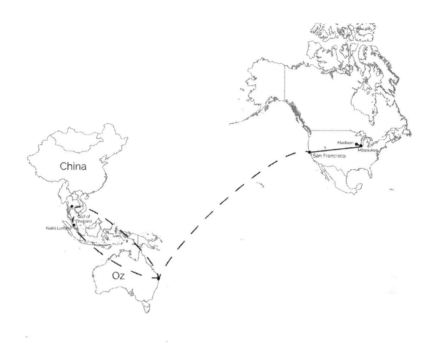

CHAPTER 15: AUSTRALIA, THE ENCORE

I took a second cross-country train to the West Coast. I found it was a fun way to spend a few days and to force the body and mind to slow down. This time my train was destined for San Francisco, where my younger step-sister Claire was set to celebrate her own 30th birthday. My two older brothers (Austin and Charlie, my step-brother) were both coming as well. It was a family affair.

I enjoyed my days on the train in the exact same way I had the first time. I read a few books, I watched movies, I napped, I wrote, and I wondered way too much about the lives of the people sharing the train.

I also vividly remember debating choices at the Amtrak snack bar, always run by a charming middle-aged goofball, that were based on trying to save 25 or 50 cents. Thinking to myself, *I sort of want a hot dog, but that's $2 and a cup of ramen is only $1.50…* before reluctantly deciding, *"I'll take the ramen, my good man."*

Between the trip to Vietnam and flying all the way home to spend a few sad weeks having my heart repeatedly flicked by the heavy middle finger of love, I ended up nearly broke. I made money fast in Australia, but without more coming in, it went just as fast as it came, and I was again down to my last $200. I just had to get back to Australia and into a kayak.

The first night after I arrived in San Francisco, I found my family, we had a few afternoon drinks, and then headed out to a big dinner to celebrate my sister. I should have been more mentally prepared—obviously the menu at a nice birthday spot in San Francisco is going to feel expensive compared to train ramen. I kept my *"harrumphs"* internal and re-committed to having a great time and celebrating my sister as I flipped through the menu mentally calculating calories-per-dollar.

I found the cheapest meal on the menu, passed on ordering more drinks, and talked to the random people I didn't know down at my end of the table. It was a nice night, and if I had a reasonable bank balance, I would have remembered it that way.

What I remember most, however, is one of Claire's friends clinking her glass toward the end of the meal, getting everyone's attention, then saying, "Tonight's all about Claire, so obviously she's not going to pay, but otherwise, everyone just throw a card in the hat and we'll split this whole thing fifteen ways!"

The price per person was about equal to all the money I had in the world, and I asked my brother to join me outside so I could say *"what the fuck"* a bunch to him.

"I ate meat loaf, while this girl next to me had a steak and a lobster... she had *BOTH! What the fuck!* They were ordering the most expensive white wine on the menu... I didn't even get a second beer... *what the fuck! FUCK, MAN!"* My brother just laughed, then covered my part of the bill and told me not to worry about it. My brother is the best. He's also smart enough to know that he's so fucking smart that he never has to stress too hard about money. If he closes his eyes and squeezes his brain hard enough, *boom*—more money.

We shared another few fuzzy, weed-gummy-filled days exploring San Francisco, riding bikes across the Golden Gate Bridge and down Lombard Street's famously steep block, stopping at Joe's Coffee, and reveling in quality family time. I left for Australia with around $20 still in my bank account, thanks to my brother and his big generous brain.

———

My last week in Byron, before heading home for the holidays to watch my one-year work visa run out, my bald, upside-down-triangle-shaped boss at the kayak company, Kurt, gave me some words of wisdom that I've always held onto. He could see I was bummed about leaving the life I loved so much in Byron, and one day he said, "Don't ferget, thee earth's not thayt big of ah playce, mate. Ye can be anywhere ye woant ta be in abowt 24 hours."

After heading to the airport in San Francisco, almost exactly 24 hours later I was back on the east coast of Australia in a bus headed for Byron, ready to take back the life I left. Another 24 hours after that, I was with a group of 20-some tourists singing Disney songs on kayaks because dolphins like music. It's true. They really do.

i. French Firecracker

My second run in Byron was a lot of the same flavors as the first, except for one very obvious difference: I was single and ready to mend my beat-up heart.

I hooked up with a girl I met at the library (in 2015—*I know!*), I dated a girl staying at Aquarius until things went a bit stale, and then I met Margaux.

Margaux was a force of nature. A self-described "witch" and French firecracker. She was a cigarette-smoking, coffee-drinking, music-singing, loud-laughing, philosophy-spitting, advice-giving, always-dancing ball of energy. She moved into Aquarius and began working on the "work for accommodation" team changing over beds. Everyone at the hostel loved her and, within a few weeks, she let me know that we were going to date. I can't say I was mad about it, since she was amazing, but I also remember thinking it was funny that I didn't really feel like I had a choice.

She would say, in her adorable French accent, *"You will be my man, Mr. Travis, just wait and see,"* as she walked by in the parking lot exhaling cigarette smoke in her Aquarius housekeeping uniform, carrying a pile of dirty dorm bed sheets with her other arm.

"Okay, I guess we'll see," I would sheepishly respond through a laugh, equal parts confused and turned on.

Once it happened, we were magnetic to one another. We played music together, laughed constantly together, slept together, moved in together, and fell fast and hard into something that felt really solid. She would come to Mokha, drink coffee, and hang out while I cleared tables and handed out drinks just so she could be around me. The owners at the café loved her, so eventually she started working there without ever even applying. *She was that type of person.*

Once, I mentioned how it would be cool to have this specific musical toy (a wooden stomp pad that plugged in and sounded like a heartbeat), which many other acoustic guitar players in Byron Bay used. That same week, I came home to find one on my pillow. Joining me in the room, Margaux said, very seriously in her accent, *"My baby gets what my baby wants."*

It was well over $300, and she was changing beds for a free hostel stay. *She was that type of girlfriend.*

I learned a lot about being in a relationship from Margaux, but I learned even more about love. She loved purely, for the sake of loving—without any reservations or expectations. It was such a dramatic and positive change from the feeling I had with Meg. With Meg, it was often hard work to get her to even smile. I knew I made Margaux smile by just being there when she woke up. I also learned how to say, "I don't like birds," in French because she would say it whenever the birds woke her up too early.

Upon hearing the very first morning songbirds of Byron greeting the day, I would sleepily say, *"Je n'aime pas les oiseaux,"* before she could, with the morning sun poking through the blinds in our little, shared hostel room. She would wake up laughing and wrap her arms around me, the smell of our morning breath mixing in the small space between us. She knew my rule about never telling partners that I loved them, to try and keep things light on my heart, but we both knew we were very much in love. Everyone in Byron Bay could see that, the dolphins could feel it.

Once, when she was leaving the café and I was ringing up her coffee, she said, "I love you" as she skipped onto the sidewalk, and I replied reflexively, "I love you too." She squinted her eyes and gave me this curious look that said she caught me as she started to laugh. I followed up by saying, "I mean, *here's your change,*" and held out the money that she was obviously trying to leave as a tip while making a dumb face; she just shook her head. For the rest of our relationship, I would whisper, "Here's your change, babe," and give her a hug whenever I wanted her to know I really loved her too. It happened a lot.

ii. Thailand Wolf Pack

Margaux and I had been dating for a few months, and things in Byron had settled back into a beautiful routine of kayaking with dolphins and whales, reading books under trees, playing a lot of music, saving up a decent amount of money again, and waking up to Margaux and the songbirds. About four months after returning, one of my closest friends, Patrick—the same Patrick of Redmond's bar in Chicago—told me to come visit him and his other close friends to wrap up his year of backpacking through Asia. He had more money still saved up than expected and invited me to come help him blow it—to basically party from Bangkok to Koh Samui and then from Koh Phangan to Kuala Lumpur.

I was doing well financially again, I really felt at peace about my relationship with Margaux, and she was really supportive of the trip. She knew I loved her and Pat.

I left all of my stuff in my room with Margaux and packed a small backpack full of tank tops, board shorts, a toothbrush, and deodorant. I checked the airport a couple dozen times then caught a ride with a few friends and told everyone I'd see them in about ten days. I had no real trouble on the way to the airport, and made it from the Gold Coast to Bangkok surprisingly seamlessly.

Once I found Pat and the rest of the boys at our hotel (yes, hotel—we were balling out, *remember?*), I opened a Chang beer and had one in my hand for the rest of the trip. We were five dudes, we were there to party, and it was my first time in Thailand. That first night, we ventured out to the famous Koh San Road party strip, I ate a scorpion on a stick, and we proceeded to all rip nitrous balloons and laugh uncontrollably the rest of the evening. My brain felt how a caterpillar looks.

After a couple nights in Bangkok, we flew down to Koh Samui and spent a couple of nights living the island life. One afternoon, we sat, lined up in five massage chairs, each getting a foot massage by a lovely Thai lady, each of whom seemed to perfectly represent the person whose feet they were rubbing—as we giggled like kids the entire time. We drank buckets of booze and ended up blacked out at a Burger King at 2 a.m., wearing paper crowns and swallowing cheeseburgers whole.

In Koh Phangan, we continued on with more of the same. Scooting around the island, drinking the brown poison known as "Hong Thong," and generally causing a mildly entertaining scene wherever we went. We liked to think others enjoyed the scene, as we would softly howl, "Oww OWWWwwww," like a bunch of half-drunk wolves into the night sky. We indulged in the local mushrooms and felt like we were dying some mornings, our internal organs making a silent plea for us to consider our actions, but we would carry on with the shenanigans when the afternoon sun began to cool. There was no reverse on this train, no hurt or self-loathing that more Changs and brown poison couldn't eventually fix.

After a few nights on Koh Phangan we all flew to Kuala Lumpur. The rest of the wolf pack was carrying on to the Perhentian Islands on the east coast of Malaysia, but I had to get back to work and Margaux. I was breaking up the wolf pack. We had a huge feast on a busy street with small stalls, fried pork steam and durian funk swirling in the street lights, and partied one last night together. I settled my various trip debts with the various drunk wolves and woke up to catch my flight the next morning, sad to leave these guys but excited to know I wasn't going to be drinking that night. I would be in bed with Margaux telling her stories from the trip. It was all, everything, and exactly what I wanted to be doing.

When I left for Thailand to see my mates, I had been warned by plenty of close friends in Australia to play it safe with immigration. The advice was essentially to delete anything from my email, Facebook, and message history that might look incriminating. Basically, anything that might make it appear that I was working since I had come back on a three-month tourist visa, which I had already extended once.

I was freaked out by the prospect of getting in trouble with an authority, the same way I have been since I was five years old, so proceeded with extreme caution and followed the advice as best I could. When the plane touched down on the Gold Coast, I was even wise enough to turn my phone off of airplane mode to catch any messages that might have come in during the flight. I did get one while in the sky from a friend at the kayak company asking me if I wanted to cover one of his paddles that week. I didn't respond—I just deleted the message, and thought to myself, *Whoa, I'm glad I caught this.* The only problem was that it wasn't the last message that would come through before I got to the front of the immigration line.

iii. Immigration Dundee

I waited my turn in the immigration line, feigning confidence and security, listening to This American Life, like picking up what Ira Glass was putting down about a Japanese reality show was all I had on my mind. After about ten minutes, I got to the front of the line, took off my hat and handed my passport to a middle-aged woman as I smiled politely. She scanned my passport and immediately took my passport out of the little box, reached it behind her, handed it to another, larger middle-aged woman and said, *"You need to speak to her."*

I muttered, "Okay," with pretend confusion, and I came around the booth. On the other side, the displeased-looking, plump woman stared at my face, then down at the passport, then back at my face. She then said a line that I'll never forget: "I neydta confiscayte yer phone. *It's a madda of naytional secyarity."*

I froze.

"Okay," I responded, pretending to be baffled about what was going on.

As I pulled my phone out of my pocket and turned it toward my face before extending it to her, I noticed two new messages had appeared on the lock screen. One was from a buddy I met traveling who I hadn't messaged with in several months.

He asked, "What's the name of that Kayak company you work for?"

The other was from my boss at Mokha Café, Moses.

His message simply said, "Paychecks are in a bit early. Come pick them up whenever you want."

My heart dropped down into my stomach as I read the two fresh messages, and then it kept falling until it came out of my asshole and hit the bright white, tiled floor of the immigration room. I hesitated, because my heart was missing, and the woman held her hand out and said sternly, "Ye cayn't touch yer phone, *thes is a madda of national secyarity."*

She looked at the phone for thirty seconds, then immediately walked me across the room to a few hard plastic chairs against the wall and said, in slow-motion, "Whait heya."

I stared at the bright white floor hunched over, mouth open with my hands folded together in my lap, focused on not puking.

After about three minutes, a six-foot-six-inch-tall man, taking long strides across the room, his shoes clicking loudly on the hard white floor, showed up with a leather face and a tight ponytail. He sat down right next to me and said, "We hev raeyson to believe yev broken the terms of yer visa. Come with mey." The Crocodile Dundee of immigration officers then grabbed my left bicep and lifted me to my feet. I walked behind him, through a busy office space, to a small grey room.

Inside of the room, there was a steel table connected to the wall, two metal chairs on either side of it, and a camera in the corner pointing down at the table. There was a locked metal door on either side of the room, and as we sat down he placed a tape recorder on the table. Immigration Dundee warned, "Everything ye say will be recorded for secyrity parposes. I strongly suggest ye du naght lie. It woant help yer situation." He pushed record and asked me to recite my name, the date, the airport I had just flown from, and the airport I just arrived in. He then stopped the tape recorder, stood up, and said, *"T'll be bayck."* It was our first of many interactions in that small, scary, steel room. I was living in a scene from Law and Order. *[Bom Bom.]*

———

I spent the next five hours of my life in that room, telling half-truths and trying my best not to cry. Before leaving for Thailand, I had deleted everything I could find in my phone that I thought would potentially incriminate me as working in Australia. The first time Immigration Dundee came back into the room he showed me Facebook photos of myself playing guitar on the street and asked me if I made money playing guitar.

I said, "I put a hat out and let people throw in change, but it's definitely not a job."

"Well, ye made money fer doing something in Straylya so yev broken the terms of yer visa. Yeh browk um rouyt theyr."

I looked at him for a moment before responding, trying to sort out if he was bluffing or not. He seemed dead serious.

"It wasn't a job. I just like playing guitar. Busking is encouraged in Byron. *There's even a sign about it."*

He stopped the recorder and left the room.

About 45 minutes later, he returned and placed a sheet of paper down in front of me. The paper was a record of my entire texting history with the girl I met at the Byron Bay library when I got back to town in early January, more than five months before being locked into this room. We hooked up for a few weeks, and eventually I tried to break things off with her in the least direct way possible. The sheet of paper was basically several weeks' worth of excuses for why I couldn't hang out.

"I'm working on the water this afternoon."

"I'm at the café tonight, sorry!"

"Taking a paddle this afternoon, *maybe I'll see you tonight!*"

Some of these excuses were real, because I was working a lot. I probably should have just said, "I'm not that interested in seeing you anymore," but I hate telling people things they don't want to hear, so instead I put nice, soft edges on our gradual breakup. Eventually I would become just some dude she used to see a few weeks ago before she even realized that much time elapsed. It wasn't the most noble breakup strategy, but it eventually worked. I never could have predicted that this string of evasive texts would ultimately incriminate me five months later. It felt like karmic comeuppance, and tasted like puke rising in my esophagus.

Immigration Dundee asked me about the texts and said, "It sure sounds like ye-wer werking frum thayse messages dunnit it?" I said that it might appear that way but I was just making excuses to not see this girl. I was trying to be chummy, giving off a casual vibe—*You know how it is, Immigration Bro! Come on, let's just all be cool here, amirite?*

He stopped the recorder after I was done lying about the text message history I had with this girl. He stood up, turned around and said *"I'll be bayck,"* as he shut the door, leaving me alone again in this scary silver closet.

He came back about 45 minutes later, and this time, with a real confident smirk on his face, along with a government laptop. "Alroiwght, well what da ye hayve to say abowt thyis?"

He turned the laptop to face me, which had a photo of me with a group of customers from the kayak company that I quite clearly worked for. I was wearing the bright blue staff rash guard, which even said "staff" on it, posing with a group of happy tourists. He proceeded to slowly flip through more than a dozen other pictures of me on the Go Sea Kayak Facebook page, posted just a few weeks earlier. He did some solid police work and connected the excuses about "paddling" and "being on the water" to one of the two kayak tour operators in Byron.

I was busted. He knew he had me. My only thought now was how to protect Kurt. Our conversation went something like this:

"It looks like you're working."

"It does look like that, doesn't it."

"Yes, it does."

"Well, I was just helping out now and then when they needed an extra guide because I USED to work there in the past... but I don't WORK work there anymore."

"Well, when you helped out, *did they pay you for helping?"*

"Yeah, you know, a little bit I guess because I was being so helpful."

"So you got paid for kayak guiding while on a tourist visa in Australia?"

"Well, Immigration Dundee... when you say it like *THAT!"*

He stopped the recorder, left the room again, but this time came back only about fifteen minutes later and with a very serious-looking document which he told me explains that my visa is being revoked and that I'll be locked up until I'm forcibly removed from the country.

———

I was handcuffed and escorted out of the airport just over five hours after my flight landed, no longer allowed to stay in the country that I had come to call home, where I lived with a girl I had come to love. I loved all three of my jobs, I loved living at the hostel, and I even loved how fucking loud the birds were every morning, but it was all over.

I was perp-walked in handcuffs to a twelve-passenger grey van in the airport parking lot. I was then locked inside with a balding older guy who would drive me over an hour to the immigration prison in Brisbane. Once inside the van, he unlocked my cuffs and immediately started shooting the shit like we were two buddies driving up the coast to catch some waves. "So, what'd they get ye fur, mate?"

At one point he said "Oy, mayte, down't eyven stress about it. This haypens to ah *LOTTA* folks, and it's naught really eyvan a big deal, mayte." It felt like a huge fucking deal, and I loved this old man for trying to downplay the first and only time I've ever been kicked out of a country. It was the first time anyone had even put handcuffs on me.

My life was centered on traveling at this point, so my mind was reeling about how getting removed from a country would almost certainly give me future problems. Australia was part of the Commonwealth; *they must all talk, right?* I wonder if I could still go work in New Zealand—*probably no chance of that now.* Meanwhile, this old bloke driving me to prison looked at me in the rearview mirror with a shrug to interrupt my internal pity session, saying, "Oyyy, don't look so fuggin' woriyed back thah mayte!" And I loved him for it.

When we got to prison, I was processed at reception. They searched my body, searched my bag, and gave me a toothbrush, then this kind-eyed woman asked me, "Do you smoke regular cigarettes or menthols?" Before I could even give an answer, I thought to myself, *I will remember this moment, that question, forever.*

I was given a brief tour, told where and when meals took place, where all the common spaces were, and was finally walked to my room. On the way, we walked past a small gym where an enormous sweaty man, covered in heavy, thick tattoos, (as well as heavy, thick black hair) was squatting racks of plates while grunting loudly. I thought, *Holy shit, that guy is scary. I bet he runs this strange little prison.*

Turned out that he was one of my three roommates.

iv. Blue Swan

My room was a tight square with two bunk beds and three other men living in it. There was a guy from Afghanistan, an Iranian guy, and a Kurdish man from Northern Iraq who was absolutely terrifying upon first impression.

I was given my one phone call, which I used to call Margaux early in the morning. She answered the phone, saying, "You didn't get in did you, I knew you didn't get in, I was telling everybody, I could feel my baby was far away from me and that something was wrong." We both cried a bit, and she said, "Baby, I'm coming to see you. I'll be there as soon as I can be."

I knew I had about 36 hours total in prison. The government handles these situations by partially blaming the airline, and putting those who get their visas revoked back on the exact same flight that they came in on, in the opposite direction the very next time it runs. This gave me a day and a half. Margaux was determined to pack all of my stuff into my backpack and whatever else she could find and then somehow bring all of it and herself to see me in Brisbane. She was the embodiment of love. She was a force.

I took a lap around the prison thinking about how lucky I was to have Margaux in my life, how weird this whole situation was, and trying not to cry. *Is this what you do with a master's degree?* I wondered, as I sat to eat some knock-off, government-funded Fruit Loops in the mess hall.

I walked back into my room after slugging the sugary milk and putting away my bowl, which is when I first realized this large Kurdish man who I had seen squatting six plates was my roommate. He was at the room's one small desk with his back to me, and, as I approached my bed, he turned with a huge smile and said, "I make art for my girlfriend, with this colorful sand! *You want to see?!*"

He was, in fact, doing arts and crafts. A particularly adorable version of arts and crafts where you sprinkle different colored sand onto glue you've strategically put onto certain parts of the paper. In this case, depicting the wing of a bird.

A few minutes later our other two roommates returned, and the Kurdish, craft-making, tattooed weightlifter said, "I heard you get in trouble for playing guitar on the street, or something like this." I responded, "Well, that was part of it I guess. How did you know that?" He rummaged in his closet and pulled out an acoustic guitar. He stretched it out to me on my bunk bed saying, *"I know about everyone here."*

A moment later, I was playing an acoustic version of "Pumped Up Kicks" for my three roommates. They sat with their faces in their hands, leaning off the bottom bunk bed across from mine, the most attentive audience I've ever played for.

In the end, my time at this prison, with these three interesting, sweet, and charming roommates has become like any other sticky memory from a hostel with a handful of people I shared a real experience with. It's actually my favorite memory like this of all.

———

Margaux somehow made it. As impossible as the journey seemed, I knew she would. She had to wait for nearly an hour after arriving for the designated "visitation hours," and then we were able to share two teary-eyed but lovely hours together. They were two hours of pure human experience.

We knew this was not our plan as a couple. We knew we loved each other. We knew this was so fucking weird—a French girl and a Wisconsin boy crying and laughing and very in love with each other at an immigration prison in Australia. So much had gone right and so much had gone wrong to end up here. So much living had happened.

I was able to look through all of my belongings that Margaux brought me, which allowed me to repack my big backpack for Asia. My curly-haired firecracker took a box that was the same size as her, with all of my things that didn't fit, back to Byron and then shipped it to my parents' house in Wisconsin, using my unclaimed paychecks from all three jobs to cover the cost. Looking back, it's a miracle my stuff all made it somewhere. Margaux was a miracle worker. She was a good witch.

———

I spent one last evening in this interesting hostel (read: jail cell) and got myself ready for a new forced adventure. I woke up early to catch my flight, which accidentally woke up my new friends and roommates. They didn't seem annoyed at all, only sad to see me go. The once-scary, large, tattooed man, who now seemed like the sweetest guy you could meet, got out of his bottom bunk across from mine and put on shorts, then offered to help. All three guys were up and there to see me out, to wish me well. I looked at my sand-artist roomie and said, "Thanks, but I think I've got it."

In these final moments together, I finally got to ask them something I was wondering about.

"How long have you been here?"

"Almost two years now...," he responded, as though it were a perfectly normal answer.

"Wait. *What?* Why have you been here that long? That seems crazy."

"I don't know—it's a problem with my visa."

"Well, when will they fix the problem? When will you know you can leave?"

"Not sure, it's a problem with my visa still, and I can't go back home."

I looked up at the two sweet, dark faces resting on their top-bunk roll bars, and gestured *What the fuck?* at them, raising my open palms above my shoulders.

"Yeah I've been here one year, and he's been here one and a half years" the young kid above me said, pointing across the room. He couldn't have been older than 25.

"What! You've all been here over a year, going on two years?"

"Yes, but the food here is pretty good. *It could be worse.*"

"Don't you want to know what's happening though? Wouldn't you want to leave?"

"Yes, of course, but there's a problem with the visa."

I shook my head in disbelief. My 36 hours at this immigration prison were immediately shaded with such a profoundly different perspective. I knew these guys were all in here longer than me, but I would have guessed a few months at most. A few years was beyond the scope of my imagination. It was more government-funded Fruit Loops than I can picture.

As I finished pulling the zippers up on my bags and looking around the room with my hands on my waist, arms akimbo, making sure I had everything, a worker at the jail stopped by and said, "Travis, *tha vayn is waiytin fur ye.*"

I turned to my three new roommates, who were now all dressed and standing by the door, and my bunk buddy asked, *"Give us a hug?"*

We shared a four-way group hug as I said, "I wish you guys the best. I hope your visa troubles get fixed."

I put my backpack on as the sand artist reached into his pocket and pulled something out. He stretched it out to me, saying, "I made this as a goodbye gift for you."

I took it into my hands and realized it was a shiny blue origami swan. Tears rushed from the back of my brain toward my eyes. I had spent the previous day pouting, thinking of my own bad luck, while he delicately folded this paper for me, knowing I was leaving and he was staying.

As I paused, taken aback by this gesture, he said, "Take this bird, and when you see it, think of us in here. We are also birds, but birds trapped in a cage. You're now a free bird again. Go fly, go explore, go enjoy the world, but don't forget your friends you met in here who are still stuck."

I gave him one last hug, and I don't think they noticed, but I wasn't sturdy enough to fight back the tears this time. Big crocodile tears had gathered in the corner of my eye by the time I clipped my backpack across my chest and left the room. I walked with my head down, feeling the fat tears break down and whisk off my cheeks, staining the grey asphalt below, as I rushed through the grounds to the silver van waiting to take me to the airport.

In the airport parking lot my cuffs were finally unlocked. I was instructed to put on a neon vest, then I was escorted through the terminal to my boarding gate by two government workers. Apparently, it was hard to tell from this get-up that I was a criminal—someone who just got in trouble because of his love for dolphins and a small surf town in Australia, and *not* a famous person. People snapped photos of me as I walked through the airport, and I laughed to myself thinking about how I couldn't wait to tell Margaux about the paparazzi. *Do these people think I'm famous?! Smile for the camera.*

I was walked onto the plane about ten minutes before they started general boarding, and I was surprisingly given a seat in first class, I think so that I could be watched more closely. Whatever the reason, it was cool. This was now my second time in handcuffs and first time in first class. I gave back the neon vest and was keenly aware of how strange it felt to be on an entirely empty plane. No vest, no guards, far from the prison, my blue swan in my pocket and my kindle on my lap—I just started to laugh. The entire ordeal was almost behind me, and soon I would just be one of countless backpackers cruising around Malaysia.

I hated Australia when I first got there. I hated that it almost made me hate peanut butter and jelly sandwiches. In the end, even though I was forcibly removed from the country, and even though beers cost way too much—I look back at my time there with acid flashback eyes and see dolphins jumping in the wake, pausing mid-air to wink and flash me a double shaka with their little fins. Byron Bay was home, and I can't wait to go back someday—but I would have to wait three years until that was even legally possible.

Meg and me during our earliest happiest days.

Part of the Leroy Espresso crew clowning around at the cafe.

Meg, a kangaroo, and me during a little trip to Tasmania.

Uluru, in the palm of my hand.

Learning about the opal mines in Coober Pedy. *This is a blower?*

My first RV road trip with this adorable couple.

Whitsunday's fingerpainted beaches.

Some of the Go Sea Kayak staff breaking down our rain cover.

Most afternoons on Byron's beautiful beach. *SPIKE IT!*

Playing my own gig at Mokha for the first time. (Photo by Matias Naya)

In Ha Long Bay at the start of our month in Vietnam.

Pretending to get along somewhere near Ho Chi Minh City.

My whole family got fitted in Go Sea Kayak gear for Christmas in 2014.

Bridge and bro shot in San Fran during my sister's 30th bday weekend.

Back on the water. Back to work.

Jay, back in the Bay, rolling one of his famous *"witche's finger"* doobies.

The Aquarius crew, my closest friends in Byron, on a birthday paddle.

The wolf pack in Thailand at a waterfall that Patrick pooped in.

Just a bunch of sweaty dudes on mushrooms.

We were having the best time before I went to jail.

CONTINENT FOUR: ASIA

CHAPTER 16: MALAYSIA & SINGAPORE

At some point during the flight, somewhere right over the Great Barrier Reef, I realized I left my Australian bank card inside of an ATM in Kuala Lumpur (KL) the night before flying back to Australia (read: the night before I was thrown in jail). I failed to realize this until I was a mile high in a steel tube headed back to Asia, back to Kuala Lumpur. I had a lot of other stuff on my mind, I suppose. I pulled out my little blue origami swan, trying to place my problems on a broader spectrum.

The blue swan helped my anxiety, but I still showed up in Asia without any access to cash at all and was forced to wait for my Australian bank card to get mailed to my Rasta-themed hostel. I had a real fear that the government would somehow drain my hard-earned money from my account since I had earned much of it "illegally."

Turns out they don't touch it, but it also turned out that it's hard to live off of a credit card alone for a week in Asia's cash-heavy economy. Luckily, I met a nice French guy who gave me some Malaysian ringgit in exchange for $100 via PayPal. It provided me with some walking-around money, which I used very sparingly.

I hung around KL eating everything, getting $7 foot massages, and visiting some of the sights until I got my card in about a week which would give me access to the nearly 5,000 Australian dollars I had managed to save over the previous five months. After opening the envelope from the bank, rushing to the ATM, and hearing the *"tchk-tchk-tchk-tchk"* of the machine count my money, I thought to myself, *Would I go back to Australia and work illegally to make 5,000 dollars before traveling in Asia, even if I knew how it would end?*

Yes, absolutely, without question.

I had seen my share of KL, checked out the Batu caves, walked through its many malls, drank on a few rooftops, and was ready to get on a bus going anywhere. The closest town that called to me was just south, a small city called Melaka. My new French buddy who loaned me money was keen to get out of the big city as well.

When we checked into our hostel I found an email from Kurt, my boss at the kayak company, that read, "I'm not worried about the goons at immigration, just glad you're doing alright and that you made it to Asia."

With the peace of mind that my boss at the kayak shop wouldn't be in any trouble for taking me back on and a brand new bank card in my pocket that worked, I was a happy dog that just got unleashed in a huge, brand-new dog park full of exciting, foreign smells.

Later that night, I was playing guitar in the common room of our hostel in Melaka for ten new friends, $5000 saved and a continent separating me from Immigration Dundee.

The highs and lows of travel, the full spectrum, the feelings that come with living hard, with trying and failing, were pulsating and swimming around me. I was equal parts exhausted and buzzing, equal parts alive and at peace.

i. Melaka Peace

I didn't have any expectations about Melaka, just a loose idea that I would spend two or three days there and then move on. Two or three days passed, and I was still happy in Melaka, happy with this new group of friends, and gluttonously enjoying the lack of expectations that the world had for me. I would wake up without an alarm, drink coffee for a few hours in cool, vegetation-covered coffee shops, go for lunch with friends from the hostel, take a leisurely bike ride to the water, have a beer with the sunset, play cards, play guitar, laugh a lot, and let go of any expectations for the evening.

I found deep peace in Melaka, and looking back, part of it is that the town has so few things to do. After a few hours, your schedule is abundantly clear. Coffee. Chill. Walk. Chill. Bike. Chill. Beer. Chill. Sleep until you naturally wake up. *Repeat.*

I've had the experience countless times of showing up in a city for a day or two and having a nice hostel worker plop a black-and-white photocopied city map on the check-in table. Before I could even drop my bags on the bed, they would say, "So, here are the top 15 things you should do in this city." It's a great intention, to show people what's possible, but I think it's much more peaceful to have no idea of what you should be doing. In those moments at the hostel front desk, I would often think, *Well, I'm only here for two nights, so thanks for making me feel like I already screwed up my visit before I drop my bags.*

In person, I would just smile and tuck the map into a specific slot in my backpack. It would eventually be added to my pile of disposable maps in a file cabinet in the basement of my parents' house in Fox Point, Wisconsin. It's where I've kept the physical evidence that all of these travels happened. I imagine a wall in my future leather-and-oak-smelling office covered in these wrinkled, small town and National Park maps, a well-placed globe nearby.

———

I took a bus from Melaka to Singapore and crossed into the future. I don't think I've ever taken more photos with my iPhone in 24 hours. Every street or alley I turned down had a different vibe, and the voice in the back of my head would say yet again, *This is cool. Take a picture.*

Singapore is at the far, southern tip of mainland Malaysia and was part of the same country just over 50 years ago. Since they gained independence, Singaporeans have been busy building an impressive, sprawling city that looks like something straight out of a futuristic movie. One of their most well-known buildings, the Marina Bay Sands, is two huge skyscrapers which appear to be connected by a blimp that landed on top of it. The blimp is a pool that you can swim in while overlooking the glowing, enormous, man-made trees of the Gardens by the Bay. It's like a real-life Asian Wakanda.

Growing up in the States, I remember hearing that you can get thrown in jail for spitting out your gum in Singapore—it was a bizarre, far-away land with crazy laws. In reality, you just wouldn't spit out gum on the sidewalk because the sidewalks are fancy and there isn't litter anywhere.

You can tell a lot about a city from its sidewalks. In Mexico City, they're old, broken, and fighting with the trees. In Lima, they're slick and covered in sea-breeze. In Naples, they blend together with meandering alleys lined with hanging laundry. In Hanoi, they smell of chicken blood and are littered with tiny plastic stools. In Lisbon, they are tiny, slippery tiles that get pushed toward ornately tiled buildings by busy trams. In Singapore, they're large and well-manicured and you would never consider spitting your gum out on them.

I only spent 48 hours in Singapore and one night in a hostel. My one night in the cheapest, most-cramped, eight-bed dorm room that I could find cost me almost $30. I met a local guy staying in my room, living in the hostel, because he said it was his best option to save some money. He had a pet hamster in the hostel and worked as a stunt man at Universal Studios Singapore. He got set on fire and fell ten stories from a high dive into a pool of water twice a day for a crowd of tourists. Despite the dramatics, he couldn't afford a normal apartment. My internal hamster wheel was also turning about economics, development, borders, and cultures. Singapore and Malaysia felt worlds apart while being a mere bus ride away and less than 50 years-post separation.

I crossed by bus back into Malaysia in the evening and stayed at a charming little hostel in Johor, just over the border, for $7 a night. I watched *Ant-Man* at a cinema in a little Malaysian mall where the crowd roared at every predictable joke and mishap, and then headed back to Melaka the following morning.

———

By the time I was finally ready to leave Melaka, the crew of friends that I had been spending a lot of time with at the hostel was ready to leave as well. Before I knew it, I had a new travel family—new people to make plans with, optimistically plowing forward into new towns and towards new adventures together.

Cheryl from the UK had studied abroad in Malaysia years ago, and she was back to revisit the sites of some of her favorite stories. She was bubbly and had big bangs that stopped just short of her eyes. There was Andrea from Germany who was soft-spoken and charmingly "nerdy," donning the type of glasses that make your eyes look huge and pressed up just behind the lenses. There was Mike Muli from Kenya who wore a baby afro, Bob Marley tank tops, and was in Malaysia because, as he said, "This is where in Asia I could get a visa being a Kenyan passport holder." It was a gut-punch of awareness about my own privilege as an American. I hadn't thought about visas for a moment since easily arranging a visa on arrival for my trip into Vietnam six months earlier.

We spent a few days in the Cameron Highlands walking through ancient, mossy forests and brand new strawberry fields before we hopped on a bus to Penang, the food and street-art mecca of Malaysia.

———

In Penang we had a local guide, Peter, a friend of Cheryl's, who was a fellow alum of the same university. The first stop he took us to was a Starbucks on the north coast. A Starbucks that he was *very* excited about. It was right on the beach in Batu Ferringhi, and as far as Starbucks go, it was pretty cool. While we drove away from it, I was holding a failed attempt at a flat white and said to our tour guide, "That was pretty cool, but I've been to a lot of Starbucks—to be honest I would rather see the weirdest or most local coffee bar you know of. The one you would think someone from America would never want to see. *Do you know any like that?*"

Locals always want to show you the "best" of their country, which through globalization and other factors tends to equate to "the most developed" or "the most American" things they know. I want to see the most local thing you know—in this case, the thing that is most Malaysian. Show me a coffee shop whose name I can't pronounce that makes coffee in a way I've never seen. The type of place that has the shop's name in the first coffee on the menu so I know *that's the one I should order*, although I can't picture it.

Our guide drove us straight from the Starbucks to a really huge mall in Penang, and that's when I realized my point in the car didn't sink in. I brought it up as gently as I could to the entire crew while we ate a delicious meal of Penang Asam Laska and other Malaysian treats at a well-loved family restaurant in the mall.

"Peter, the Starbucks was cool and the mall is fine, but I would love to see some parts of Penang that I would never find without a local's help, and that don't remind me of anything in the States or anything that I'm used to. I'm out here exploring and not at home because I want to see something new—*something different.*"

"Oh, so you don't like this mall and you want to leave, *lah?*"

Cheryl jumped in. "No, I don't think that's what Travis is saying, it's just that these things are nice and comfortable, and we understand you're proud of them in a way, so you want to show us that Malaysia has nice things, but we don't need nice things. We're used to malls and Starbucks and stuff."

"Oh, so you want to see something totally different, *lah?*"

"YES! That's what I'm trying to say!" I chimed in as I watched Peter's mind work through the request—processing what he perceived to be the nicest things in his country, not matching what his new international friends were interested in.

After a few minutes of contemplation and a course change in the conversation, Peter interjected with a smile and said, "I have a place. It's just outside of Penang, but it's worth the drive."

———

That night, five of us loaded into Peter's four-seat car and took off from our hostel in the Georgetown neighborhood. I tried to find a radio station in the front seat (the benefits of being a big dude) as we drove out of Penang and onto the long bridge that connects the island to the mainland. Listening to music, being silly in a packed car with new friends, driving to a mysterious destination—*this is what I wanted.* Not to be in the stale AC of a bright-white mall, a thirty second walk from Zara or two different Starbucks.

We drove for about 40 minutes, and the three in the backseat were starting to question whether the haul was worth it just as we pulled into an unassuming driveway with tables and chairs out front and a kitchen tucked behind a big roll-up garage door.

I couldn't read the sign—*it was perfect.*

It was a restaurant that made only one thing: Tom Yum soup. You could pick your type of noodles, the type of meat, veggies and other ingredients to add into the soup, and then hand the bowl you were filling with your favorite raw things to the staff there. They would bring it back as a tangy, spicy, and incredibly satisfying soup minutes later. I went for seconds and tried a different, even spicier broth—we did drive 45 minutes after all!

Tom Yum is still my answer to the frequent debate topic of *favorite type of soup,* and it's almost certainly because of this experience.

After the drive home I laughed and cried while catching up with Margaux, sitting on the porch of our hostel in the graffiti-covered Georgetown neighborhood of Penang.

I normally hate talking on the phone but was on a roll, so I called my Dad to tell him I was in Asia. He asked, "Oh that sounds interesting. Are you staying for good or just a short trip before you go back to Byron Bay?" I waited a beat, thinking of the best words to choose, but in the end just said, "Dad, I can't go back to Byron Bay."

It wasn't a fun conversation. The drama of the situation was over two weeks old at this point, and I was well adjusted to my new reality, to the serious nature of what had transpired, but my Dad was not. I could hear his concern through the receiver. I could hear him picturing me in dirty elephant pants, surrounded by garbage and mangy street dogs, all alone, and so I tried to reassure him, "I am fine. I was planning to leave Australia pretty soon anyway. I am with friends. I am healthy. I have a good amount of money saved up. Please don't worry, Pops."

When the conversation ended, I was relieved, but I could feel a small worry settle in my stomach. This was the first time in my years of traveling I didn't have any sort of distant plan. There was no Alaska, Hawaii, or Australia where I could go make money on the horizon. There was no grandma money. There was just the money I had saved up in Byron—a place I was now banned from returning to—and a credit card in my wallet. I was also now thirty-one, which is the official cut-off for most work visa reciprocal countries. I even got a personal email from the friendly government in New Zealand confirming I was several months too old to apply.

————

Our last night in Penang I met a young guy named Calum from Wales, and before our first conversation ended, I knew I had found a friend. We went and drank at a liquor store that set up tables on the street in front of it, and somehow sold beers for half the normal rate. Alcohol is taxed heavily because Malaysia is a predominantly Muslim country, and drinking is legal but in a way that feels a bit frowned upon. The man who worked at this "discount bar" was huge, shirtless, and had a single, thick white hair growing out of a mole on his chin that was at least 10 inches long. I resisted batting it like a cat.

When I returned to Penang over three years later, I found this illegal bar again, and bought a beer from the same plump man, with the same impressive mole hair, maybe even slightly longer. *What had he been doing the last three years?* I wondered. *Is he proud of his mole hair? Should I touch it?*

One winter when I was back home for Christmas and my annual pilgrimage up north, I stopped into a Chase Bank branch in Milwaukee. "Bank stuff" was always on the "USA List," which I kept as a note in my iPhone. I was sorting something out with a new credit card and talking to a nice banker, a middle-aged black woman who was extremely friendly and talkative. She was really interested in my story and extensive travels, but at one point as we were talking she said, in a loud curious whisper, *"Doesn't it get old, all the traveling? Do you ever get bored with it?"*

I looked at her name on a little wooden sign across from me on the front of her desk, the same desk she had likely been coming to sit at every Monday through Friday for five years or more, and didn't know what to say.

"Not yet," I finally said, as I smiled.

I think about that conversation all of the time, and I wonder if she's at the same desk where we had the exchange. My gut tells me that she most definitely is.

ii. Langkawi Haystack

Calum decided to join a few of us on a trip to Langkawi. Cheryl and Mike planned to spend more time in Penang, and we would meet them after for a trip to the Perhentian Islands, Malaysia's best-kept secret and the spot of the *"cheapest snorkel tour in the world!"*

You could take a ferry from Penang straight north, up the west coast of Malaysia, to Langkawi. After spending nearly $5 per beer everywhere we'd been in Malaysia, I was excited to drink duty-free dollar beers in a tropical paradise. The government made the entire island duty free to reinvigorate tourism, which worked for us.

When we got to Langkawi, I was keen to rent a scooter, but it was raining, and there were three of us, so we realized it would be both cheaper and drier if we rented a small car. We had a few hours before sunset after sorting out the rental car, so decided we should try to do one island thing before checking in somewhere. We set out for a waterfall that we found on Google Maps and knew nothing about, whipping our new rental car through palm-covered roads as the rain dissipated.

Monkeys were shaking the leaves and screeching in the trees above us as we pulled into the dirt parking lot. As soon as we stepped from the car, a man in the parking lot, standing with some authority, yelled over, "Change into your swimsuit if you have one. *This place is good for swimming.*" We were walking into this totally blind, but in a flash we were stripping off our shorts and changing into swim trunks, giggling in the shadows of monkeys. We excitedly hiked the 15-minute path to the waterfall, and we could hear the rushing and falling water well before it came into view. When we rounded the last corner and could finally see what we'd been hearing, we all had the same immediate reaction—we celebrated, howling into the jungle punching our fists into the air. It was one of the biggest waterfalls I'd ever seen in my life, and you could run around and swim in all of its many pools and showers. We were kids again, exploring a new setting for unbridled fun. My face hurt from smiling.

After we swam for about 15 minutes, I had an unprompted, instantaneous sinking feeling and called out to Calum, *"Do you have the car keys?"* He called back across the waterfall with the most logical response possible.

"No mate, *you drove.*"

Right. I did drive. I also have no recollection of what I did with the keys. Maybe I left them in my pants when I frantically put my swimsuit on in the parking lot. Maybe the car is still unlocked? *They're probably just sitting there in my shorts. Yeah, for sure.* The back of my mind also asked a very logical question: Are they in this massive fucking waterfall somewhere?

The sun was starting to set and with the keys missing and taking over my thoughts, I could no longer enjoy this tiny slice of wet heaven, so decided to hike back to the car to investigate. Calum and Andrea followed.

The car was locked, but my shorts were in plain sight on the backseat. I was so certain the keys were in the pocket. We tried to break in, and the man working the parking lot helped us try to break in as well with a clothes hanger he had just for the occasion. We worked on it for nearly 30 minutes, losing more hope and daylight with each attempt. I felt like a fucking idiot. The monkeys laughed and shrieked their judgments.

A Chinese family in the parking lot, drying off and packing the trunk of the last car in the lot, seemed curious about our situation, so I went and talked to them. Luckily, the father spoke perfect English, and without much context, he offered to give us a ride back to the rental agency.

Thirty minutes later we had traversed back across the entire island and were sitting outside of the place where we originally rented the car. The shop was closed, and we were out of options. Our bags and clothes were on the other side of the island, trapped in a rental car. We didn't have our wallets or our belongings and it was now fully dark, as dark as the sky with a week-old moon gets. I was also very aware that it was entirely my fault. I was trying to remain positive but found myself continually mumbling, *"I'm really fucking sorry, guys."*

As we sat there in front of the closed rental agency, dealing with this reality we hadn't imagined, a security guard walked out of the closed mall then locked the door behind him. I asked him if he knew how I could contact the rental agency, pointing at their windows, and gave him the ten-second version of our situation. The universe winked at me, and this guy was apparently a good friend of the guy who ran the rental agency, so once he heard our predicament, he was keen to help as much as he could. After a few phone calls, we got in touch with the right guy, who was ten minutes out but on his way. Something finally went right and I felt the knot in my chest loosen slightly.

He showed up with a spare key and we thanked him profusely. I thanked my Mom in my mind as well. We reassured him, "No worries, we're pretty sure it's just locked in the car," when he informed us that, if the original key was lost, it would be a $200 fee for the replacement. It was a smart key, which meant it had electronics and chips of some sort inside.

We took an expensive taxi back across the island and found ourselves back with our rental car, optimistically opening the back door. I pulled my shorts out and grabbed the pockets. I pulled out my backpack and looked through it. I looked on the floor of the car, all around the backseat. It felt good to hold our wallets and phones, but the key was still nowhere to be found. My stomach sank and the knot tightened again as I realized where it must be—*one of the 15 massive swirling pools at the base of the waterfall.*

$200 was a lot of money for me at this time. I was making choices between staying at $7- or $10-a-night hostels. I was filling up on free hostel breakfasts and eating street food most days. I would carry a flask of whiskey to the bars. I would force strangers to help me cut my hair. I was the epitome of a budget backpacker. $200 would be a massive kick in the financial dick.

I asked the guys if we could come back the next morning just for a bit, so I could poke around with my diving mask and see if I could somehow find it. The odds were low, but even the slim chance of saving $200 seemed worth the effort. They were fine with it. They were incredible friends throughout the entire ordeal. I was the one fucking up and they hit every speed bump with me, chalking it up to "travel," "this type of shit happens," and "it'll be a good story." These are the travel friends you want to make. This is the type of friend we all hope to be in a tight spot.

———

We checked into a small room in a little beachside village at a place called "T-Star," and finally got some well-earned rest. The next morning, after making the most of free breakfast, we drove straight back to the crime scene. I threw my snorkel in the car, ready for a real-life Easter egg hunt with high stakes.

We got back to the waterfall, and the fellas just enjoyed the scene. Calum sat on a rock with his legs crossed, entering into a meditative state. I spit in my mask, washed the lenses in the bubbling water, slapped the strap across the back of my head, and slipped into the first pool. When I opened my eyes underwater, it was clear for a moment, then filled with a billion tiny bubbles that blurred my vision, as water dumped from pool to pool in a never-ending energetic flow.

I tried my best to look through each of the pools I remembered romping around the afternoon before. Checking the rocky floors of the pools, using my hands to feel around the areas where my eyes couldn't see. After checking the four main pools quite thoroughly, I started to lose hope. It was as akin to "looking for a needle in a haystack" as it gets, and the mic-dominant, eternal optimist inside of me started listening to the soft-spoken realist: *"You made a mistake. It's gone, it's okay,"* it told me.

After 45 minutes of intense searching, I decided to drift down the base of the waterfall a bit from where I was swimming the day before, following the flow of the water, wondering if that's how the key would have drifted as well. I ended up in a pretty deep pool about 40 feet from any pool I had swum in the day before, and the first time I dove down I came up holding a pair of reading glasses. I set them on a rock and went back down. This time I came up with a pair of sunglasses. I didn't really want either of the glasses, but my hope was back as I thought—*this is the pool where lost things wind up.*

I kept diving down into different pockets of the pool, and in less than ten minutes I had found five pairs of glasses. I held my breath, went back into the moving water and scanned the rocky bottom. This time, between explosions of bubbles, I saw a small black triangle sticking up in the pebbles.

As I grabbed it, I realized it was a key.

I looked at the logo through my goggles, through the bubbles—**S, for Suzuki.**

It was *MY KEY. I FOUND THE FUCKING KEY!* I shot up out of the water holding the key high in the air and screamed through laborious breaths, "I FUCKING FOUND IT! *HOLY SHIT I FOUND IT!*"

I broke Calum's meditation, and he started cracking up. He Gollum-scurried across the jungle towards me, saying, *"No way, no way, no way"* over and over again as he hopped from one rock to the next. He took the key from my hand and said, "Holy shit man. I really thought there was a zero percent chance of you ever finding this, but I was just trying to be a good friend and happy to come back here and chill for a bit. When you put your snorkel on I thought you were absolutely mad. *You lucky bugger!"*

———

We cruised around Langkawi in our rental car for a couple more days drinking cheap, duty-free beers and exploring new beaches and dense nature. My smile was permanent. I felt like I had made $200 with my incredible key-finding luck. Even the dollar Tiger beers tasted better because they were essentially free, based on my mental math gymnastics. The lows can hurt and often come unexpectedly, but the highs can make you feel like the luckiest person on Earth for a day.

We took a ferry back to the mainland and bought overnight bus tickets to the other side of Malaysia, where we would meet up with our other friends for a trip to Malaysia's best set of tropical islands.

Pro tip: An overnight bus cancels out the cost of a day's accommodation, so getting comfortable on overnight rides is one of the best things any backpacker-on-a-budget can do to extend their travels.

I fell asleep on the bus blissfully, smitten with my life, the future, and the idea that my physical being would still be traveling as I dreamt. Overnight buses are the closest thing we have to teleportation, and I grew to love falling asleep with a good book and waking up to a different climate in a new town.

iii. Mother Earth's Arm-Length

After securing ferry tickets, we were processed through a little port, paid additional "island taxes," and boarded a small skiff to the Perhentian Islands. The islands are quite far out to sea from the coast, which is part of how they've stayed so beautiful and pristine. A mother earth's arm-length away from the pollution and grime of the mainland. Our ferry was basically a small speedboat with a prop motor, and even cruising at a pretty good clip it would take well over an hour to get to the two small, tropical dots of lush land. The captain was chain-smoking cigarettes as he steered our ship toward the islands, knowing exactly where he was from years of driving the same route.

When his cigarette got to the end he would simply flick it off the side of the boat and begin fumbling in his breast pocket for the next one. After watching him do this a few times, I made eye contact and a gesture meant to instigate the thought process: *Why are you doing that? Why wouldn't you just leave the butts in the boat and get rid of them properly later?* He seemed to partially understand what my body language question was and made a gesture back like, *What, the ocean? The ocean is huge...* (or maybe *fucked anyway*), and he carried on flipping cigs into the beautiful blue sea as we pushed forward. For the rest of the ride I played out different versions of the full conversation I couldn't actually have with our captain.

Our crew rented a couple bungalows on the far side of the island which connected to the more popular and populated beach by a 15-minute jungle path. I loved the little trail and walking back to our quiet side to escape the daily fire-show and beach-party energy that lasted late into every night. Each night we were there, we would buy a couple small bottles of rum, lay in the sand, and watch the fire spinners perform. The fire from their poi or staff was the only source of light outside of the moon and stars.

We snorkeled in the day, hiked to the high point on our island, and passed the few days doing whatever it was that pleased us most. *What would make me happy* was the internal dialogue pushing the days along and helping us make choices.

The last night we spent on Perhentian Kecil, the smaller but more populated Perhentian island, we repeated the same evening tradition of drinking small bottles of rum and watching the fire show, a tradition that seemingly lasts 365 days a year if you live on the islands. I fell asleep nice and toasty from the rum but found myself tossing and turning in the night. When the sun rose and the rum wore off, I woke up keenly aware that something wasn't right.

I had changed bungalows the night before, and this new bungalow had a very serious bed bug infestation. I woke up to find my back, shoulders, waistline, neck and even part of my face entirely covered in small red bite marks. I couldn't have counted the number of bites if I tried. They were pushing over a thousand if I had to offer a guess. *They must like the taste of rum,* I thought, as I looked over my skin in the mirror, hungover and itchy.

I packed my bags and got myself out of the bungalow and back across to the other side of the island. That morning we all said goodbye to Cheryl, who got on an early ferry to head back to the mainland, and ultimately back to her real-life in London. I joked about the bites, hiding my frustration, anger, and fear as we all said our goodbyes. The fellas and I found a new hostel to check into.

I tied my backpack up in a thick black garbage bag, trying to prevent any bed bugs that might be in my things from getting out, and I got into my bunk bed, desperately needing a nap.

I should also point out that I was severely sunburned on my back from the previous day's snorkel tour. I had hundreds of bites, I was painfully hungover, my back radiated heat—oh, and *I was also very sick.* The three straight nights of drinking bottles of rum and smoking bad weed had shot my immune system. I was coughing and blowing my nose without pause.

I was on an island paradise that most folks will only ever get to see by Googling "the Perhentian Islands," and all I wanted was for time to speed up: for my bites to heal, for my sunburn to cool, for my nose to stop running, and for my brain to stop jumping on the trampoline. I didn't make any new friends that night. I just waited for time to pass. *High highs. Low lows.*

iv. The Sun Finally Set

When Michael, Andreas, and I got back to the mainland, we stayed in a small town with a major bus station, and I healed. I talked to Margaux on the phone and fell in love with her energy and French accent again for the hundredth time. I also threw all of my belongings on the black roof of the hostel, tied up in a black garbage bag, and just let them bake in the sun for an entire day. The friendly local who worked at the hostel told us about an outdoor market and food court that was having a massive celebration for Ramadan. I didn't quite understand what that meant, but I wanted to, so we walked in that direction.

As soon as we got to the outdoor area with colors, smells, and food stalls everywhere, I felt in the air that *something was different.* I grabbed a pink dragon fruit juice, a nod to the farm days and an excuse to talk about dragon fruit, then walked around the markets as I scanned for details and evidence of what was strange. I grabbed some street meat and ate crispy pieces of pork on a stick, scanning the crowds and vendors, watching them prepare food and mingle with one another. The sun was in its last hour, and the three of us slowly worked through different stalls tasting things in small portions to maximize the number of new, intriguing, and delicious foods we could roll around on our taste buds.

As the sun finally set, I realized immediately what I couldn't put my finger on since we arrived. Ninety-five percent of the people at the market weren't eating, drinking, or consuming anything for the first hour we wandered around—they were just there waiting.

The collective joy of hundreds of people finally getting to eat and drink for the first time in over twelve hours was visceral. I couldn't communicate well with many people there, but one middle-aged man, with a kind, weathered face and a purple baseball cap, told me, "It's Ramadan, and that's why you can see everyone so happy to eat now. We waited all day to enjoy." I've never once in my life waited while awake for twelve hours to eat or drink. I've done a three-day, green-juice fad diet, but even then I was pounding green sludge every four hours to put something in my system. It felt antiquated. It felt other-worldly—this foreign belief system, this other culture whose gods and religious scriptures could get masses to go hungry in their name.

This was my first extended time spent in a majority-Muslim country, and I took note of certain glimpses of that truth reflected in my surroundings: the 5 a.m. call to prayer, the different formal wear, indents on foreheads from years of kneeling—head down on a rug, *praying hard*. Waiting for the sun to set in order to eat or drink was just one example in a world where the signs of a different belief system could be found on passing faces, hanging on the walls, and down every street.

I couldn't help but wonder how different my life and closest-held beliefs would have been if I were born to a family in Malaysia, India, Namibia, or any other part of the world. This was the first thought that broke my little 11-year-old brain and began my religious disillusionment back at that tender, early age. I vividly remember not being able to reconcile the idea that if only Christians get into heaven, then every baby born in India and every other country where they don't believe in Christianity have no chance to get into heaven. *That can't be right. That cannot be the way God would have let this play out if there is a God.* I resigned to feeling like there probably just isn't. I still firmly believe that to this day, and claim agnosticism as a form of intellectual humility. I am 99% sure there isn't a god, but I'll leave some room to be wrong in the naive hope that everyone else will as well.

As I left the market, I was wondering if the Muslim folks who saw me and my two friends eating while the sun was still up thought, *Welp, there goes their chance to be saved* or maybe *those boys just don't get it*. Maybe those who noticed our presence at the market, being fairly easy to spot, just thought, *I wonder where they're from?* as they surmised at a glance the enormous gulf between the way we approached this market, this world, and ideas of religion and faith.

On the thirty-minute walk home from the market, as I thought about the lines that both divide and connect humanity, a guy pulled his car over near us and asked if we needed a ride. He had a round, smiling face, perfectly manicured hair combed back, still appearing to be wet, and a friendly accent that accompanied the impressive amount of English he knew. We trusted our gut and took the ride. We had a twenty-five-minute walk cut down to a five-minute drive, and learned that our new friend was a professional photographer as he showed us photos of happy couples at their weddings on his phone.

Our crew consisted of a Kenyan man with an afro, a skinny Austrian guy with glasses, and me. I think he found us to be intriguing subjects, and before he let us out, he asked if he could take us for a photoshoot the following day. Of course, we accepted.

———

The next day we spent the morning posing in a neatly laid out pine forest, where teenage trees were planted on a huge grid, perfectly spaced, perfectly manicured, still growing and filling the space between themselves. It made for a brilliant backdrop as our new friend made us feel famous and beautiful.

"Now turn your face slightly."

"Look up a bit."

"Now take a step forward."

"Yes, that's it."

I still have the Chang Beer tank top I was wearing that day.

I had found my stride again as a solo traveler, bouncing around from place to place, new best friend to new best friend.

I had shaken off the sticky stress and anxiety residue of getting kicked out of a country, and I was trying to just be present. Make one plan at a time and not worry about *"the future."* I did, however, have one piece of my life that didn't feel as free as the rest.

My heart was still with Margaux, and I felt it weighing on my travels. We hatched a plan to meet in Bali, and I knew going into it that I would have to say things with my face directly to her face that she would not want to hear. I needed to be fully free, and I was starting to believe that long-distance relationships were just set-ups for sadness, angst and jealousy.

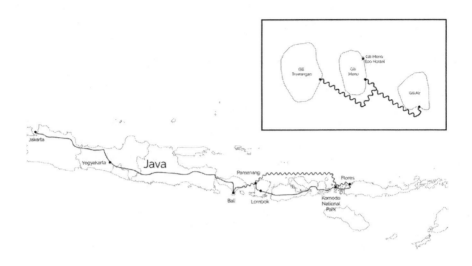

CHAPTER 17: INDONESIA

I got myself from the northeast corner of Malaysia back to Kuala Lumpur on an overnight bus ride, and, after one forgettable night in KL, I was back on an AirAsia flight—this time of my own volition—to Bali. I rented a scooter so I could pick Margaux up at the airport and we could feel free together. I spent a few days in Vietnam 6 months prior as a beginner scooter driver: one with Meg, one alone, and both fairly uncomfortable. I was a very confident cyclist, extremely capable on two wheels, but I was still feeling out the scooter below my body weight, leaning, turning, and stopping as one.

I was also still acclimating to Asian traffic, to being comfortable as one sperm in the sea of sperm-motorbikes. Driving in Asia is more like assimilating to a school of fish than following rigid traffic laws, largely because the laws that do exist are often regarded as mere suggestions. It's also for this reason that if you see a young kid at a hostel anywhere in Asia with bandages on his arms and legs, nine out of ten times it'll be the result of an overzealous scooter lesson without a teacher present.

On the way to the airport, I got pulled over by a local police officer and paid a $20 bribe. Well, he called it a ticket, but it didn't feel like that and I never actually saw any slip of paper with foreign scrawl. As the officer was intimidating me, a ten-year-old drove a scooter past us on the sidewalk with no helmet on, *but a 30-year-old wearing a helmet without an "international license" was the real issue.* I was starting to understand Bali rather quickly. I paid the bribe and let what felt like a legal robbery wash over me. I was too happy to see Margaux to be disgruntled.

I picked up my lightning-bolt of a girlfriend, and we drove straight to our place in Kuta. We checked in and locked ourselves in our room for the next few hours until we were so happy, satisfied, and tired that it was a struggle to feed ourselves. Our sheets even looked exhausted, splayed across the bed and onto the floor. We had a photo shoot in our hotel bathroom mirror, smiling at seeing our tan, naked bodies together again, touching again.

For the next week we cruised around on the scooter, checking out temples and markets and remembering why we were always so happy together in Byron Bay. We moved to a beautiful place surrounded by rice fields in Ubud, a small town with hippie-yogi vibes made famous by its feature in the book *Eat, Pray, Love.* We did two of those three things in Ubud. We spent an afternoon getting crawled on by monkeys at the famous monkey sanctuary, where you can hand out bananas to thankful monkeys. I saw one tourist trick a monkey and hand him an empty banana peel that appeared full. The monkey opened it, looked baffled, then screamed and scratched him and I thought, *Yeah, that's what you get, man. Don't try to trick these dudes. All they want are bananas!*

During our adventures I ended up paying one more $20 bribe to a cop while we were cruising around the north coast of the island. We were in the middle of one of those perfect travel days, on a scooter in a sunny, foreign country, stopping at volcanic craters, temples, coffee plantations, and markets. I didn't let the twenty dollars rob us of our unbridled joy that day, but I did file the offense away in my *what the fuck, Bali* mental file cabinet.

———

After Ubud, we moved back to our posh $10-a-night hostel in Kuta where we first made love. On our last full day together, we decided to go check out the only really famous temple on the island that we hadn't yet visited—*Uluwatu.* It was south of where we were staying, just an hour's scooter ride away.

As we cruised the one road heading south from Kuta down to the small peninsula where this world-famous temple was built over stunning cliffs, I noticed a police stop ahead of us. Lots of scooters were cruising straight through and I thought to myself, *Look confident, just keep cruising.* As I neared the police stop, an officer stepped out in front of me and waved me off the road.

I nodded and slowed down, veering onto the dirt shoulder, my shoulders slumped in defeat. My bike was about to fully rest when something took over me, and I *ripped* the throttle. We took off again in a cloud, streaming from the shoulder back onto the road, getting the scooter up to full speed as fast as I possibly could. I didn't have time to look behind me to see if I was being chased, so I just drove as though I was.

Margaux screamed, *"Baby, what the fuck are you doing?! Why did you do that? You crazy, baby!"* She was upset but also laughing and shaking me and full of the same adrenaline that was coursing through my body. I ripped down the road as fast as I possibly could, and, ten minutes later when we were driving on smaller, winding roads, my stress level finally dropped. As we approached the temple there were no cops in sight. Margaux was still slapping me on the shoulders every few minutes, saying, *"Baby, I don't believe you. You're just crazy."* She was half laughing, half actually upset.

When we finally pulled into the scooter parking at the temple, I threw my helmet in the seat hold and immediately darted into one of the twenty souvenir shops that lined the parking lot. I was a wide, nearly 6-foot-tall, white guy wearing a brightly tie-dyed tank top that a friend had given me in Australia, and there was only one road back to Kuta. I needed a disguise.

I sorted through the tank tops and eventually found a white XL Bintang beer tank top with a little red logo on the left breast. It wasn't until I finally put it on that I was able to take a deep breath and fully relax into the temple vibes and beautiful afternoon. I have a lot of tank tops (read: too many), each with a story of some sort, but this was the only one purchased as a disguise to evade foreign police.

The temple was beautiful, and so was the drive back. I cruised right past the police stop this time without so much as a nod, eyes straight ahead, tie-dyed tank top buried in my backpack.

I dropped Margaux off at the airport the next day with a tearful hug and a knowing look that we would never be this way together again for as long as we lived. When we returned from Uluwatu the night before, we had a conversation that changed everything.

i. Breakish Up

Margaux was a lot of things, but she wasn't subtle. She let me know pretty clearly, most days, how much she wanted things to work out for us. Her own belief in the power of love was enough to make me think *maybe she was right*. It felt like that alone might be enough to carry us through this distance and forced time apart. It felt like it might be enough to start a war if need be.

I told her I wanted things to work out too. That was true. We sat on an outdoor stairwell, and I tried to carefully choose my words to convey my love for her without saying "love," along with my fears and reservations about carrying on with long-distance without saying, "Let's break up."

I told her that I was optimistic about our future but "maybe we should not promise each other anything." As soon as the words left my mouth, I knew everything was different. She didn't respond, which was the worst possible response. She slowly lowered her head into her hands, then she just started crying. She let me hug her while she did. She knew I loved her, but she also knew at this moment that it was over. Everything we had built and the dream we had conjured—in which our love was an indomitable force that we would protect at all costs—wasn't coming true, *at least for one of us*. Once the toothpaste is out of the tube, it's impossible to put back in.

I knew I needed to speak the truth, and that was the most gentle way I could think to word it, but it broke my heart to make Margaux sad. It broke my heart to shatter a love with the one person who believed in the idea of love more than anyone I had ever known.

We still spoke most days in the following weeks, and we even saw each other months later in Bangkok, where we shared a night of tears, drinks, deep conversations, and amazing sex. We fell back into being us for moments throughout that night, which, as soon as they were noticed, would be followed by a heaviness that drowned out the conversation. The silence that followed was deeper than the ocean. Our night in Bangkok was fleeting, but at one point our love was so expansive, our future was together, and we could effortlessly ride the wave of time like the dolphins of Byron Bay.

ii. Swiss Mushrooms

I caught myself replaying our conversation over in my mind, sprinkled with images of some of our best moments—cuddling in the morning sun of Byron, riding a scooter through rice fields just days before—that interrupted the weight of each word as I recalled them. Bali felt like broken love, and I was in the mood to move, to distract myself.

I was also in the mood to do some hallucinogens.

I took the ferry to Gili T, which is well known on the backpacker trail as a place to find fresh mushrooms. The Gili Islands are three little dots off the coast of Lombok, a slow, four-hour ferry ride east from Bali.

I got to the quaint little dock and carried my backpack up the fine white-sand beach, greeted by locals and horses tied to colorful little carts. There are no cars or motorized vehicles allowed on the Gili Islands, which is a huge part of the island's charm. Gili T, the largest and most famous of the three, has a perimeter you can run in an hour-long morning jog.

I found a nice-looking hostel in the middle of the busiest stretch of the main drag on the island and checked in. I was pleasantly surprised that my dorm mates seemed like fun guys. It was a group of four friends from Switzerland, who dressed nicer than your average backpacker and seemed like pretty straight-laced fellas. I was getting a *strictly beer* vibe, until one of them said, "So I heard you can find mushrooms on this island pretty easily. *Have you ever done mushrooms?*"

I responded, perhaps a bit too eagerly, "*Yes!* I love mushrooms. I was hoping to find some tonight, are you guys looking to do some too?"

One of the other guys said, "Yeah, I think so. We haven't really done them before but we're hoping to try here. This seems like the place!"

I immediately made it my mission to make sure these four guys had the best first mushroom experience, or at the very least to make sure they would *have* a mushroom experience. After we all grabbed a simple sunset dinner together, I turned on my drug-finding spidey senses that I developed with Brian finding blow in every conceivable situation in South America.

I apparently give off the vibe of someone who would do drugs, because I'm always targeted by the *"lookie lookie"* guys on the corner anywhere I go in the world. I can be walking with a group of ten close friends or three people I just met, and, if someone is trying to sell some weed or blow, he'll single me out, stare right into my face, and give his best pitch for recreational drug use.

"Charlie. CHARLIE."

"Weed. Blow. Ecstasy."

"You need something man?"

"Good blow man, try before you buy!"

"You wanna get high, *maaaaannnnnnnnn?*"

We walked the narrow, car-free lanes of Gili T, taking in the island vibe, looking for the magic mushrooms. After about fifteen minutes, a short, shirtless guy with wild surfer hair said *"mushrooms"* directly into my face as we passed, so I turned. Before I could respond, he added, "Very fresh. Picked today." I made an inquisitive look, and he said, "Let me show you." Without saying a word, I was in the middle of a drug deal.

While the others loitered casually in the narrow street, I stepped into a dark alley with the surfer guy and he pulled out a cone-shaped brown wrapper from his backpack. When he peeled it back, there was a large pile of fresh, wet mushrooms organized in a tiny, trippy bouquet. They were still wet and in their most natural form. We negotiated the price and I ended up getting an entire cone for the five of us to share, which seemed like a reasonable amount. I walked back to my new friends a hero.

———

We had a few beers, and, as we sat looking at the water, I casually unfolded the paper cone then threw a cap in my mouth and chewed it up. It tasted like mushrooms—like something that had grown on poop.

I handed out a few stems and a few caps to each guy, and we all chewed fast and swallowed hard, shooting expectant glances at each other like the 'shrooms were going to work instantaneously and our faces would just start melting off.

We ordered more drinks and waited for the magic to kick in. Everything everyone said started to get funnier, and lights started to trail as I dragged my vision across the beach bar, scanning the other travelers and the ocean just beyond them. We finished our beers and walked the street until we ended up at a big multi-floor bar with EDM music blaring from the speakers. I love being on drugs around people I don't know in a foreign place. I can just enjoy it all, without fear or care of judgment. I was wandering the levels of the place, enjoying the high as it started building in waves, the music and lights becoming more and more dreamlike with every song. After about ten minutes in the bar, I lost track of the Swiss guys, but I wasn't stressing it. They were on their own journey, *maaaaannnnn.*

I found another friend whom I had met at the hostel earlier in the day, and I told her that those Swiss guys and I were all on 'shrooms and that they were pretty strong. *We should find those guys,* I decided. She wandered the hectic bar with me, then the streets a bit, but there was no sight of them. I got pulled into new conversations and different moments, and the urge to find them dissipated as quickly and strongly as it rose. I wasn't too bothered either. I just figured maybe the craziness of the throbbing EDM and hive of activity was too much for a first trip. I pictured them in my mind's eye laying on mattresses, having a drink, staring at the water, and laughing at everything.

I stayed out talking to random humans, connecting with people in the way drugs always seem to assist with, dancing, and drinking beers slowly until the sun came up. I tripped hard, and it lasted around six or seven hours. I sat with a younger local kid around a beach fire as the sun rose, talking about life, talking about *what really matters, maaaannnnnn.* When I decided to finally return to the hostel, I crept across the dark, palm-covered grass and into the room to catch a few hours of sleep before checking out.

As soon as the door opened, I noticed the guys were also still up, and before I could say, "How was your night?" one of them said, "We talked about it and decided you're not allowed to sleep in our room." I was still a bit high, and this came as a very unexpected buzzkill.

———

"What are you talking about? I'm definitely going to sleep right there," I said angrily, pointing at my bed. The same cross alpha of their group said, "We know you're fucking with us. You didn't even take any of those mushrooms. You're just trying to rob us when we sleep, so we decided that you can't sleep here."

This is the exact point at which I realized they did not have a good trip. They became paranoid and spiraled into some super-negative groupthink about the American guy they met who helped find them mushrooms and was maybe *too friendly, maaaaannnnnn.*

I reminded them, as I attempted to smooth out my scalp with both palms, "I ate the mushrooms right in front of you, what the fuck are you talking about?!" At this point, I started getting upset. The accusation was infuriating. I was trying to help them, trying to be the catalyst for the best travel night of their lives, and, in turn, they surmised that I was a trickster and a thief and that I couldn't sleep in the bed I paid for. *Fuck that.*

"What do you think I want? I have my computer right there. I have clothes. I have my phone," I whisper-shouted as I waved my phone around. "I don't want your shit, and I'm not leaving this fucking room because you guys are bad at doing drugs. *Fuck this shit!*" I finished ranting as I walked toward my bed. My resolve to finally sleep was stronger than theirs' to kick me out.

I crawled under my sheets and turned off the light, as I suspected the alpha of their group started to realize maybe he was being a huge asshole and insanely paranoid for no reason. My actions were not those of a guilty fellow. I shouted into the black room, "You guys fucking suck at doing drugs," as I laid in bed before drifting off to sleep.

A few hours later, I woke up to the sound of them all packing and sneaking out of the room with the heavy air of shitty decisions wafting around the bungalow. I sarcastically said, "Really nice to meet you guys! Great night! *Pleasure was all mine!"* as they moved their bags onto the front porch. When they had all their stuff outside, one of the guys in the group I had really liked twelve hours prior popped his head back into the room and said, "Hey man, I'm really sorry about that interrogation last night. We all got super paranoid. I don't know why we thought you were going to mess with us or something. I'm really sorry, man."

His sincerity made me soften immediately. I smiled at him and said, "You guys really suck at doing drugs. It's supposed to be fun. I had a fucking great time until I got back." He laughed and said, "Yeah, maybe you're right. Safe travels, man." I wished him the same and immediately fell back asleep.

If you Swiss guys ever read this, I hope you've all tried mushrooms again and had a better, more peaceful trip—but if I had to guess I'd say you probably didn't, which might be for the best. *You definitely suck at doing drugs.*

iii. Bamboo Basketball

At this point, with my Australian money slowly disappearing, I decided to start looking for ways to make it stretch. I had heard about a website, *Work Away*, from several other travelers I had met on the road. I paid the $20, two-year membership and poked around the site, looking at the various volunteer gigs being offered all over the world.

It was essentially a Craigslist for travel jobs, where the roles were all volunteer-based, and, in exchange for 20 or 25 hours of work a week, you would get a free bed and maybe a free breakfast. I just wanted to keep the travel adventure alive, so I would be happy to work for accommodation and keep my Australian money from pouring out of my bank account like an above-ground pool with a catastrophic leak.

After searching the website for "Gili Islands" to see if there were any gigs posted, I found one in the most unexpected place—Gili Meno. The three Gili Islands are a short boat ride from Lombok, starting with Gili Air, then in the middle Gili Meno, and finally the most famous of them all, Gili Trabanang, or Gili T, furthest out to sea.

My big night on Gili T was pretty par for the course, which is how the island gained its reputation as a backpacker haven for partying and diving, much like the Utila of Indonesia; the type of place backpackers go for a weekend and stay for a year. Gili Air is the second-largest of the islands and a bit calmer. There are still mushrooms to be ingested but also a lot of yoga and meditation happening. It's the wiser, older, hippie uncle of the young and crazy Gili T. Gili Meno is for honeymooners. *That's pretty much it.* It's the smallest of the three islands, the least visited, and when people do stop there, 95% of the time it's a romantic couple looking for a relaxing island paradise, looking to escape the crowds rather than join them.

There was one hostel though, Gili Meno Eco Hostel, and they were looking for volunteers. I sent them a note and showed up a day later, ready to help out in exchange for a free hammock and some pancakes.

If money were no consideration, I would have stopped for a night at the Eco Hostel, imprinting the strange bamboo structures and homemade vibe of the only hostel on this island into my travel memories as an interesting stop. One short paragraph of the Indonesia chapter of the Asian section of my mental travel book. But money *was* an issue, and since they were looking for volunteers, I took half a look around and decided to call the place home indefinitely.

One of my favorite guiding principles in life has become structure breeds creativity. In this case, my structure was that I was slowly going broke. Money was a pressing issue; I could see the light at the end of my travel tunnel, and what might be on the other side scared me. *Would it be a desk job?* Fuck, I hope not.

As is the backpacker's way, however, money being an issue didn't cause me to stop. It just prompted me to get creative. Work Away led me to the Eco Hostel, and I would make this chapter the cheapest and hopefully most fun one yet. This imposed structure led to getting very creative, *often with bamboo.*

———

My life quickly became a strange routine of eating shitty pancakes every morning (FREE THOUGH!), working with bamboo and power tools in the morning hours, and then taking a quick lunch at Pak Man's. Pak means "man" in Indonesian, so his place, which didn't even have a sign, was basically "Man Man's." (Don't worry, we made him a sign before I left, complete with Pac Man ghosts).

He became my favorite local on the island immediately, and every day he set out a lunch of "rice and other things," which is called "nasi campur," a staple of Indonesian cuisine. It cost about one dollar, it was tasty, it filled me up, and Pak Man was a great host. He would even give you incredibly painful back massages with his strong, small hands if you were lucky.

In the afternoon I would normally snorkel out in front of the hostel, where I would more often than not find a sea turtle or two and swim around with them for fifteen minutes before heading back to shore. I would also normally take on more fun work(ish) projects like painting signs, hanging swings, making games, or just clowning around with the other volunteers and local staff.

There were other volunteers at the hostel, and my two immediate, closest friends were an Argentinian couple, who were both beautiful. They were fit, kind, hard-working, and the kind of couple I would have happily accepted a non-sexual (read: sexual), third-party role in. There were also a few young local guys working at the hostel; Zy, Rossy, and Ali were the perfect crew of young Indonesian best friends. They were living their best lives, partying as much as they could, working as little as they could, and embracing the slow island life. The mission of every day was to do as little as possible and see who could chill the hardest while getting yelled at to work the least.

I was doing some writing while on the island and published my first article to the BuzzFeed community page, which earned a great reception. It got passed around the internet a bit, and it was the first thing I created in a while that gave me a sense of pride. *Maybe I could write about my travels…like a blog or a book or something,* I thought to myself. Then I filed that thought away next to an idea for a rom-com movie script I've always had (read: still have) and the prospect of opening my own hostel someday, which I still hope to do.

In the first month I spent at the Eco Hostel, I built a gigantic swing that swayed over the ocean, I built a basketball hoop out of bamboo that I was obnoxiously proud of, I built some new bathrooms including compostable toilets, and I contributed to *the world's largest bamboo hammock structure!* This was the Eco Hostel's attempt at a claim to fame. It was a three-story bamboo structure that was open-air, and could, eventually, if completed, hang up to 60 hammocks in dorm-style rooms, where you would sleep soundly outside, swaying next to other strangers, knowing your valuables were in a well-constructed lockbox just behind you. I made those lockboxes as well.

One night the crew was in a particularly goofy mood, and we ended up creating our own advanced communication platform. In other words, we hung numerous lengths of twine, each with a paper cup at both ends, throughout the main common spaces of the hostel and up to the star deck. As we let some fresh magic mushrooms from Gili T digest in our stomachs and enter our bloodstream, I thought about how important my first adult phone number used to feel. I still remembered the angst I felt around giving it up.

I got my first cell phone at age 17 through AT&T (read: soulless corporate overlord) and the nice lady at the shop suggested a number ending in "1983," my birth year. *I was proud of that.* Leaving for South America I paused the number and recovered it upon my return. When my phone was stolen in Cancun the second night of my second big trip, my cool personalized number went with it and I never looked back. In hindsight, the amount of importance I placed on keeping that number seems really out of balance with how unimportant it proved to actually be. Phone numbers really don't matter, if you choose not to let them, and I haven't had a proper phone number since waking up that morning in Cancun. Besides, they aren't nearly as fun as cups on strings.

———

I loved the hostel work, although it paid—well, nothing. It paid in pancakes, I suppose, and a free hammock, but that was all I needed to be content. The family at the hostel ("La Familia," as we called ourselves) would sweat together in the day then drink rice wine together in the evening. There was a local man across the island, a five-minute bike ride away, that made rice wine in a little bamboo shack in his backyard. I would bike over to him in the afternoons and fill empty, one-liter, plastic water bottles with the concoctions he fermented. Nobody had lost their vision yet, so we just kept drinking the sweet poison.

The white was strong and tasted like paint thinner, but the red was a bit sweeter—the one I preferred. Both were tough on people new to the hostel, but, at some point, backyard-rice-wine from a recycled water bottle became as normal as a Miller High Life and shot of whiskey at home in Wisconsin.

We are all much more malleable to our circumstances and surroundings than most of us realize. This realization comes when everything changes and you find yourself shirtless, wearing atrociously dirty basketball shorts, drinking rice wine most evenings with ragged travelers and 19-year-old Indonesian kids, sleeping in a hammock, feeling totally at home. *This is what you do with a master's degree.* Definitely, *this is what you do.*

The vibes at the Eco Hostel were great, except for one person: the owner. The land, and eventually the hostel that was built on the land, was owned by an English family. Ben, the son of the primary owner, who managed the hostel most of the year, was kind and understanding. He was an easy guy to get along with, although I don't think I ever considered him a friend because he kept a bit of distance between himself and the volunteer crew. His mother, on the other hand, walked around the property silencing conversations, evaporating them like a glass covering a candle. Her judgmental eyes darting around as she walked, everyone anticipating that they might get yelled at for something unexpected.

She left a wake of bummed-out people in her trail whenever she showed up at the hostel. You could tell if she was on the property by the vibe in the air as soon as you woke up in the morning. The staff, the volunteers, the guests, the birds—everyone was a bit tense, and the seashells we walked on felt more like eggshells, as we couldn't fully enjoy our island paradise without her harshing our collective mellow.

———

Most days while at the hostel, I would sneak off to buy a coffee and use the internet at the restaurant of one of the fancier hotels, just down the road from the hostel. I would check in with Margaux, and do the devil's work of reassuring her that we were alright, reassuring her that Bali wasn't our last time together, although we could feel through the phone that our futures were no longer tethered together. She told me she loved me; I told her I put an envelope of change in the mail for her. She sent me naked pics in red lingerie, and I returned the favor in kind, my sexy photo attempts always themed as dirty-backpacker-bamboo-chic.

During one of these WiFi sessions I stumbled across a Facebook ad for the travel startup Remote Year. I scrolled its amateur website and learned that Remote Year was bringing together digital nomads (read: folks who can work from anywhere) to form travel communities that would move together from city to city across the world for one month at a time for an entire year. It was brilliant. It felt like the future. It looked like they were in the middle of their first trip and maybe gearing up for a second or third.

My immediate gut reaction was a deep *Fuck that's a good idea—I should have thought of that.* I decided to send a cold email to ask if they were hiring. The money constraint felt more real every day. Even though most days I was spending less than five dollars, it certainly wasn't sustainable and I needed to figure something out. *If you can't beat 'em, join 'em,* I thought as I hit send. I closed my computer and packed my bag to head back down the sand path to the hostel. There were some new bamboo bathroom fixtures that needed to be finished.

A few days later, sitting at the same fancy, honeymooners' resort, I got an email back. It was from a guy named Jesse Gross, who was apparently in charge of Remote Year's enterprise team, which meant absolutely nothing to me; I'd never heard of an enterprise team.

Jesse's actual email read:

> Thanks for your inquiry. Could you please send over your resumé with a brief paragraph on why you could be a good fit? I can forward it to the relevant person and have them reach out when there is an opening.

Here is my word-for-word response, typos and all.

> Thanks for getting back to me. I've attached my resumé below, actually two of them. One is from my professional background in youth development and nonprofit management. The other is my guiding resumé, which has been the primary work I've been involved in the past few years while living and traveling abroad. I think both relate to working with a program like Remote Year.
>
> Why I think I would be a good fit...
>
> I am a believer in traveling. After finishing a master's degree in nonprofit management in 2012, I decided to begin a new two year program of my own creation. A master's degree in traveling, self-discovery and learning about the culture, ideas, people, and magic that make up the world. It's been extended to a three year program at this

point. I have been fortunate to land on my feet along the way, and I the last three years have been the best of my life. I would love the opportunity to help facilitate the learning, self-discovery and pushing of personal comfort zones that travel naturally allows for. I think the idea behind Remote Year is brilliant, and being apart of of a start up organization with a mission to get more people out into the world and having the type of experiences I've been fortunate to have would be a dream. I also think my skills and personality type would be ideal for a program or guiding type position with the company. One thing I know about myself for certain at this point in my life is that I am at my best when I'm accountable to other people. As a guide or as a youth worker, I really enjoy having a position of leadership where I am relied upon and looked toward to facilitate group bonding, personal growth, and good times. I have also learned over the past few years of traveling, that I am a much happier and productive person when living and working in a community. I think this is one of the most brilliant parts of remote year, and I know I will thrive in this type of community setting. Beyond my love for travel and how perfectly the program fits my passions, I have a great deal of relatable experience. I have been a group leader, programer, and tour guide for my entire adult life, and it's what I do best. I think I could be an asset to your growing organization, and I think it would be the perfect opportunity for myself to continue to grow, learn and travel.

Thanks again for getting back to me. I hope this finds you well!

Sincerely,
Travis King

I felt good about what I wrote and genuinely certain that I was a good fit. I sent it off with a little prayer from my regular spot at the fancy resort down the road.

Partway into my time at the hostel, a new volunteer showed up with long blond hair and tattered pirate clothing. He was a German backpacker named Clem, and he was a living embodiment of the expression, *"I'm not here for a long time; I'm here for a good time."* He fit into La Familia immediately and worked reception at the hostel most days, which basically meant smoking cigarettes while sitting on a particular stool. He would always talk about opening his own hostel over red rice wine at night, and we would all say, "Yeah, that sounds cool, Clem."

Of all the conversations I've been in where people, myself included, talked about opening their own place, it turns out Clem was the most sincere and driven. A few short years later, I visited Lost in Never Land, Clem's pirate-themed backpacker haven on the coast of Cambodia in Otres Village.

iv. Alpha Monkey

After a month of a routine that got incredibly familiar and with dirt permanently packed under my fingernails, I decided to get off the island for a while. The hostel, the local boys, Pak Man, the sea turtles, a crew of built-in volunteer pirates and friends—they would all be there if I decided to go back.

I took the ferry over to Gili Air for a few nights. I had a less memorable but equally powerful mushroom experience, and hopped on one more short ferry ride over to the main island of Lombok.

As soon as I arrived on Lombok, I realized that one thing was wrong, one thing was missing. While on the ferry, I remember thinking, When was the last time I saw my bank card? I searched my wallet and the pockets of the pants and shirts I'd recently worn. Pockets of my trusty bags I'd hauled all over the earth. I searched them all again, and a deep sense of dread settled inside of me. No fucking way did I lose my card, again!

I couldn't find the Australian bank card that I needed to access my cash, the only card I had that could access any cash. Somewhere between Gili Meno, a mushroom night, and this ferry it went missing. Thankfully, I had a little emergency money tucked away, a lesson I learned on my first trip crossing that border into Bolivia. It was around $60, so I wasn't entirely fucked, *yet*.

When I arrived at the first hostel I found on Lombok, in the small town of Pamenang near the Gili Island ferry port, I was thankful to meet an American backpacker. Not just any American backpacker, but one who also used Chase Bank. As we had beers on the front porch of the hostel, I casually dropped into the conversation, "You don't happen to use Chase Bank, do you?" He did, so I explained my situation, transferred him $100 with a WiFi connection and a few buttons on my phone, bought him a beer, and had roughly the equivalent amount of the local currency after a quick hike to the ATM. At this point, I had around $150 dollars in rupiah, the Indonesian currency, and a credit card that I could use for relatively few things. The lost-card-stress faded like hot shower condensation from the mirror after the bathroom door swings open, so I decided to rent a scooter.

Most days traveling we are forced to sort out directions through an unfamiliar city, find the right train in a station labeled in what appears to be hieroglyphics, or problem-solve our way out of a situation that seems pretty dire. Traveling forces us to push our brains beyond blindly walking through habits and routines, and that has to be good for our mental health and acuity. There's not a day that passes while traveling when a little riddle isn't solved or a new path isn't walked, and simultaneously a new neural connection must be formed. I'm no brain doctor, but I'm guessing there's some science to back up this belief.

Routines allow us to sleepwalk through hours, afternoons, long-stretches of driving, or even full days of our lives, but traveling is the anti-routine. Even working at the hostel on Gili Meno, each day brought a new puzzle: amateur plumbing, cooking with foreign ingredients, communicating with a granny, or buying a new type of rice wine.

————

Outside of feeling ready to get off the little patch of land that was the hostel, I also needed to extend my tourist visa if I wanted to stay longer in Indonesia, to see more of it's 17,500 islands (not a typo). I had to make it to the middle of Lombok, to Mataram—the only big city on the island—where the immigration office would need a passport photo and some money to let me stay an additional month.

I rented a scooter for a few days and explored the island in what had become my favorite way—on two wheels. Muslim Lombok is much less internationally famous than its Hindu neighbor Bali (the only Hindu-majority province in Indonesia), but it's equally as beautiful. Rolling through lush green hills on a scooter with tropical foliage and wild monkeys greeting you from the trees and roadway railings, it's hard not to wonder, *Why had every traveler in the world heard of Bali, but most folks couldn't even tell you what country Lombok Island belonged to? How come tourism is on a totally different scale a short ferry ride away?*

I stopped at the very top of a mountain pass, the high point on the northern edge of the island where the road opens up a bit and there's a place to pull off. Covered by towering tropical trees, the road dipped downhill through an endless palm forest on either side. Before I could kill the ignition on my scooter, lots of little, curious friends started coming out of the jungle. As I looked for some peanuts I had stashed in my backpack, ten monkeys turned into twenty, which turned into forty. I was handing peanuts out one at a time to some cute, brave monkeys who walked straight up to me, hands out. I was occupied by their little humanoid hands grabbing the peanuts one at a time and didn't notice a bigger alpha monkey approaching from the back of the group, just three meters away now. He screeched and showed his teeth to catch my attention and my reflex was to throw the entire bag of peanuts over all the monkeys' heads, while echoing the alpha's feral screech. They turned to scramble for the scattered nuts, and I hopped back onto my scooter in a flash. I drove off giggling uncontrollably downhill through a beautiful, tree-lined jungle road as monkeys howled in the distance, wrestling for my peanuts.

Later that day I booked a cruise to Flores, an Indonesian island which was a few days boat ride away. The travel office took a credit card, thankfully.

When I say cruise, I don't mean an all-inclusive mega-ship with a swimming pool on the deck. I mean a boat where twenty backpackers would be crammed together like sardines, packed into a room with little mattresses sleeping side-by-side with complete strangers. I was told a week earlier by an English lad at a hostel that taking the "backpacker ferry" was the biggest mistake he made on his trip. I was told multiple times that some people loved the experience and others hated it. I loved being on a boat, so I figured it was my type of mistake to make.

v. My Type of Mistake

The next day I met the twenty other brave folks who signed up for a four-day, three-night voyage, floating with strangers from Lombok to Flores. Somehow, almost the entire crew on the boat spoke native Spanish, so I was the odd man out.

There was a group of guys traveling together from Spain, a group of friends from Chile, a few other couples on board, and me, a gringo who spoke present-tense caveman Spanish. *You want beer now?* The only other two on the boat who seemed happy and able to speak English were buddies from Java. Two twenty-year-old Indonesian guys who smoked heavy clove cigarettes and were quick to laugh.

I knew from the moment I saw the small boat why some people complained. I also knew that I would love the next four days. I read books, drank beers, played my little guitar for my new Spanish-speaking friends, goofed around with my buddies from Java, and flirted a lot with one of the girls from Chile.

She had a beautiful, freckled face with strawberry blond hair, and I found myself wanting to be around her all the time. It was a crush like those I had in high school. In my mind, I played it cool, trying to make her laugh and be her pal. I'm sure to everyone else I seemed like a dopey boy with a crush on his babysitter, following this freckled beauty around the boat and being overly interested in everything she said.

I was still talking to Margaux before the cruise, but couldn't reach her for the entire duration. I still cared about her very much, and, with her witchy powers, I had the feeling she knew all the way in Australia that I had a secret strawberry crush.

We finally made it to Komodo National Park and, after we checked out the weird gigantic lizards—really dinosaurs with strange double dicks (let's call them what they are)—we parked the backpacker's ferry in the port of Labuan Bajo.

The group made plans to get dinner at a well-known pizza place in town that night, and we all broke up to check into various hostels and hotels. The crew from Santiago had a room at a nice little hotel, and I checked into the cheapest, dirtiest hostel I could find. I needed money to keep this Asian fun going and my bank account was going one direction. It was the kind of place where you fall asleep with your fingers crossed, hoping you don't wake up having been the secret midnight cheesecake for a bunch of bed bugs.

After checking in, my crush asked if I wanted to go see her hotel. She told me she was going to nap and wanted to know if I wanted to nap too. My tongue then unraveled onto the floor like a cartoon dog's and I might have yelled *"AWOOOGA!"* I can't fully remember. I followed her through town and up a hill, my heart pounding in my chest, the front of my brain yelling "TAKE A NAP TOGETHER—*come on, this is an obvious sign, dude!"*

The walk was probably eight minutes, but it felt like an eternity. I weighed my genuine desire against my sense of self and integrity on some type of scale in my mind. Could my physiological truth that I wanted this woman outweigh my desire to see myself as a good guy? After all, I was still someone who felt a bit committed, spoke regularly to a woman he cared about, and really didn't want to make his witchy French girlfriend sad (even if we had de-committed to some degree and lowered our love-dot on some pretend chart about relationships).

I tried to play it cool as we got closer to the room. Once I got inside, I dropped my pants immediately then pulled her shirt up over her head, and we started making out passionately.

Just kidding: I did that thing again where I lie to you because I think it's funny.

In reality, we entered the room and I certainly acted weird as my mind raced a million miles a minute. Her roommate was already asleep in the king-sized bed on the far end of the room facing the wall. My crush crawled into her own bed and motioned to me, so I took the two-foot strip on the edge right next to her, moving like a robot. She rolled toward me, then smiled, and for a moment our faces were twelve inches apart in the same bed—I didn't know what was going to happen.

I said, "SLEEPY TIME," because I'm smooth as fuck and a born player. Then she rolled over.

Our bodies were close enough that they were touching, which I liked, but I guess the scale tipped toward trying to be a good guy, and I never did anything beyond lie perfectly still. For the next 90 minutes I didn't sleep for a second, I just laid with my eyes closed, trying to breathe like a normal person—which I had somehow forgotten how to do—and desperately trying for some reason to gain the reputation of "someone who is good to nap with." If anything was ever going to happen between us, this was certainly the moment. The moment passed. It felt like I had been holding in a fart my entire life.

A day later, my Chilean friends and I went on two mind-blowing dives together, and a day after that they left town. My strawberry crush and her travel pals continued on their path, eventually leading back to Santiago. Years later I found out through the magic of the internet that my Chilean crush and the Chilean guy in their traveling threesome became a couple later on that trip. A few years after that, they even got married. Maybe it was all for the best, even if it required me to breathe like a fucking crazy person and remain perfectly still like a weird, broken robot for over an hour that day.

vi. Nudi Shark Movie

The two dives I went on with my Chilean friends were by far the two best dives of my entire life. I'd been on over 70 dives up to that point, the majority off Utila, but I didn't know the ocean could be so alive in such a condensed space, so saturated with secrets. I was noticing it on a microscopic level like I never had before, and on a macro level (read: shark) I was more blown away by the things I experienced on two dives than on the previous 70 combined. I knew before surfacing from the first dive that I was willing to go into debt for more. *This is what credit cards are for,* I confidently reassured myself as I watched sharks enjoy their breakfast on the second dive of the morning.

On the first dive of that day I was separated from my friends who were less experienced divers. This meant I could go visit one of the most famous sites in the area for sharks. You had to be an advanced diver or beyond for this particular site because the current was incredibly strong. Imagine a toddler standing in a parking lot during monsoon winds; you'd want someone with more general standing experience for those conditions.

Our dive instructor briefed us on the dive: "Once we enter, and everyone gives the okay, we will begin to descend straight down. Follow me only a few meters to the spot, then find a rock and hold on. Once you have your spot and a good grip, *enjoy the shark movie.*"

Twenty meters below the surface, holding on for dear life as a current tried to rip my grip loose over and over, I watched more than a dozen sharks feed on a huge school of delicious-looking fish. I'm not sure what type of fish they were, but they reminded me of the large, monotone, fish-colored kind you'd see on ice in the seafood section of a fancy grocery store.

The next dive was less challenging but equally wild. Two days later, with my Chilean crush long gone, I went on my fifth and sixth dives at Komodo. I saw five different nudibranchs on the first dive (basically sea slugs, which are incredibly rare and hard to spot) and went on the most adventurous and difficult dive of my life on the second.

Our Divemaster gave the dive brief and told us to follow him, reminding us this dive was for advanced divers only. We would stop at a huge crevasse to watch a school of barracuda, then we would carry on farther down into a huge bowl, cross it, then wait and see what happens. "Just try to stay close behind me." The way he finished his brief with a sly smile and a side-eye had my brain hula-hooping.

After the barracuda, across the bowl, I was about two meters behind the Divemaster and all of a sudden I was in a washing machine. Once I gathered myself I realized I was in a current flying somewhere between 15 and 20 miles per hour through the ocean. I also realized I was laughing hysterically into my regulator. The scene from *Finding Nemo* where Crush, the surfer sea turtle, rides the speedy current with eyes half-open like the little stoner he is flashed in my mind as I flew.

I left the island with a few hundred dollars of credit card debt and a mind full of vibrant images and visceral memories—memories of a specific quality and saturation that the ocean had never quite provided me with before or after. I was grateful to Indonesia for reigniting my love for diving; moreover, I was happy to know that a backpacker cruise where you sleep like sardines on a shitty ferry was certainly my type of mistake.

———

I took a series of small vans and ferries back across the islands to Lombok—taking over thirty hours total—and eventually made it back to the hostel where I had stayed before I knew Komodo dragons had two dicks. When I returned to the hostel in Pamenang, near the Gili ferry port, I was eager to find the owner whom I befriended when I arrived and who was doing a favor for me. He had given me the hostel address so I could ship my special package from Australia.

When I walked into the hostel, he was behind the desk on the phone. He immediately interrupted his own conversation, put the phone down on his desk, grabbed an envelope and said, "Your special package came today!" Inside I found a fresh yellow-and-grey Commonwealth Bank card. I would have waited for days and weeks longer if needed, but thanks to my new friend I was free to go. He was so kind that he single-handedly raised my positive feelings about all of his countrymen. All of my memories of Indonesia are full of people who I didn't know very well, but I now imagine are just as kind. We all have the power to do this, I suppose.

After I got my magical bank card with its fresh magnetic strip, I marched down the windblown street, trash lining the edges, to the closest ATM. After a pregnant pause, breath stuck in my throat, my Australian-earned money began clicking through the inside of the machine, eventually pushing its way out through the little doors' rubber lips. I breathed a deep sigh of relief, took the money into my hands, and looked up at the Indonesian sky while laughing to myself. *Don't let this happen again.*

For a traveler in front of a new ATM in a foreign country with an empty wallet, the *"tchk-tchk-tchk-tchk"* of an ATM is the sweetest noise in the world. It means cold beers, street food, and a hostel bed. It's the whine of the line running out of a fishing rod on a real live one. It's the sound of further adventure.

vii. Java's Blue Eye of Mordor

I returned to Gili Meno, played with power tools, got covered in dust, drank copious amounts of rice wine, swam with the sea turtles, and found myself feeling ready for something new after two short weeks.

I loved my life on the island at the Eco Hostel, but I knew that the days I had in Asia—and the days I had as a young, confident backpacker who could stumble face-first into any country to find new friends and adventures—were numbered. So many names and places on the map still represented mystery, which never sat well with me as a kid paging through National Geographic in our suburban basement. Now that I was so close to so much that was new to me, I had to go see more.

At the time that this feeling was rising, there was a friendly backpacker—let's call him Andrew—at the hostel. He was from the UK and seemed the quiet type—the type with a quality camera around his neck and pants that could quickly convert to shorts. His color palette was a combo of various beiges.

Around the nightly bonfire, I shared with Pirate Clem and the other members of La Familia that I was off in a couple days, that I was sniffing for something new. Andrew approached me over free pancakes the next morning and asked where I was planning to go. I told him that I had a flight to Manila out of Jakarta in about ten days, so I was pointed in that direction, toward Java.

He asked if he could join. I didn't know him well, and he didn't generate much emotion in me in either direction, so I told him, "Sure, let's do it." It would feel better to leave a tight-knit hostel family with one beige mate than alone with two backpacks.

We ferried together, across the water that separates Lombok from Bali, and took a shuttle bus to Ubud. Although I fed the monkeys their bananas, hid my knees from the temples, and enjoyed the lush, peaceful bubble of Ubud again, I was still itching for something new, and my mini-cat-calendar pages were flying off the proverbial wall.

We organized a shuttle bus from Ubud that would board a short ferry and continue on to Java, specifically to the base town of a volcano that Alex was excited to see. The crater of Ijen was described to me, by our tubby driver, as "looking into an eternal blue flame, like seeing the blue eye of Mordor." I was interested, and only slightly less so when informed our tour would leave at 1 a.m.; it needed to be black-out-curtains dark to see the blue flame, and this hike wasn't some short ramble.

———

The next morning we were carrying our exhausted bodies along a severe trail cut into the side of this volcano at 1:30 a.m., wearing bandanas around our faces to ward off the intense sulfur smell. The volcano purged the vile gas—smelling of rotten egg salad—from every crack and crevice; it circled in the air, choking our small group and blinding tourists with walking sticks.

We carried on pushing for the finish, pumping our legs toward Mordor. Every three minutes of the two hour hike, a different flip-flop-wearing Indonesian man would pass us, carrying a stick behind his neck off of which dangled two plastic buckets filled with rocks. Our friendly Indonesian guide let us know, "*Sulfur is stinks, but it very valuable!*" He kept our mind off the harsh fog, sharing with us how sulfur is used in various cosmetic and beauty supplies, and this volcano is both a tourist stop and an active mine for the locals in the area. As he pointed to one of the humbly sized men walking by in flip-flops and torn, dirty clothing, he explained, "*They do three times each day, up and down, make maybe $25 or $30 dollar a day.*"

I stopped feeling sorry for my nose, and I let the sweat run. We made it to the glowing blue flame, to the stunning turquoise lake at the center, and took photos with our lovely pint-sized guide at the water's edge. We took photos with Andrew's nice camera, holding an average-size bucket full of sulfur blocks on our necks, feeling the weight of the miners' daily lives for about seven seconds. We decided that just one trip up, down, and back was enough for today.

After leaving Ijen and recovering lost sleep, we carried on west, toward Mount Bromo, Java's favorite child of a mountain. It was bigger than I could have imagined and older than Java itself. We covered ourselves in its space dust, got lost on its ridges, and stared into its mysterious holes.

The geology minor side of me was a cup overflowing, but I was ready for civilization. Andrew and I spent a few more nights together in

Yogyakarta and saw its famous temples, and I decided I didn't really love his company. I didn't strongly dislike him either, but I found myself in the unfamiliar position of wanting to be free of my travel mate, grateful for my impending solo flight.

In the same way that travel allows one to take risks in romantic relationships, it gives freedom to try unexpected friendships as well. Far more often than not, those risks will work out, but, even when they don't, it's barely a flap of the butterfly's wings in the annals of your travel diary. It's a board game someone bought you that you don't like playing.

I left Andrew in Yogyakarta for Jakarta (similar name but very different place—the capital in fact) and stayed with Gamal, one of my clove-smoking mates from the backpacker ferry, who was already back to normal life in Jakarta. Through a series of Facebook messages, he invited me to stay at his family's beautiful compound tucked in a well-to-do neighborhood in the grey city that I was happy to be flying out of rather than into.

After a few drinks at a bar and a single night's sleep, I woke up and thanked my mate and his family, told them how lovely it was to know people in this intimidating city, and waved goodbye as their driver escorted me to the airport in a freshly-waxed, black Cadillac SUV.

CHAPTER 18: HONG KONG AND THE PHILLIPINNES

I flew from Jakarta to Hong Kong to catch a ride on a boat I found through findmycrew.org. There was a yacht captain I messaged on the site who was headed from the Port of Hong Kong to Manila. In exchange for sweeping the poop deck—or whatever boat jobs they might use me for—I would spend five days at sea working on my beard and thinking of pirate jokes. I had never done anything like this, but loved being on a boat so was stoked for the opportunity.

When I got to Hong Kong I reconnected with an old travel friend from England—let's call her Gwen—who I knew was now living in Hong Kong through Facebook. She let me crash in her apartment while she house-sat a much nicer place for an extremely rich friend up the hill towards Victoria Peak. Her apartment in the dry-food neighborhood of Hong Kong was actually owned by a small parakeet. Well, at least the parakeet had the alpha ownership of the small, fifteen-by-fifteen foot box of an apartment. After Gwen helped me get settled, I spent most of my time in her apartment on the bed, while the parakeet made random squawking circles four feet above me at lightning speed. I'm not fluent in bird, but he was definitely squawking some version of *THIS IS MY APARTMENT, BITCH!*

My first three days in Hong Kong were spent wandering around by myself and meeting up with Gwen, who was a graduate student in the city, to find temples, eat noodles and drink cheap local beers from plastic cups. I was also continually messaging my new, rich yacht friend, who had been out of touch ever since I landed in Hong Kong.

On the third day, Gwen and I did sex.

She was a beautiful, English-raised Indian girl who I had impressed with my average folk cover songs back in Lake Atitlan the night Nick and I made $100 each. She had an amazing body and boobs that made me want to be a painter, but she didn't like to kiss. The sex was wonderful and confusing. I was a King Kong, chest-pounding sex monster when she reached climax, but a dopey boy who gave a heart-felt Valentine's day card and didn't get one back when she wouldn't return a kiss. We would have gotten on quite well as travel mates exploring her new home city if we had never shared that first semi-unrequited kiss that led to full-on penetration. Either way, she made my few days in Hong Kong way more local and sexy and I was grateful to have a good friend in Hong Kong. Fantasizing that her cleavage was the setting for a tale in which horny little elves lived was a bonus.

On the fourth day, my rich yacht owner friend wrote me to explain that he had actually crashed his yacht in the Hong Kong harbor, which is why he'd been out of touch the last few days. He offered to buy me a flight to Manila since my ride (read: his boat) sprung a leak, and he felt bad that I had been waiting around for a message from him for days. He was also yacht-owner rich, so I accepted the free hundred dollar flight which he booked for the next day.

———

I left Gwen's apartment early on my fifth morning in Hong Kong and said goodbye to my parakeet roommate. He replied, *FUCK OFF,* back. Four hours, three public buses, two security checks, and one airport McDonald's double cheeseburger later, I was frustrated and tired, walking around the concrete jungle that is Manila, wondering if I should have just stayed on Gili Meno until the end of my visa. *I'd probably be eating lunch with Pak Man right now,* I imagined.

I'm sure if you stayed for some time, or knew where to go, Manila has its share of hidden charms, but upon arriving with no connections and no plan, Manila can't help but make you think, *How do I get the fuck out of here?,* as soon as you exit the airport.

I stayed one night in what, looking back now, was certainly a sex hotel; I'm not sure if it was the red-and-black leather motif or the hourly rates that make this seem so obvious in my memory. On my first full day in the Philippines, I was very excited to take a bus north from Manila to Banaue and Sagada to explore some rice terraces, find some waterfalls, and spelunk in some caves. I also chewed betel nut for the first time north of Manila, and let me tell you, it's exactly what you would imagine dried slugs, lime, and crushed betel nuts rolled into a leaf would taste like—*delicious!*

It produces a sensation comparable to caffeine or nicotine in small doses, closer to that of cocaine if consumed in large amounts. For me, it just turned my mouth red, produced a lot of red spit (A LOT), and caused me to laugh at myself for being so shit at consuming this interesting rural drug. I was trying to fit in with the locals, and although I failed, I did make them laugh while red drool dripped onto my Skid Row tank top.

The first person who shared their betel nut with me was our caving guide. A few buddies whom I met at the hostel I checked into were also interested in exploring some of the local caves, which is the primary reason this rural part of the Philippines is on the traveler map. We tried to negotiate the price down to no avail, so paid whatever it was for a trip into the caves and met our local guide bright and early the next morning.

As he told us about the trip into the caves and shared his betel nut, he said, "These caves can be very dangerous. Sometimes when it rains, hard water floods the caves very fast and all the guides work together to rescue trapped tourists. Sometimes water can be two meters high throughout the cave system and that is even scary for us guides. *It's not a joke.*"

Even after these words of warning, we strapped on some helmets with headlamps, as betel nut courage tingled our cheeks, and crawled through an opening no larger than a hula-hoop into an intricate and winding cave system that we wouldn't exit until 90 minutes later. No rescue team was needed, but we felt like adventurous, thrill-seeking bad-asses when we were finally back out in natural light drinking a beer. We passed on a second offering of betel nut.

I took a bus back to Manila after four nights in the rural north of Luzon and jumped on a boat to Leyte. I didn't have any real clear direction in the Philippines—outside of knowing that I was slowly going broke—so wherever Work Away had opportunities, I decided to chase them. The one I got a response from right away was with Hands On, an international NGO that rebuilds homes and communities after natural disasters. Tacloban, the largest city on the island of Leyte, had been hit by the largest recorded tsunami in the history of the Philippines less than a year before, so the organization set up shop to help with the rebuilding efforts. I had spent close to a year rebuilding in the Gulf Coast after Katrina through AmeriCorps NCCC, a national service program in the States, so I knew I loved the work—the sawdust-smelling, sweat-through-shirt-wearing, dirty-face-having, swinging-a-hammer work.

i. Hands On Tacloban

Within a week, I felt at home living at the Hands On camp. I was a work-crew coordinator because of my previous construction experience, I started an "egg collective," and I had plans to play an acoustic fundraiser at a café in town.

What is an egg collective? Oh, don't get me started. It was a group of six of us who each took one of the work mornings, Monday through Saturday, to cook all six eggs for the collective in whatever way you chose. Otherwise, our one-egg ration would take up to five minutes each to prepare, log-jamming the breakfast line for the over 50 volunteers on site. It still might be the best idea I've ever come up with in all of my days traveling or volunteering. We ended up with a waiting list for the collective a few days after the first morning it started.

I was proud of the egg collective, but the thing I became most proud of from my time in Tacloban was my brick-wall-making prowess. After a week on various job sites—especially one where we were converting a space into a community center—I could lay bricks, mix the perfect spackling concrete, whip concrete with my trowel onto the wall, spread it out in big repeating circles, and end up with silky-smooth walls that would be ready for paint only days later. I was the only volunteer on our site that the local builders trusted to finish walls, and honing this ability made me feel like I had a special bond with the local guys, despite our inability to properly communicate. Smiles, shoulder slaps, and pointing go further than you might expect at a construction site.

———

While in Tacloban, I was committed to the work and constantly tired, but still absent-mindedly checking my email and sporadically perusing the internet for any leads that came up for an actual job. I was throwing myself into ten hours of heavy construction a day not only to help out a very worthwhile cause, but also to stretch what little money I had left. Figuring out how to make more money sometime soon was a slowly rising concern, one I approached like someone ignoring the weird, growing stain on their ceiling. During one of these WiFi sessions, I found that I had received a response from Remote Year after sending off my typo-riddled email. After another quick exchange, I had a Skype interview scheduled with one of the founders.

Two days later, I showed up after work at a café with decent internet, sporting my nicest party shirt and weird mohawk poof (terribly finger-combed down to one side), and attempted to be the guy that had a master's degree and years of legitimate, relevant work experience—as opposed to the guy who made his own cocaine and loved mushrooms. I am and was both.

I was so out of practice interviewing that I couldn't tell how it went, but I thought I did alright. I thought I was, at least, myself.

I was invited to a second interview, with the other founder, which I took from the same chair about a week later in a different party shirt but with the same stupid hair. I told him how I had never seen a job description that seemed written for me until I found the Program Leader role for Remote Year. They wanted someone with group-leading experience, a leadership- and community-development background, along with extensive travel experience. I wanted to yell through my computer—*Show me someone else who has more of these things!*—but I decided that being friendly and calm was a better approach.

They said they would be in touch. I decided against telling my Dad about it, worried that if things didn't go my way and I went back to being a dragon fruit farmer or ended up trimming weed to make ends meet, it would just break his stressed-out lil' heart.

In the end, I spent a few weeks in Tacloban working eight-to-ten hour days, six days a week, spending money only on rum, beer and cheeseburgers in the evenings; I left after nearly three weeks with new life skills, new friends, a new lead on a job, and only a couple hundred dollars less in my account. It was a fruitful few weeks, but I wanted to see more of the Philippines before leaving the country.

———

After a quick ferry ride I was on the island of Bohol, looking for adventure and new friends. I found some immediately. At this point in my travels, I was really good at spending time alone and even better at finding company when I craved it.

I've only ever traveled alone, meaning I set out for a trip alone. One of the most common questions friends and family ask me when I'm back in snowy Wisconsin is, *"What is it like traveling alone, don't you get lonely?"*

My honest response is, *traveling alone is basically getting somewhere alone, then trying immediately to make it less lonely.* Human connection is a tribal and ancient need, and it's that need for it rising in my chest, begging me to fill the void, that I love about solo travel—not the being alone part. Solo travel forces you to be open, to be curious, to take risks, and to discover for yourself that the culture of travel will reward you time and again when you make the effort. On the road, it's encouraged or even expected that you walk up and ask, *"Hey, can I join you guys?,"* when you see a table of people drinking together at a hostel. In Chicago, if you walk up to a table of people drinking at a bar and ask, *"Hey, can I join you guys?,"* you'll most likely get a very different response, and it may even appear as though someone farted terribly, wrinkling everyone's faces in anger and confusion.

That constant invitation for new human connections is one of the things that unites all travelers. It's a secret pact (the secret handshake is a slap-dap) between those on the road, wanting to put new, international characters inside their most vivid memories. We buck the norms of minding our own business to introduce ourselves and ask "how did you get here?" which leads to an infinite range of futures with that person, from simply sharing a drink over stories of the road to co-creating the next, best tall tale.

ii. Talking Boners

On Bohol, I met an Asian-American guy—let's call him Van—who brought up "fucking chicks" in less than ten minutes of knowing him. I still don't quite know how to deal with these macho dudes who attempt to bond over being weird toward women.

The guys who are like, "What do you give her?," nodding at a girl walking by. "I reckon a 6."

I've always just responded like, "Yeah... yeah, I guess so, mate." If I had to guess, I'd say I think about sex more than the average guy, but I always find it strange when dudes just turn into talking boners and then look at you with huge boner eyes like, "Right... RIGHT! SEX! FUCK YEAH, MAN! *SEXXXX!*"

"Oy, I'm gonna fuck someone ragged tonight."

"Yeah, that girl's a 5, but you know, two 5s make a 10, mate!"

"Aw, she's looking to get stuffed tonight, ye, mate!"

Yes, all of those were meant to be read in either an Australian or British accent. They're not the only culprits of this transformation, but those are the only two voices I do in my head when impersonating someone who is a talking boner.

Van and I had a few beers at a beach bar somewhere along Danao Beach and rode our scooters back to the off-the-track hostel where we were staying. We grabbed a few more beers and then met a young, thick, beautiful, round-faced Norwegian girl with long blonde hair. As soon as, let's call her Leah, got up to head to her room, Van looked at me, jumping his eyebrows up and down, and whisper-shouted, *"I'M GONNA HIT THAT, MAN!"*

We had picked up another couple of new friends and were all four or five beers deep when she rejoined the table. After another beer, we decided to head off from the hostel toward a karaoke machine that was set up on the main road connected to our hostel's long entrance. I'd never seen a roadside karaoke stand before arriving in the Philippines, so I was eager to inquire. On the way, I yelled out, "I'll meet y'all there. I'm just going to pee quick!" I didn't realize at first, but Leah, the thick Norweigan girl, followed me, and soon we were washing our hands in the dark next to each other in the middle of nowhere on an island in the Philippines.

Maybe it was the exotic setting, or that Margaux and I had been talking a lot less, or that I hadn't had sex in well over a month, or maybe it was Van being so sure that *HE* was going to "hit that," but I made a move, and all of a sudden we were pushed up against a bamboo door making out passionately under the sexy hue of a single, dim light bulb.

We paused after a few minutes, laughed sheepishly, and I said, "Let's go find the crew, huh?" We held hands as we walked out of the darkness, and she flirtatiously said, "Yeah, but let's also definitely do that again later, okay?"

––––––––

The Philippines love Jesus, Jollibee restaurants, huge colorful trucks, and *Kara-motherfucking-oke*. To this day I've still never encountered a road-side, arcade-game-style, karaoke set-up outside of the Philippines, and they aren't at all hard to find there. Filipino people, when their schedules allow, will pull over, post up, pop a few coins in a karaoke machine, sing their hearts out, and be on their way again. On the night I first partook in this incredible invention, we had a few locals join us and sing as well, and I vaguely remember doing an inspired and slurred version of "Umbrella" by Rihanna. Under ma *uhm-ber-ela-ela-ela-ay-ay-ayyy*. Montell Jordan as well— since I was trying to impress my new make-out buddy.

We all drank ten beers and sang ten songs each. It was an excellent night, in large part because the round-faced Norwegian girl and I definitely had sex—a lot of it. We actually had really incredible chemistry on the mattress, but, before the end of the next day, I was starting to doubt if we had any other type of chemistry, compatibility, or even the possibility of having a decent conversation.

Van, Leah, and I hit up the Chocolate Hills and saw some tiny monkeys with anime-style bulging eyeballs, hanging onto trees, looking around their environment like stressed-out stuffed animals. We lost Van and ended up taking a ferry to Cebu in accidental-couple mode. I was actively trying to island-hop around "God's sneeze on the map," from booger to booger, so I could feel like I saw at least a handful of the countless islands that make up the Philippines. Cebu was supposed to be nice, and it was supposed to have whale sharks. Utila has whale sharks as well, but in all of my trips out to sea from that little island, I never got to catch a glimpse of one of these beautiful, underwater monsters. It was towards the top of my nature bucket list, highlighted in bright pink with a small note next to it—something about how I had terrible luck with these big buddies.

iii. Underwater Zoo

My new Norwegian running mate and I took the ferry over to Cebu City, which, much like Manila, causes the immediate reaction of how quickly can I get out of here, so we jumped on a bus south toward Oslob, where we were told we could see whale sharks, *"for sure."*

That "for sure" part should have set off some red flags, but I was too stoked about the prospect of finally ticking it off my imaginary list and too tired to really consider it because of, you know... all the sex I was having.

We crashed in a terrible hotel room that was the classic bed-inside-a-square style, which is common around Asia. It was fine, and we had a door we could close, so we did the only thing we were good at doing together. We also sorted out what we had to for the next morning to experience the whale sharks, which boiled down to "go to that big sign over there," about a two-minute walk from our hotel. It almost seemed *too* easy.

We got our tickets the next morning and were put in a queue waiting to be called down into a boat. We were certainly not the only people there to see whale sharks, and something felt fishy about this "ocean nature experience."

We were tied up in life jackets and placed in a rowboat, then told to wait for further instructions. After we made it about 20 meters offshore, the rowboat guide told us "we are here," as the other guide was dumping buckets off the back of the boat. The buckets were full of krill, and the sharks were all around us now, enjoying the effortless meal. Any guarantee to see something in nature comes with a caveat, and this place's dark truth was that none of this would be occurring naturally this close to shore; it's a contrived human intervention so that tourists can see whale sharks and I can effortlessly tick a dumb box. Such an experience is accompanied by deep shame for participating in something that isn't right, for breaking the rhythms of nature.

I was there already and pot-committed, so I lifted my knees back and James-Bond-rolled off the side of the boat, then I opened my eyes to see the largest marine mammals I'd ever swum alongside. They were majestic and beautiful, but their eyes seemed sad, the ocean somehow seemed cramped, and the scene was manicured. They were elephants in an underwater zoo.

We got out of the water and had some more sex while still covered in the ocean's salty tang that you could taste with every kiss, then we packed our bags, checked out, and wandered out front to get the bus that would pass by on the main road.

––––––

As we got toward the end of the hotel's drive, I saw a bus turn the corner at full speed, and my heart dropped. Buses came by Oslob every few hours and my flight back to Thailand was later that afternoon. There wasn't much margin for error, but apparently, I thought there was time for salty sex.

I ran to the end of the driveway, and a guy with a scooter saw the look on my face and immediately offered, "Do you want to try and catch it?"

He yelled for his friend nearby to come help, and my round-faced Norwegian lover hopped on his bike following just behind as we ripped down the road chasing a huge bus, the weight of my backpack swinging us dramatically around each curve.

After about five minutes of this daring, high-speed scooter chase, we got behind the bus, and, after another full few minutes of honking and waving, the bus finally noticed us and pulled onto the shoulder.

We quickly gave some cash to our scooter friends who saved the day, boarded the bus, apologized awkwardly to everyone already seated, and then giggled our faces off as we sat down next to each other in the front row. It's not how I would ever choose to catch a bus, but the entire rest of that bus ride, and boarding my flight to Bangkok later that day, I had the biggest grin plastered across my face; my cheeks hurt more than the scratches down my back. *No mud, no lotus*, in the immortal words of Thich Nhat Hanh.

No truly great stories are born from things going as planned.

CHAPTER 19: THAILAND

I left Leah behind in the Philippines. I was ready to be solo again. I was ready for better conversations and to make plans without considering anyone else. I would miss the sex, sure, but not much else—and who knows, maybe we'd cross paths again. She had mentioned future plans in Thailand and beyond, and those serendipitous run-ins while backpacking are more common than one might expect.

I arrived in Bangkok for the second time, now without Pat and the rest of the Wolf Pack, and checked in at Born Free, a cozy hostel in a neighborhood about a fifteen minute walk north from the chaos of Khaosan Road. I paid for a few nights and spent a few days exploring Bangkok in a new way. Less partying, more massages, fewer scorpions, more mangos. I visited temples, explored the corners of my neighborhood, got my teeth cleaned for $20, and spent some time trying to figure out what was next.

Pro tip: Southeast Asia is the best place in the world, in terms of quality for value, to get your teeth worked on. I haven't had my teeth worked on anywhere else in the world in the past five years, and I've spent a total of less than $200, without insurance, keeping my pearly whites healthy. Apparently, Colombia is the place to go if you want a new butt or tighter face skin.

I was still floating around on a budget with my Australian money, but was checking my bank account with my butthole clenched. I was down to my last thousand dollars, and every cent felt precious. Every dollar was a can of beer, every two dollars was delicious, street-cart pad thai.

While in Melaka, I had heard of a place from another traveler, a beautiful, wide-open place up near Chiang Mai called *Mindful Farms*, where you could volunteer and stay for a few dollars a day. After finding their antique farm website and exchanging a few emails from Born Free, I took the next night bus straight north. I had been partying my way through Asia, so along with trying to be thrifty, I was also keen to change up my day-to-day routine. I was excited to be a healthy farmer again, but I wasn't quite prepared for just how different it would be from the Maui Dragon Fruit Farm.

I got myself north to Chiang Mai and spent the day wandering its perfect square of an old city—two kilometers east to west, two kilometers north to south—filled with numerous, ornate temples and complete with a moat, dilapidated castle walls, and ancient stone gates situated at all four cardinal directions. I tried khao soi for the first time at a street market, licked all the plastic clean, and spent one forgettable night in a hostel before finding the right "red truck" the following morning. I needed the truck that drove the road about an hour north out of the city to the farm's drop-off point. Turns out this truck was a yellow one. As I sat on a truck bed's bench with my bag leaned against me, I started chatting with a younger French guy who was sitting directly across from me. He was the only other non-Thai person in the truck.

It didn't take us long to realize we were both on our way to Mindful Farms, and I felt an immediate sense of kinship. I wasn't alone on this adventure. Friendships form fast while traveling, but I had a feeling that Alex was going to be a true friend, a brother, my French Brian, my beardless Jay, even before the end of the hour-long drive.

What qualifies as a conversation starter in terms of proximity? What are the limits and guidelines for when "we're both here" is enough to justifiably start a conversation? If we're in the back of the same truck driving into Thailand's countryside to work on the same farm, then yes, *of course*. It would have been weirder if we didn't talk. If you're on the same bus or airplane as someone, I think that's enough. Staying in the same hostel? What about on the same island or in the same city? On the same planet? Same bungled but beautiful attempt at the human experience? Why does that not feel like enough? I think it should be. Why can you not walk up to a table of strangers at a bar in Chicago and ask to join them? I think you should be able to. *The hostels in Chicago are probably the only places in the city limits where that type of bold behavior is welcomed*, I thought as we bounced along in the back of the truck.

Alex and I were dropped off on the side of the road and followed the general instructions we were both sent via email, which took us through rice fields, over two little wooden bridges, and finally down a dirt road that ended at a farm. We were home.

i. Mindful Farms

We walked up to the farm, where we found a charming Indian-American who seemed like the senior volunteer and was really warm in welcoming us into the small community. The farm had about eight or ten volunteers at any given time, and that night we met everyone as we helped prepare the vegan meal we would all share. I was also reminded that there was no smoking or drinking on the farm. There was no garlic or onions either—the two vegetables intense enough to be considered a vice, apparently.

I took it as an opportunity to let my liver recover, to let my lungs rest, and to eat a lot of leafy greens, some of which I picked myself from the farm. I would be my healthiest self.

After arriving at the farm, I got sick immediately, probably from my body feeling genuinely confused. It couldn't make what's-what of all these various, leafy greens and liquids that didn't get me drunk. Luckily, it was the perfect place to recover and my body acclimated. The fresh air and organic food filled me with all the right things to get myself back to health, and the daily schedule was quite relaxed.

We would wake up and prepare ourselves a green breakfast, grown from the farm, so it resembled lunch and dinner almost exactly. Lots of bright green and earth-tasting salads. After breakfast, we would do an hour of yoga, and once stretched out we would all work in the garden or on various farm projects until lunch.

The afternoon was set aside as leisure time, time to just enjoy living on the farm, to smell mother nature's musk. I would generally read, nap, wander, and journal with most of my downtime. Sometimes I would just sit and think. My iPhone was reduced to existing solely as a camera, and it was nice to just leave it in my room after snapping a couple cool photos of the farm. Finally, each day would end with us having dinner together, meaning we would chop, prepare, eat, clean and put away everything as a team, then meet in the meditation hall for a session led by Pi Nan, the former monk and founder of the farm.

This was my first foray into meditation, and those twenty minutes of each day, when we would sit cross-legged and attempt to clear our minds, were as long as twenty minutes can be. I felt every second and struggled through each collection of sixty. The pain in my hips would interrupt the random thoughts in my mind, then I would think about how I'm terrible at meditating, and that would happen in reverse again, on loop, until the sound of the meditation bowl would ring out, and I was put out of my misery. The first night I remember thinking, *Maybe I'll get better at meditation. I'm going to stay awhile.* I did not.

We would also *not* smoke weed, we would *not* drink beers, we would *not* spend any money, and we would certainly *not* stay up past 10 p.m. There was nothing to spend money on and nothing to do after the sunset. This time is highlighted in my memory as much by what was not happening as what was, like the white spaces of a painting or the absence of music in a purposefully hollow song.

Pi Nan was starting a vegan restaurant and health food store along the country road, a short walk from the farm, the same road Alex and I were originally dropped off on. He had a passion for veganism and living a healthy, happy life and wanted to share the same types of food and raw lifestyle that he enjoyed with his entire community. When I got there, a basic outline of the building was laid out. There were some foundations put in, some roofing beams, but no walls and no actual roof yet. He already had piles of bricks and cement mix waiting to be transformed into a wall—a thing I was now skilled at thanks to my time at Hands On.

I quickly became Pi Nan's favorite worker. I put up most of two entire walls over the next week. The restaurant was taking shape. My health had entirely rebounded, and I was feeling my absolute best. I was full of vegan soup, I could easily touch my toes for the first time in my life thanks to daily yoga, and I had sweat out a month's worth of booze and toxins building those walls in the sun.

———

At the start of one of our meditations, about a week into my stay, Pi Nan asked if anyone would be interested in taking on the challenge of a full day of silent meditation. This would mean no talking and no working, he explained. I thought about it while the twenty-minute meditation slowly passed by like sand struggling to get through the opening of an hourglass, one grain at a time. Before going to bed, I told Pi Nan that I thought I would do it. *"I've never done anything like that, so yeah, I'm in,"* I told him.

In my mind, I would just read or journal all day and pass the hours in the shade of a tree, taking in the beautiful open spaces of the farm. After expressing my interest, however, I was told, *"Silent meditation means no book, no writing, no anything but your own thoughts."*

The next day, I sat alone, eating breakfast, counting the seconds, realizing just how long of a day this would be, realizing just how distracted we generally keep ourselves from our own thoughts.

I walked in the creek adjacent to the farm, counting my barefoot laps up the creek and back down, thoughtfully picking which rocks to step on in the clear, cool water. Noticing each dragonfly, each noise the river produced, and each gentle gust of wind. Time crawled forward like a confused baby in a boring baby race. Lunch was the next event of the day, the one thing that I had to look forward to, but it arrived and passed in the same quiet, lonely, stoic way as breakfast: the same spread of vegan salads eaten in a cross-legged position, alone under a tree.

In the afternoon I decided to lay in a forest of pine trees a short walk from the main farm. I lay down, looking up at the pine trees, and tried to ease my mind into a wandering, carefree state, enjoying the freedom that accompanied the nothingness. I was lying under the trees for maybe 45 minutes when I had the thought of returning to the creek, to go visit the dragonflies and count my laps.

As soon as I had the thought, I popped up and began walking briskly— taking the most efficient path through the pine trees directly toward the footpath that led back to the creek. I was methodical, quick, and full of intention. I was trying to get there in the fewest steps.

All at once, I found myself laughing out loud and laying back down in the pine needles looking at the pine trees' underarms from below. I had nothing to do all day. In fact, there was nothing I *could* do all day—that was the goal, yet I was still trying to save time. I was still in a hurry. I took off like there was a dragonfly emergency, and I was the dragonfly ambulance.

I realized in that moment just how deeply programmed I am. How my default settings have me treating each day like a checklist and each week like a race to finish. I lay under the pine trees a while longer, then slowly walked back to the creek at some point, still laughing at myself, wondering how many ways my programming manifests itself on a daily basis.

I made it through the rest of the day silent, and it felt like a huge accomplishment. It was something I hadn't done since I spoke my first word, and I suppose that's part of why I wanted to do it.

ii. Happy 32nd

After ten full days on the farm, my birthday was fast approaching. Alex was ready to party, and I was ready for a meal that wasn't a bowl of freshly mashed-up vegan food, so we decided it was the perfect excuse to return to Chiang Mai. We ate pad thai, bought some hooch, and started drinking at my hostel, knowing we deserved to ingest any amount of poison we wanted to put in our pink, healthy bodies. Alex had checked into his original hostel in Chiang Mai because he had a free night there for some reason, and I got a bed back at my original hostel because we didn't coordinate properly.

The night snowballed into finishing a bottle of Hong Thong, the brown Thai liquid, which says *whiskey* on the bottle but certainly isn't. We went to the North Gate Jazz Club, we drank more, and later that night we jumped into a tuk-tuk and were led to "the last bar open," at around 2 a.m. by a friendly driver.

Alex and I made eye contact while being led through the front door of the bar (read: brothel) and gave each other wide-eyed looks of concern and disbelief. We both shook our heads in unison, freed ourselves from the grip of multiple women who were attempting to drag us through the entrance, and ran back to the tuk-tuk laughing.

The driver was amused by our immediate return and started laughing as well, as I said, "Man, that wasn't a bar." He responded through his laughter, "Yeah, but they sell beer. I thought you would like it." Apparently, that's what a lot of white guys are after in Chiang Mai, and he thought he was helping out a birthday boy. *He was not.*

We had him drop us back at my hostel, where we heard music coming from a dive bar across the street, just behind a rolled down metal door that was left up about a foot from the ground. We got on our stomachs, turned our heads to the side, shimmied under and immediately tried to act cool, wasted and covered in dirt.

The bartender and the fifteen or so locals looked at us as the record metaphorically skipped. Alex yelled out in his French accent, *"It is my friend's birthday! He turns 32! We just want to drink!"* I showed the bartender my Wisconsin driver's license and then we played pool, drank Chang beers, and shouted things we had no chance of remembering at each other until some unknown point in the night when they finally closed the place for real.

Alex, being the caring friend he is, took my exactly thirty-two year old self up to my dorm bed and tucked me in as we laughed and felt like champions for somehow partying this late in a town where everything shuts down at midnight. He closed my door, went down the stairs, and found that the front door of the hostel was locked. There was no one at reception, my bedroom door was locked, and the lobby was a ghost town. I was already snoring deeply, sawing down a tree in my dreams, with my mouth wide open. I was little help.

There's video-surveillance footage of Alex, with a butter knife, drunkenly shoving it between the two doors, then sitting back down on the floor, leaning up against the wall, hands on his head. He was trapped in the hostel foyer for about three hours, and, in the first hour of sunlight, a normal person on a normal schedule finally left the hostel (using her keycard) to get breakfast, and Alex stumbled into the streets of Chiang Mai, glowing in the morning sun. He told me later the next night that it took him another two hours to find his hostel because he was still so drunk and his phone was dead.

My instinct on that yellow truck when I first met Alex was right: a true friend, indeed.

The next day I checked my email and followed up with messages about certain roles with G Adventures, Trek Bike trips, and Remote Year. Remote Year scheduled another Skype interview, and, like a jury deliberating a long while, I couldn't decide whether another interview was a good thing or a bad thing. I tried not to worry about it. I thought to myself, *Worst-case scenario, I go home for the holidays, stay with my parents for free, and start looking for any old job back in Milwau…no no no, fuck that*. Okay, I was worried.

Still trying to be brave and fearless, but in a whole new way all these years and adventures later.

CHAPTER 20: MYANMAR

At one point on the farm, Alex and I made a plan to head to Myanmar next. It was a place we both wanted to go and after seeing so much of Southeast Asia, I had internalized a goal of going to each major country on the backpacker trail. I never said it out loud, but I was getting so close to that end anyway that I thought to myself, *It would be silly if I made it to nearly every country over here, but didn't see Myanmar!*

Myanmar (formerly known as Burma) had opened itself to travelers only recently, and it was still a more difficult process than just showing up on a plane or bus and purchasing a tourist visa on arrival, which is how the majority of countries in Southeast Asia handle their tourists. It's the best system for both sides, in my opinion. The government makes some money on visitors, as it should, and many countries' passport holders aren't put through bureaucratic hoops or put off by the price tag. To me, it's always felt easy, fair, and mutually beneficial for both sides—a true win-win.

Myanmar did not have this system, but we were told that in Bangkok we could go to the embassy of Myanmar, drop off a passport photo, fill out some papers, pay some money, and pick up a visa later that day. This also sounded relatively easy, it just meant we would have to return to Bangkok before heading to Myanmar.

We took a bus down the next morning and followed the plan. After stopping at the embassy in the morning, we spent the hottest hours of the day drinking beers and waiting for the building to open back up after lunch so we could retrieve our passports, which would hopefully include a new visa sticker.

———

That evening, we were on an overnight bus that would get us over the border sometime in the middle of the night, then to Yangon (formerly known as Rangoon), the capital of Myanmar, by the following morning. I have a vague memory of getting woken up, shuffled through a line holding my passport, then getting ushered back onto the bus where we continued toward the capital. I was blissfully asleep in the back of a bus driven by a complete stranger, careening down highways, passing cars, and taking turns as fast as he could on what one can only assume was far too little sleep for that amount of responsibility.

There's a lot of trust placed in the universe—as well as in complete strangers—while traveling, which at some point feels like the same thing. My Dad thinks about this while I'm traveling way too much. It's the foundation of his general and irrational level of unease, but I love it. If I am meant to get to Myanmar safe and sound on this high-speed overnight bus ride, wonderful. If not, that's just the universe at work.

We made it. The universe loves me.

———

Myanmar was different. It smelled different, the food tasted different, the temples in Yangon looked different, and the culture, in general, felt like something brand new. The language was impossible for me to pick up, and even "thank you"—ကျေးဇူးတင်ပါတယ် or kyaayyjuutainpartaal—felt like something I would never wrap my mind around.

Written out, the language looks like a series of beautiful loops with various, unique features. Every sign was a beautiful mystery, and ideally it included a picture as some sort of clue. More than any other time crossing a border in Asia I thought to myself, *This place is something else entirely.*

Myanmar was still getting used to hosting travelers and tourists, and people's curiosity felt genuine. When someone asked, "Where are you from?" it wasn't to initiate a conversation in hopes of selling you a tank top or tour. It was a genuine question driven by a real sense of wonder.

"This is probably what traveling back in the 70s would have felt like or something," I said to Alex as he looked at his phone to find us a place where we could get lunch. After lunch, we took an ancient train around the city, just because it seemed like an interesting thing to do. It was, and we never even got off.

We saw temples, ate food, had some broken conversations at Shwedagon Pagoda with a few younger monks, and finally figured out how to say "thank you." One of the young bald men adorned in a burnt orange robe with gold trim told me it sounds a lot like a rushed *"Jesus Tomato."* Some version of a fast *"jeszu tomaade"* became my way of expressing gratitude going forward, and after its first usage my success with it grew on itself.

ii. Jesus Tomato

After a few days in the capital we got ourselves on a bus straight to the fairy-tale town of Bagan. Leah, my Norwegian lover, and I were still in touch and she was in Myanmar now apparently. She would be meeting us in Bagan, which was exciting for my dick, but made me nervous in another way. I found her annoying from the second day we spent together, but I'm not really great at confrontation and didn't quite know how to break up with someone I was just sleeping with.

Bagan is the world's largest archeological site with more than 2,000 temples and pagodas. It looks like something from Dali's imagination. Everyone bikes or takes electric scooters around the expansive site to explore, so Alex, Leah, and I rented a few pedal bikes and took off down the dusty road toward what looked from the map to be an *infinite* number of temples. They were uncountable—a photograph of a swarm of bees.

Every road we turned down was lined with pagodas and temples. Alex, looking back at me waiting at a crossroad shouted, "Where should we go?

"I don't think it matters," I responded with a shrug.

There are a handful of more-famous temples scattered across the acreage of the World Heritage Site, but the real magic was just in getting lost among the countless structures. Red-brick forms, mostly pyramid-shaped, timeless and unaware of our presence. Piles of evidence of so much past labor and love, of entirely different priorities than how I've lived my 30-some years. *Man, this place is something different,* echoed in my mind.

The next morning the three of us woke up early and took in the morning hot-air-balloon launch, a daily occurrence for the more wealthy travelers visiting Myanmar. We rode our bikes as the sun was just breaking the horizon and found a small temple to perch on top of, taking in this otherworldly scene.

"Jesus Tomato!" I slowly whisper-shouted as we watched hundreds of hot air balloons rise into the burnt-orange sky above thousands of temples.

Alex and I are both the type of people who can carry on a conversation with a statue, but that morning the three of us sat in silence, just breathing and watching the scene unfold. None of us said it out loud, but I knew we were all thinking, *Aren't we fucking lucky?*

As romantic and tempting as it was, we never even asked about prices for the hot air balloons; I knew by looking at them that it was out of my budget. Later that day, I walked to a cash machine and checked my balance. I saw that I had just over $100 left, so I took a deep breath, punched in my code, selected to withdraw $100, and waited for my favorite sound in the world. Except, in this instance, it never came.

I tried the machine next to mine and attempted to take the equivalent of 80 Australian dollars, just in case the conversion was my issue.

Again, nothing happened.

I tried a third and a fourth time.

Nothing.

I decided to check my account balance again after the numerous failed attempts, which is when my heart dropped. It showed I had just taken out $100 and had nothing left in my balance. I immediately contacted my Australian bank who could do nothing about it because as they said over a broken Skype call, "What if you did get the money, and just called to say you didn't? It's an issue with the bank in Myanmar, good luck."

Fair point. Thanks.

This is how I spent my last $100 in the world, by failing to actually get it from an ATM. Luckily, Alex was there to spot me, and I started living off a credit card and the generosity of friends from that point on. A dozen or so people going forward let me transfer them money from a credit card that I couldn't turn into cash, in exchange for the cash they did have access to. I'd never really been in debt in my adult life until this day in Myanmar.

At least I could have feisty sex in a ragged budget hotel room with a round-faced Norwegian to take my mind off of it.

————

Later that day, I checked my email for responses from any of the travel-related jobs I had been applying for. Nothing came back for weeks now from G Adventures, and a job with Trek Bikes as a guide for cross-country bike tours that originally seemed promising started feeling less and less likely as their hires were normally much younger—they were all college kids. My focus narrowed in on Remote Year. They were at least still responding. From my dirty hotel in Bagan, I found this email from Trish at Remote Year in my inbox:

Travis! How is everything?

Agree with you heavily on Thailand...going to pretend the Taylor Swift comment didn't happen.

As I mentioned, we've all really enjoyed getting to know you via Skype and our fun interview guides...but we'd love it even more to have a chance to meet you in person. So, how do you feel about a quick trip to the south side of this lovely country for a couple of days? I think sometime in the next two weeks is best for us—do you have any timing or scheduling constraints over that time? Let me know and we'll get a flight set up and plans sorted out :)
Looking forward to seeing your shirt collection in the flesh.

Below is my previous email that I sent off back when I was in Thailand. I include it for context about the Taylor Swift line, but also so you can get a real-time glimpse of just how uncool and needy I was being at this point. I said *"ants in my pants"* in a real email to a real person I was trying to win over.

Hey Trish,

Sounds amazing! I really like the islands here. I really like Thailand in general, despite a lot of people saying it's too touristy or whatever. I find it such a charming and beautiful country. I think it's like pop music. Sometimes pop music is popular because it's just really good. Thailand is like the Taylor Swift of countries is what I'm trying to say. (Yes, I really like Taylor Swift.)

I know you're really busy so I'm trying to calm the ants in my pants. I'm just really excited about the possibility of the job so keeping my cool has been a bit of a challenge. Anyway, take your time (island time!) and I'll be looking forward to hearing back from you at the end of the week.

Cheers,
Travis King

Most of the first Remote Year crew was together on the seventh month of the first Remote Year trip, in Koh Phangan. They knew I was in Myanmar and were happy to cover the cost of my flight there to vet in person this prospect they couldn't agree on.
They wanted to fly me in and put me up for a few nights so I could meet everyone on the team. In about two weeks, I would be there in person to shake hands, smile, and dial-up the charm.

Long term, I was stoked about the prospect of a dream job, and in my current state, I was just ecstatic about a free flight.

My weird party shirt collection had impressed them, but the jury wasn't done deliberating, still wanting more evidence of who I was. At least I was still in the running for this job that started to feel like my only glimmer of hope.

If Remote Year was the founder's baby, I was a high-school kid getting grilled on what my intentions were with his now-teenage daughter, and I was *definitely* trying to fool around with her—but in a mutually beneficial way.

iii. The Slow Boat

Alex and I would roll our eyes at each other every time the Norwegian girl annoyed us, which was most of the time she spoke.

"Did you know Norway is the only country with a government benefit to give fishermen a tax break?" (Eye roll.)

"Oh, you went to New Zealand? People talk about how beautiful the fjords in New Zealand are, but Norway has many more beautiful fjords." (Heads drop.)

I thought that the average American was a little overzealous with their love for the United States, but if my small sample size is at all representative, Norwegians are proud of Norway on another level. It was an annoying level.

The three of us spent two full days on our bikes in Bagan collecting memories and photos of temples that I could never find again. In a quiet moment, at the end of the second day, Alex and I planned our escape. Well, to clarify, it didn't start as a conversation about ditching the Norwegian girl, but, as we discussed how we could take the slow boat up the river to Mandalay from a small port nearby, we both began talking about the idea like it would just be the two of us.

We didn't realize just how sneaky and intentional we were being until the next morning. We were slowly creeping around our room, collecting our bags, and shuffling out the door at 4:30 a.m. as the Norwegian girl slept soundly in bed. When the barely audible *"click"* of the door closed behind us, we scurried down the hall and out the front of the hotel. We began laughing uncontrollably as soon as we were on the dusty street in the still-dark morning.

I've never run away from anyone in my life in this fashion, let alone a girl I was seeing, but, in this instance, it felt like the prudent thing to do. I didn't want to have an awkward conversation about how we decided we didn't want to travel with her anymore.

"Why do you want to go without me? Don't you like me?"

"No, I find nearly everything you say incredibly annoying."

"But don't we have fun in bed?"

"Yes, but it's starting to make me feel like a terrible person that we're hanging out all day but the only thing I like about you is the sex we have. Well, and how you say *'wegetables'* instead of 'vegetables,' because I really like that, but it's besides the point."

I felt like this version of ripping off the band-aid made sense that morning. A clean break. While I'm not proud of it, I don't regret it. I'm in favor of getting out of relationships that don't serve you and knowing who in your life is participating in ways that are positive and who might be leaching on your good vibes to fuel their own shit. If we're the product of the seven people we hang out with most, sometimes cutting to six makes sense.

———

As Alex and I paid for our ticket at 5 a.m. and loaded onto the rickety wooden boat, I was oddly proud of myself for doing something that felt out of character. I'm a natural people-pleaser, and I knew running off with my French best buddy wasn't something that would please the girl I was sleeping with, but deep down it's what I wanted to do. I'm non-confrontational by nature as well, so this was how I chose to avoid the conversation but take action for my own happiness. She had done a ton of solo traveling (she bragged about it a lot), and I would never see her again, so, I figured, *what was the real harm?*

On the boat the strange sense of dubious pride was overtaken by a strange feeling in my entire body. That morning I woke up feeling a bit off and as soon as I was on the boat I felt the chills shake me to my core as sweat started rolling down the back of my neck and over my stomach. I asked someone who seemed in charge if there was a place I could lie down, miming that I wasn't feeling well and using small English words. They pointed at the wooden floor of the boat.

As I made it clear to the elderly man selling snacks on the boat that I was feeling ill, he pointed me to a single, shoulder-wide mattress on a bench in a small room at the stern of the slowly moving ancient boat. I lied down on a thin mat covering the bench slightly more narrow than my shoulders, wrapped myself in a blanket, and looked out the window while falling asleep, just as the sun began to break the horizon line.

I was in and out of sleep, both freezing and sweating, for the next 24 hours. Between naps, I would glance out of my window with a forced smile and think, *I'm somewhere in Myanmar.* The boat ride was a full two days long, and I didn't move from that mattress for the entire first day of the trip, relying on Alex to bring me bananas, noodles, and water every now and then.

———

By the next sunrise, I had some of my energy back, and I could finally leave my mattress and take in what was happening on this boat. The first thing I noticed was a giant pig. The entire boat was one floor, which had nothing of significance separating different parts of the boat. There was a paper-thin black roof held up by old wooden beams, and hammocks strung to and fro by various passengers as a place to rest—an upgrade from the only other available option: the patchy wooden floor.

There were no seats and no windows besides the one in the small room I just spent 24 hours in, and noticeably no other travelers besides Alex and myself. We were proud of this fact. It's hard to get off the traveler's trail, but by getting on this old wooden riverboat to Mandalay with a giant pig, we had definitely done it.

Every now and then, the boat would just slowly crash into the muddy bank of the river, and large sacks of small things, people, and animals would be moved on and off the boat at a frantic pace. With the looping letters and indecipherable language, Alex and I had no idea where we were or what anyone was ever saying. The one person we could communicate with a bit was the old man who ran the boat's unofficial snack shop, which kept us alive for these two days. He had bananas, chips, cookies, packets of coffee, and cups of noodles, along with a tea kettle and a small flame, so those five things are what we ate for two days. I passed the rest of the day reading while trying and failing to be comfortable.

At one point, the boat crashed against a certain muddy riverbank with a small wooden walkway jutting out into the water. The snack shop guy looked at Alex and me, and then said, *"Mandalay!"* in an adorable, excited voice. We jumped up, thanked the old snack man, strapped our backpacks across our chests, and jumped off onto the little wooden walkway. We could have been anywhere in Myanmar, but we trusted the snack man, and apparently, this was our stop.

iv. Wisconsin License Plate

Mandalay is the old capital of Burma, the site of old kings and a British overthrow. It's full of historically significant landmarks and dipped in ancient sauce. It was also very full of garbage, street dogs, and a sense of deep economic inequality. Alex and I spent two days in Mandalay biking around with a few friends we met at our hostel. We stopped by random temples and fortresses and rode up and down the unpaved dirt roads that lined the river. We had an unpolished and unobstructed view of what life was like for people living with next to nothing. We looked wide-eyed at them, trying to imagine their lives. Seeing four white guys biking down their dirt road away from the city, they looked wide-eyed straight back.

The last thing we both really wanted to do in Myanmar before leaving was a trek from Kalaw to Inle Lake. Although tourism had really begun only in the last ten years, this trek was known and talked about at hostels throughout Asia. Outside of seeing Bagan, this trek was the one thing I knew I wanted to do in Myanmar even before arriving, and I only had about five days until my flight back to Thailand to go win my dream job.

We took an overnight bus to Kalaw from Mandalay and assumed we could just figure out the trek when we got there. After enough travel, it was easier to make this assumption my default setting and suffer the consequences if a tour was full or the hostel was booked, which seldom happened. Before the end of my first trip in South America, one clear takeaway was that it was all easier than I ever imagined. The world was set up for me, and I could stumble around eating the best food, seeing the best things, and staying at the nicest hostels, all without really trying—and high as hell on cocaine when I wanted. If anything, that sense of ease was even more pronounced throughout Asia. Everything felt set up to accommodate the traveler. Everything in English was slightly misspelled with the perfect mix of charm and sincerity. *I'll take the chinken spagetti and a pinopple juiz.*

What we weren't anticipating was that the seven-hour overnight bus that was meant to arrive around 7:30 a.m. would actually take only four hours and drop us off at a random corner in the dead of night on the outskirts of a small town. With our phones without service and the beautiful swirls of the two closest street signs proving absolutely useless to us, we just picked a direction and started walking in the dark. Things were easy to sort out in Asia, but sometimes the execution was suspect or the outcome unexpected. Sometimes you'd get a *pinopple chinken and a spagetti juiz.*

———

Luckily, within the first fifteen minutes of wandering around, we found a place to stay that let us split an open room. We caught a few hours of sleep and woke up at 8 a.m., determined to start the hike that day. There were multiple touring agencies taking travelers on roughly the same three-day, two-night hike that ended at Inle Lake: Featuring floating villages and traditional fishermen in small boats using the same methods and ancient traps for generations, seemingly posed and ready for a *National Geographic* photo shoot to stumble upon them.

We booked a hike leaving later that morning at 10 a.m. at the first office we walked into, joining four other hikers and our two guides. I don't remember the four other hikers at all, but our two guides were 16-year-old girls who were more badass than I'll ever hope to be. They carried an insane amount of food and gear and happily hiked ahead of us for three days straight.

They would prepare our breakfast, lunch, and dinner and serve it with a smile, seemingly proud to provide local food that they made for six complete strangers. Burmese food is largely an assortment of different types of salads, so most of our meals were an assembly of tomato, bean, egg, and other small salads, which we would ravenously eat after doing nothing but walking for the previous four hours.

The hike was wide open and beautiful, and it felt so good to just be single-minded. No distractions, just a trail and one foot after the other. I couldn't check my email and see that nobody wanted to hire me or that my Dad was still questioning all of my life choices. I was just walking, breathing, and exploring somewhere new.

At one point on the hike, I looked out over a ridge to never-ending, checkered, earth-colored farm fields, many of which had cows wandering through them, others growing corn. I thought to myself, Looks like Wisconsin. I found myself thinking this often throughout my travels. The world is divided up in states, countries, and continents based on lines and borders we've agreed and disagreed on over time, but a lot of it is just grass, trees, corn, and cows. A lot of it looks like the top of the Wisconsin license plate. It looks like home to me.

On each of the two nights of the trek, we stayed at a homestay, which was the floor of a large room with a thin mattress, pillow, and a rough blanket. After a long day of walking, I found it perfectly comfortable, and I blissfully fell asleep. On the second night, our homestay was in a very small farming town that became the unofficial last stop of the trek for every company and everyone hiking from Kalaw to Inle Lake.

It was a strange microcosm where travelers and locals seemed to be in harmony, each respecting and benefiting from one another. It was a stripped and scaled-down oasis of what traveling can be at its best. We ate with our host family, then had a few beers with some other travelers in front of a little corner store where the local kids watched us hang out with rapture and wide-eyed curiosity. I sat in the front of a wooden ox cart, sipping a beer, sharing stories from my years on the road with fellow travelers, realizing just how long I had been gone, and taking a moment to see it from someone else's perspective.

A tall Belgian guy asked, "So, do you ever want to go back and live in the States?"

"I don't know, maybe someday. It's not that I don't like home, but there's just *so much* to see," I said, trying to sound thoughtful. That was the truest thing I could think of saying. It's still all that comes to mind.

On the third morning, we hiked out of this lovely farm town, and after four hours of rolling hills we finally saw the finish line—we saw Inle Lake. Our crew of eight was loaded onto a long narrow wooden boat, with eight small folding chairs in a single-file line. As the single-stroke engine ripped alive with a pull from our driver, we took off down narrow lanes of water, mapped out in squares exactly like the roads of a small gridded suburb. We eventually hit the open water of the lake, and our driver blasted the throttle. I dropped my head back into my hands, looking up at the sky, so grateful that I was exactly where I was. At that moment I wasn't stressing at all about my bank account or my uncertain future. *This is definitely what you do with a master's degree,* I thought as I smiled to the clouds passing overhead.

————

Alex and I had one last night together in the small town of Intha at the northern end of the lake. The next day I would be on a bus all the way back to Yangon to catch a flight out to Koh Samui, and we knew we would likely never see each other again. Thick as thieves, making every single choice together one day, entirely different life paths the next. It was the traveler's way, and we both knew it.

When we checked into our room that night, I opened my email and found a flight confirmation into Koh Samui, from which I could ferry to meet Remote Year on Koh Phangan, the next island over in the Gulf of Thailand. Optimism and positivity swelled inside of me. I was going to nail this weekend-long interview. I was going to travel home for the holidays with news of conquest and victory.

We walked around Intha trying to ignore the unpleasant truth that this was our last meal together and focused instead on enjoying the bond that we had earned. We finally picked a small, colorful restaurant and ordered a variety of salads and noodle dishes. As we sat there, drinking a cold Myanmar-brand Myanmar beer, reminiscing over memories from the farm, the bus rides, my birthday, the hike—two girls walked into the restaurant, and I froze.

My mouth hung open, eyes wide and pushing, like they would rather leave my skull than stay and see this.

Later that night, Alex couldn't stop laughing in his bed just two feet from mine as we tried to fall asleep, repeating, "Ah, you should have seen your face when Norway walked in. It was priceless. I can't fucking believe Leah is here. You'll never get away from her! *She's going to follow you back to Thailand, man!*"

Ko Pha Ngan

Haad Rin
(Lots of neon)

Gulf
of Thailand

Ko Samui

CHAPTER 21: KOH PHANGAN

I arrived in Koh Samui directly from Yangon, spent one night in a hostel, and the next morning got myself to the ferry port on the north side of the island. From there I boarded the slow boat over to Koh Phangan, a giant Buddha further north over my shoulder.

I rented a scooter right in front of the marina where the ferry docked, finally feeling fully comfortable ripping the throttle in Asian traffic, a confident sperm wearing fake Ray Bans. I strapped my backpack across my chest and shot down to the far southern corner of the island where the first-ever Remote Year group was a few weeks into the seventh month of their year-long trip around the world together—just past the halfway point. I gave myself a pump-up speech in my mind as I cruised south toward Haad Rin.

Who has more group leading and travel experience than me?! Who!? THAT'S ALL I'VE EVER DONE! I'm perfect for this. This job was made for me!

I got to the resort where everyone was staying for the month and met up with some of the original Remote Year team: Trish, Hannah, Jesse,

Dave, and one of the founders, Greg. Sam, the other founder, was away sorting out plans for the following weeks, trying to stay one step ahead on the Remote Year Monopoly board. I checked into my room, which was the nicest room I had stayed in at any point during all my years of travel. I was so used to twelve-person hostel dorms that I felt out of place and very alone within minutes of being in my private suite. Sitting on the bed, I wondered what "settling in" looks like for other people, resort people, old people—*me* when I'm an old person.

After dropping my bags and picturing myself eighty years old, I joined everyone on the team working from a café nearby. I had an hour-long sit-down with Trish, the operations manager for the first Remote Year group and the person with whom I had communicated the most leading up to this weekend. The conversation flowed naturally, I did well not to bring up Taylor Swift, and every time I made her laugh I tallied it in my mind on a scorecard that needed a certain amount of ticks on it for me to feel confident I was going to get this job.

Later that day I had a coffee with Hannah, the community manager of the first group, and I tallied a few more points in my mind with a little mini-golf pencil every time I made her laugh or thought I came off as charming and sincere. Hannah and I were fast friends, and I quickly turned every filter in my brain off and just told her exactly what I thought and what I was nervous about, rambling about my last few years. *Was not having a full-time job for so long a concern?* I wondered aloud as I thought about all the many Skype interviews. I successfully avoided saying *"please, oh please Hannah, just give me the job,"* but my body language screamed it.

She assured me this was all just part of the process and that she had a good feeling about it. The conversation ended with her telling me, "You should know before the end of the weekend, for sure."

The job of a program leader for Remote Year, specifically the community manager side of the role, was large but relatively vague early on:

Take 70 adults around the world for a year.

Make it good.

Try to make sure people don't leave.

Plan fun things.

Create a strong community.

Make t-shirts. *Maybe tote bags.*

Got it? Good!

Hannah made sure I realized that there wasn't really a playbook, that they were making it all up on the fly with every new day, including today. Essentially, the small team was building the airplane as it was flying, currently somewhere over a Thai island.

I was ready for the challenge, and I really needed the money, so if they had told me that my group would be 150 people if I got the job, I would have said, "Yeah, cool, why not 200? *Let's do this!*"

I took a long walk on the beach that afternoon with Greg, one of the two founders, hoping to make a good impression and rambling about all my past work and travel experience; trying to score points, trying to convince him—*It's me you've been looking for. Give me a shot!*

I couldn't get a read on Greg. I gave myself zero mental checkmarks.

Sometime during that afternoon, Reid, a participant on the first program, a hulking, viking-like man with long hair, asked me, "Did you know it's the full moon party tonight? It's like you planned this all out for yourself perfectly." In fact, I had no idea it was the full moon party, and I didn't know whether to think *cool* or *oh no* so I landed on *okay, weird.*

That evening, I brought a handful of my travel costumes, wigs, and outfits into Trevor's room, one of the natural leaders in the first group. I outfitted a few people in my strange garb as everyone pre-gamed for a big night, and just shrugged, saying, "I don't know. I'm weird, I guess," as a response to Trevor rightfully asking, *"Why do you travel with all this stuff?"*

i. Full Moon Fiesta

The majority of the group that was in town, some thirty people, all descended onto Haad Rin for the world-famous monthly party. We grabbed buckets full of brown poison and go-juice from the little beach stands, trying to get to a mental state where neon everything, loud EDM music, and a beach full of drunk strangers could be the setting for a great night.

At some point around 10 p.m., most of the group went off to a bar in the far corner of the beach that was known to sell magic mushroom milkshakes. I love mushrooms, and milkshakes—especially Oreo ones— and I flirted with the idea for a tenth of a second before immediately realizing this was all part of the job interview and that I should probably not ingest reality-altering illegal drugs. I hung out with the crew while they did, hoping to appear chill and non-judgmental, to maybe even play the role of sagacious guide for a bit.

While most people's pupils started dilating and they ascended to a different level of the party, up the invisible escalator to floor two, I took that as my cue to leave. I wandered away from the group about an hour after the milkshakes were consumed without a word, looking for a place to have one last chill beer before calling it around midnight. I wanted to be bright-eyed and bushy-tailed the next morning.

I ended up finding a couple of local guys playing guitar for a small crowd, and I joined in with a loose drum they had at their feet. After a few songs, I was handed a guitar and was in the rotation, leading this newly-formed street band through some of my favorite crowd pleasers. Music is a universal bond, so after playing a half dozen songs with these two guys, we were a group of friends looking to get into more trouble together. After the street performance wound down, the younger of the two guys said, "Let's go find the reggae bar, *wink-wink*." Well, I don't think he actually said *"wink-wink*," but it was implied.

After a short walk, we were in a hazy Rasta-themed bar, a strangely common bar theme for a country that has scarce amounts of and serious punishments for weed. But if you looked hard enough you could find it, and on this particular night we did. I hung out with my new friends, time floated away on the sea breeze like the ash coming off of our joints, and at some point I realized it was around 4 a.m.

I was a pretty seasoned partier, so I wasn't too worried about the time. I figured I could bust it home, sleep until around 10 a.m., wake up, pound some coffee, pour on some more charm, and take off at the end of the afternoon before the group had their big, travel-family Thanksgiving—a perfect excuse for me to graciously leave. *I wasn't part of the travel family, yet.*

––––––––

The resort where everyone was staying was a short five-minute walk from all the bars of Haad Rin, and right when I was about to turn up the main road toward home I thought—*No, I'll take that secret little beach path through the bushes back to the resort to make sure I don't run into anyone!*

I carried on toward the ocean, and having found the path in the darkness, turned right and started slowly making my way up the beach along the hidden footpath, pushing brush out of my way as I slowly made progress—stoned, drunk, tired, and with only the full moon's light to guide me.

I was about halfway down the path, halfway home to my private suite, when I heard someone yell, "Travis, hey, is that you? Don't you play guitar?" I turned over to see Trevor holding up a guitar, sitting on a cushion on the porch of the single little beach bar off this path.

"Yeah, come join us," shot up as a chorus from the ten or so other people with him and, at that point, I couldn't pretend I didn't see or hear them. I was trying to make a good impression on these exact people, so I made my way over to join them on the porch, water lapping on shore below the wooden beams. I sat down, grabbed a beer from the cute, older man serving the group, and took the guitar in my hands. The next time I thought about what time it might be was when the sky began to lighten. A few people from the group had snuck away at this point, *but not me.*

I decided to stick it out to the bitter end during the most important job interview I had ever been on. I was really committed to the cause because, when I finally went to bed, I realized that it was just myself and a Russian guy named Boris left. I really liked Boris, but it turned out he wasn't even in the Remote Year group. I think after that night Boris would have hired me for *something*, but I couldn't remember what he did for work, or even what he looked like.

I successfully snuck like a drunk ninja back to my room unseen, peering through the bushes and noticing that some of the group was already at the breakfast buffet around 9 a.m., waking up at a normal time to eat breakfast like normal people.

———

I slept a few hours until noon, then got up and tried to casually reintroduce myself to the happenings of the day, passing knowing *"whoa"* glances at Trevor and some of the other folks who were at the small, ocean-side bar when the sun came up.

The next four hours passed without incident. I had another chat with Trish, where I believe I managed to not give away the state my brain was in. I chatted with Jesse, Hanna, and other members from the community, ready to laugh at anything anyone said.

As the group began divvying up responsibilities for their Thanksgiving feast, their 100-pound feisty, beautiful, Italian community leader Hannah was running the show with unquestioned authority. I took a quick moment to thank her, saying, "It looks like you all have a super fun night ahead of you and a lot to get ready. I'm going to take off so I'm not in the way. Thanks again for everything."

I thanked Trish and reassured her that I really wanted this role. I said goodbye to the rest of the team that I could find, and then mercifully got myself on my scooter, strapped on my backpack, and ripped back up the coast toward the ferry port, hoping I wouldn't fall asleep at the handlebars. I checked into a hostel near the port and went to pass out, anxiously thinking, *Did I just fuck that up?* right before my brain turned off. I still had no idea what the Remote Year team thought of me, or if I smelled like a dumpster to someone else.

The next morning, when I was finally fully recovered, I sent a note to the entire team expressing that I still very much wanted the role and the challenge, writing as though I was already far away, when in reality I was just a fifteen-minute scooter ride north.

I was deeply worried I had fucked up, but I also had no idea how obvious it was to anyone else that I was an absolute wreck on Sunday. I was told that I should know if I was hired by the end of the weekend, so at least the outcome wouldn't weigh on my mind for too long—*or so I thought.*

———

I took a ferry to Koh Samui and onward to the mainland. I got on a bus toward Bangkok, and through all of it I couldn't shake the thought that I had screwed up my future. My phone wasn't connected, but, at every bus stop and every café, I would connect to WiFi in hopes that there would be an email ending the looping anxious thoughts tumbling around in my mind. I was trying to tell myself I'd be fine either way, but, in my most honest moments, I really deeply wanted this job, and there wasn't a backup plan.

If I had to return home for Christmas in just over a month to the barrage of *"what's-next-for-the-world-traveler"* questions without having an actual answer—or any money to fund a vague plan where I take off again on a one-way flight somewhere—that would be the end of it. The adventure would be over.

I would have to update my LinkedIn and start scrolling on monster.com from my parents' desktop computer in Fox Point, Wisconsin. Almost four years of non-stop travel would end with no real answer to *what did it all mean?* I wanted to feel like it was building toward something. Even just to say, "SEE, DAD, I had a plan all along."

Taking a job in the nonprofit sector and moving back to the States would be an all-out admission that my travels weren't adding up to anything. The new countries and years of adventure were all just a long vacation, a weird travel phase of my life, not a core part of who I imagined I was becoming.

CHAPTER 22: CAMBODIA

Once in Bangkok, I hatched a plan to get myself to Cambodia as fast as possible. After a quick $7 foot massage, some street noodles, and a wander to the transit station, I got myself on an overnight bus toward Siem Reap. Cambodia and Laos were the last two well-traveled countries in Southeast Asia that I had yet to explore, so with just over a month before heading home for the holidays, I at least had a general direction to head in. Hopefully, the new surroundings would occupy my mind long enough to keep me from just staring at my email inbox.

We crossed the border in the early morning, and the now-familiar shuffling off the bus into a line, sleepily holding my passport, just to get back on the bus, was becoming a ritual I loved. We passed into the country on foot, meeting the bus on the other side of a long bridge that would drive us the rest of the way toward Siem Reap. Cambodia's entry visa was a brightly-colored, full-page sticker that cost around $35, and I remember proudly thinking, *My passport is getting so full*, then gently letting that thought go again.

When we got to Siem Reap I didn't know where I was staying or what to expect. I just knew it was the town of Angkor Wat, one of the most famous temples and tourist attractions in the entire world. The town itself had clearly developed around the temple to meet the demand of the thousands of visitors every year; its offerings were dictated by capitalism, by who was going to spend the big bucks. Whatever brought in money was built, so there was a booming bar street. In fact, the entire town of Siem Reap had a way more intense party vibe than I had anticipated based on my mental image of ancient temples at the border of a small Cambodian town.

Naturally, I checked into a party hostel, and within the first ten minutes I was spinning a big wheel to determine if I would take a shot for free or not. There were black and neon lights, loud EDM music, and an array of backpackers from all over the world. There was a huge shot tracker chalkboard with flags down the left axis, and I was proud (read: a fucking moron) to see the States was slightly out-drinking the UK. After I had a few drinks and my tongue loosened up a bit, I started jabbering to these two younger Swedish guys near me at the bar, each with smooth baby faces, both blond, one with a ponytail.

They had also just arrived in Siem Reap by way of Phnom Penh, and together we made a plan to not let this night get away from us, but rather to go to sleep early and try and make it to sunrise at the temples the next morning. Seeing Angkor Wat at sunrise is what you're supposed to do when visiting Siem Reap, so before we got too sucked into the party vibe, which was blasting electronic drum beats and obscuring our vision at that very moment, we decided to set alarms for 5 a.m.

———

We met in front of the hostel that following morning and grabbed one of the fifteen tuk-tuk drivers waiting in front of the dark, five-story building, hoping for a chance to be an Angkor Wat guide on that particular day. We made it to the ticket office as the night sky just began to lighten, and, after getting our one-day passes, we jumped back in the tuk-tuk and rushed over to the main temple—the site of the famous sunrise photo.

As we sleepily walked up to the temple, feeling but not really seeing a crowd of people around us all moving in the same direction, a short man jumped in front of us and said, "You guys need coffee. Come to Spider-Man Coffee at stall 21!" He then pretended to shoot webs from his forearms. I told him, "Maybe later, but we are in a hurry." He saw how much I liked his Spider-Man shtick, so he made me promise that I would get a coffee from him after sunrise.

I promised.

Ten seconds later, a small woman jumped in front of us and said, "James Bond Coffee, License to serve…*coffee.*" She then shot finger guns at us. I was also amused by this, but I couldn't make the same promise to this sweet woman.

We made it just at daybreak to the spot—the one with reflecting lotus pools in front of it, framing a beautiful image of temple spires shooting both north and south under the hazy purple dusk of night mixing with the bright orange sky of the first sun, morning dew still fresh on the grass.

After sunrise we went to Spider-Man Coffee and realized each coffee stall had a hilarious gimmick. I wondered out loud to my Swedish mates how it got that way. I reckoned, "It must have just started with one entrepreneurial person, and all of a sudden *'Batman Coffee'* was getting all the business so everyone else had to follow suit. So strange, but I can't say I hate it. I love Spider-Man Coffee. It's definitely more memorable than Stall 21."

We spent the rest of the afternoon wandering all the most famous sights around the grounds. There's the "Tomb Raider Temple" made famous by Angelina Jolie, with massive trees growing around and through the ancient structure in every way nature could have conceived of over the years, exhausting every option.

There's the Khmer temple of Bayon, with beautifully carved faces growing moss on every edifice, smiling back at you while you get lost among the winding stairs and countless sweaty visitors.

After a day of exploring temples—even at arguably the most famous and significant temple complex in the world—you realize a temple is a temple, and it's hard to stay interested or push on in a new direction. We covered well over 80% of the compound, but we were sweaty, thirsty, and ready for a beer.

That feeling led us back to the tuk-tuk and into a three-day bender that I couldn't have seen coming.

i. Three-Day Bender

Siem Reap is fun—unexpectedly fun. After checking off this major travel bucket-list item, I apparently felt like I deserved 100 beers. The seeing-new-things part of travel was always enough for me to feel full, to feel like I did something worth celebrating every single day.

The Swedish boys and I were getting loose back at our hostel and joined forces with some other backpackers from a variety of countries, keen to make a night of it. I was in the familiar position of partying hard and realizing I was a good six or seven years older than everyone else in the circle. At this point, it didn't phase me for a second, and I was pretty good at blending down—always flattered if age came up and some nice lad from

England was like, "Fuckh off, *yah tharty-won!* Well, you fugin' look goud, mate."

We ended up dancing on tables to Drake and 90s hip-hop classics at the famous *Angkor What?* establishment of Pub Street. It was perfect. I woke up the next morning well after what check out time would have been, and, with an expanded network of party friends at the hostel, the first thing I did was pass a knowing hungover glance to a few people already at the bar before joining them for a beer. This cycle carried on for three days.

My third consecutive night dancing on tables at Angkor What?, I ended up getting friendly with a cute brunette from the UK, also probably about seven years younger than I was. We danced together for a few songs, but then I lost track of her. I was lost in the spinning energy of this dive club with ambient green light and names written in Sharpie all over the wall when a girl pulled me aside and gave me the "you take care of her" best-friend speech. It took me a moment to figure out who she was talking about. I didn't realize sex was already my predetermined fate, but it clicked when I saw her friend just beyond her shoulder. I assured her not to worry. I kept dancing with my new partner as we began a sloppy, dance-floor make-out session.

———

After the bar closed we wandered back to my hostel where we started getting frisky on a tucked-away couch just off the huge, open rooftop bar. Things were escalating and pants were being unbuttoned when she asked if I had a condom. I knew I didn't, having noticed a few days earlier I was out. I told her not to worry, that I would go grab one and be right back.

A minute later I was jogging down the street in my flip flops, wide-eyed, looking for any type of corner store or late-night shop. I found a 24-hour place and happily grabbed condoms from the guy at the checkout, who knew exactly what was going on despite our language barrier. I ran back to my hostel at full speed, carrying my flip-flops in my hand.

When I made it back to the couch, we ended up getting entirely naked before we realized we couldn't have sex in this open common space, so we snuck, clothes piled up in our arms, to the closest bathroom. Once we locked the door behind us, things escalated quickly.

The condom lasted all of five minutes. We stayed locked in that bathroom for about an hour. At one point I was just fully lying on the dirty, hard, tiled floor, hoping this could simultaneously last forever and also wondering if I even *could* finish at some point with this amount of booze in my system.

The setting for some of my best memories of carnal, animal sex is a hostel bathroom. I finished at the perfect moment and dropped my head back on the hard tile floor. I'm telling you, "Never try, never know."

As I woke up the next morning with images from the night before flashing in my mind and a three-day hangover mounting, I realized I needed to get out of Siem Reap and far away from Pub Street. It was too much fun. It had a hold on me.

My email inbox said nothing of importance, which I discovered over a terrible but essential coffee.

I ran into the Swedish guys who, I could tell, were thinking the same thing. They told me they were planning to get a bus later that day to southern Laos, a place called 4000 Lakes that was known for being super chilled out.

"That sounds perfect. I'm coming with you guys," I told them in a scratchy, barely audible plea for help. I thought of Brian at the start of my travels, and how he told me he would be joining me to Salento's towering palm-scrapers.

ii. 4000 Lakes and No Pages

I had about twenty-five days until my flight left Phnom Phen for Hong Kong. I had already booked my flight back to the States months before out of Hong Kong after I found a $550 one-way flight into Chicago. A quick Google search for "cheapest city in Asia to fly back to the States from" led me to this simple choice.

> Pro tip: Look into the cheapest airports in each region for cross-continental flights when one-way solo traveling. Hong Kong wins by a mile going from Asia to the States.

I figured that I could travel through Laos, see a few major stops along the way, get a feel for the country, and still make it back to Cambodia a few days before I left. Laos was the last country in Southeast Asia I hadn't stepped foot in that I really wanted to see, so I felt like it only made sense to go, even if briefly. Who knows how many more chances I might have? Who knows what sad eventuality next year might hold?

On the way to the Laos border, I started wondering—internally at first and then out loud—whether I would be allowed into the country after realizing my passport didn't have any fully free pages left. I wasn't sure if Laos issued a full-page visa like many countries in Asia. I asked the cute French girl next to me what she thought, and after paging through my passport she didn't exactly reassure me.

We started chatting about life and travel. She was running a blog for solo female travelers, and I could have listened to her talk in her accent forever. After we chatted for 20 minutes, I finally asked her what her name was.

"*Margot*," she said.

I dropped my head back and started laughing as she asked, "What, why, why is that so funny?!"

I explained to her how I just got out of a relationship with a different cute French girl named Margaux whom I met in Australia; how her name was spelled differently but pronounced the same. How Margaux was still in Byron Bay but that long-distance was just too hard on us. How I missed her but knew that I needed to be single.

After I rambled, she slyly snuck in, "Did you just call me cute?"

We chatted for a little while longer, and eventually she told me she really needed some sleep and dozed off. I said, "Yeah, of course," trying not to let on that I never wanted our conversation to end.

After our lunch stop, she switched to a different bus to head to a town called Kratie, to see the rural Mekong lifestyle and the river dolphins that lived there. I had never heard of Kratie, but it sounded interesting and I love dolphins, so I joked with her that maybe I would see her there in a day or so if things didn't work out for me at the border.

She responded, taking my concern earnestly, "I'm staying at this hostel called the Silver Dolphin. *Maybe I see you?*" Her accent caused my heart to go BASE jumping inside my body. I smiled and waved goodbye as she climbed into another van.

Our bus carried on for another few hours as I slowly flipped the pages of my passport, hoping a new page that was stuck together would magically appear.

At the border, it took about five minutes for me to accept that it was hopeless—that this entire bus ride led me somewhere I couldn't go. When I got to the front of the line at this small immigration shack, the man flipped through my book and handed it back to me without a word, and just shook his head side to side.

It was *"no"* in every language.

Not only does Laos issue a full-page stamp, but the Cambodian visa I had was also a single entry visa, so I would need another full-page stamp to get back into Cambodia for my flight, which there was definitely no room for. I was a full two pages short of the plan I had confidently set out to execute that morning.

I said goodbye to my Swedish friends, goodbye to Laos, and waved the bus off as it kicked up dirt and plowed forward into a new country, a place that would have to remain a mystery to me because of the number of pages in a small blue book—and the fact that I gave myself a Machu Picchu stamp nearly three years earlier in the last page of my passport book. I did it by choice; I thought it would be a fun little souvenir. The dominos are set up in mysterious ways sometimes.

———

I turned around, clipped my backpack back on, and went to sort out what I was going to do that night as the sun began to quickly drop out of sight, darkening the sad scene of an immigration booth that I couldn't get past on a dirt road in the middle of northern Cambodia.

I found a single guy who had a scooter and spoke "little English" and, after fifteen minutes of trying to negotiate with absolutely no leverage and no other options, I gave the guy $20 to drive me fifteen minutes back down the road I just took the bus up.

I spent the night as the only guest in the only guesthouse in a one-street town. The strange hotel seemed to exist entirely for people who end up in my situation, and, dire as my situation was, I was thankful for the bed.

Nobody in the one-street village spoke English, and they seemed a bit terrified by me when I did, motioning for me to go away and speak English somewhere else. After about thirty minutes, I convinced a kind-looking older woman with deep wrinkles to feed me a bowl of plain white rice, using lots of crude sign language (read: my finger was almost in the rice). I spent the night re-reading a Dave Eggers book on my Kindle and watching movies from my hard drive.

In the morning, I woke up bright and early to stand on the side of the road in front of the strange hotel with my thumb out. I figured buses had to pass by here, as it seemed like the only road into and out of Laos in this rural part of northern Cambodia. I was right, but the first few buses heading south didn't have any interest in stopping; they didn't even slow down. It was eventually noon, and I was covered in dust, hungry, losing hope fast, and starting to worry.

Sometime just after midday, I saw a fourth bus coming the right way and without properly considering the possible consequences, I actually stepped out into the road this time, determined to make it stop or run me over. The bus driver decided against killing me, and, as I jumped into the door, he showed me how full the bus was—every seat was taken and some people were already standing, but I didn't care. I had money, and I needed to leave this place. When he could see I wasn't fazed, he said, "Phnom Penh." I gave him the equivalent of $10 and stood on the stairs near the door with a huge gill-to-gill smile, a happy shark. I was off—I finally had some positive momentum.

———

On the way toward Phnom Penh, I started thinking about dolphins and the French girl, Margot, who spoke in this familiar way that made me melt. I felt a warm curiosity and a strong pull toward her but didn't imagine I might actually see her again. In general, when I'm traveling, my instincts with people feel sharp and first impressions can tell you a lot about someone. I knew she would almost certainly still be in Kratie, and I even knew the name of the place where she said she was staying—*Silver Dolphin*.

When the bus made its stop to let some people off to "change bus for Kratie," I lied to the bus driver and said that's where I was actually going, and, before I could think twice about the choice, I was on a new bus for a small rural town on the Mekong Delta, following an instinct and a beautiful French girl with whom I had spoken for less than thirty minutes.

An hour later, from the middle of Kratie where the bus let me off along the Mekong Delta, I was told by a tuk-tuk driver that the Silver Dolphin was a five-minute drive up the road. I paid the man a few dollars, and we shook off the curb as he ripped the throttle, speeding away on three wheels.

I checked into a dorm room and threw my stuff down on an empty bottom bunk bed.

At the check-in desk I noticed a sign and small menu for a roof-top bar, so I looked for some stairs going up. When I made it to the top, I was back outside, and immediately made aim towards the view at the far railing.

I stopped mid-stride and looked over when I saw a petite brunette having a beer at a table all alone. She looked up, and we made eye contact. We both smiled, then Margot started laughing as she said, *"So you didn't get into Laos?"*

I melted at her voice, her casual way.

After a stunned moment, I laughed and said, "No, apparently you need room in your passport or something like that. Anyway, I'm just glad I made it somewhere after last night, and I'm really happy to find you."

She invited me to join her so I grabbed a beer and we started into a conversation that was full of laughter and flowed easily, just as it did only a day before. I told her the story of my strange night in the confusing hotel in the middle of nowhere. How I kept trying and failing to use crude sign language to tell people I was hungry until an old woman finally just gave me a bowl of white rice like I was an annoying street dog. At some point, I wasn't even listening to myself as I retold the story, I was just looking at her smile and noticing the creases her eyes made when I really made her laugh, the way her full lips puckered after she finished swallowing a sip of beer. How she would put her hand over her mouth or on her cheek, her eyes wide, to show she *really* couldn't believe me.

I knew before I finished telling her the story that I was glad I didn't make it to Laos. I was perfectly happy at this table trying to make this beautiful French girl laugh, hoping to make her cover her face again and again in the most precious way.

———

About an hour into learning more about Margot, the blog she was writing, what her life back in France was like, and where her trip had taken her, I felt my phone vibrate with a text message.

I flipped it over on the table, still listening to Margot, but my reaction must have given away that it was important, as she stopped mid-sentence and asked, *"What!?!* What does it say?"

Over the few beers we shared, I had told her a bit about my travels and how I was heading home for the holidays like I had done every year since I left, but also how I was pretty low on money after getting kicked out of Australia and bouncing around Asia for so long; I seemed doomed to get stuck at home this time.

I told her about Remote Year, and that I was really hoping to get a job with them.

I told her about the full moon party, the looping doubt in my mind, and the hourly email checks.

I looked up, wide-eyed, and said, "It's Trish from Remote Year, that travel start-up I was just telling you about."

"What does it say?"

It just says, "What are you looking at right now?" I told her with confusion as I slid next to her to show her my phone.

Sitting in the same corner as her now, shoulders pressed together, staring at the luminescent glow of the screen, we both laughed as I slowly typed, "I'm looking at this river in northern Cambodia that is supposed to have dolphins in it. I think you know this, but I love dolphins."

I showed Margot the phone, getting her head-nod approval that it was a good response.

I looked at her with uncertain bravery and, making the same face Dougie would to mean *the ocean, huh?,* I hit send.

Both of us were staring at the phone now.

We watched as the three dots bounced up and down, waiting for Trish to respond.

Why did she want to know what I was looking at?

What does that question even mean?

A message appeared and my eyes focused in to read:

"Well, I hope it looks better now that you know you got the job as Community Manager for Remote Year's third group."

I looked at Margot, confirming that what I read was right, and as time slowed down I could hear her yelling, "Oh my god, congratulations!" her face so sincerely happy. Time pulled away from me and the music bent, then snapped back all at once, and I jumped up and let out a primal scream that had been stuck in my chest for the last two weeks as I waited to find out what my future would hold.

I did a flailing lap around the bar and hugged our Cambodian bartender—I hugged another table of Cambodian guys up on the rooftop patio, shouting incoherently the entire time, as they kindly obliged while flashing incredulous looks at each other.

I finally returned to Margot still fully in shock.

She looked into my eyes and in her charming accent asked, "Do you want to kiss me?"

I didn't say anything—I just leaned in and kissed her deeply and softly, holding the back of her head with one hand and pulling her closer to me with the other. It was the perfect kiss and, in all my travels, the most perfect moment.

Maybe I did have a plan all along. Maybe it was all leading to something—to this exact, heart-bursting moment on a rooftop bar in rural Cambodia with yet another Margot.

iii. Cambodia Is For Lovers

Margot and I slept together that first night in Kratie—more than a few times. We took a scooter adventure around Kratie together the next day to find the dolphins, already falling into a fast and effortless love. I adored the way she spoke, how she ate, how she would hold me from behind as we drove the dirt roads—hilarious and adorable questions being shouted to me over the sound of the wind as we searched for our next stop. I had never had such a strong feeling so fast about a woman in my life, but there was this giant dolphin in the room, so to speak.

Before we even kissed, I had told her of my plans to head home for the holidays, and our first kiss was essentially a celebration of landing my dream job—one that would dictate everything about the coming year. We ignored this invisible truth as well as any two new lovers could, and just enjoyed each day that we had to explore Cambodia together.

We traveled south to Kampot where we slept in a treehouse, then over to Sihanoukville. We took a ferry to Koh Rong, where we shared a bungalow on the beach for a few carefree, easy days in which my sole goal in the world was to make this beautiful French girl smile. We held beach puppies, ate fresh fruit, swam in the neon blue ocean, swung in hammocks, and made love in our tiny bungalow, not worrying about the credit card debt that was accruing more with each meal.

It already felt paid off.

When we got off the island, we made our way to Phnom Penh for our last few nights together. Our unbridled happiness was periodically interrupted by reminders that our days were fleeting—organizing transport to the airport, our final dinner, and ultimately our final morning together. After having beautiful, slow, and intimate sex—the type of sex that's only possible with a certain level of trust and comfort—we both got teary-eyed in bed, knowing we weren't sure when or if we would ever share a bed together again.

She rolled over on top of me and wiped a tear away, looking into my eyes, mocking me in her French accent, "Oh no, look at my big, strong American. He's not crying is he?" An image of laying in bed with Lisa in that brick room in the salt flats on our last morning together flashed through my mind. I wondered where she was, and I hoped that she was as happy as I was in that moment.

I could have died right then—I was madly in love with a girl I was leaving, headed home to see my family and closest friends whom I missed dearly, and had landed my dream job. I would finally have something meaningful to tell everyone back home about my future plans.

For the first time in my adult life, I couldn't wait to tell my Dad about my travels—what had happened and what was going to be. *This is what you do with a master's degree*, I thought to myself holding Margot close, lying in bed with tears landing on my chest. *This is exactly what you do.*

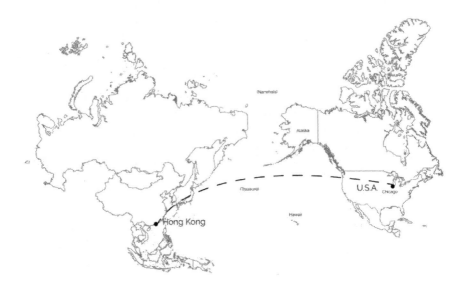

CHAPTER 23: HOME AND THE FIG TREE

There's an excerpt from The Bell Jar by Sylvia Plath that I think about all the time. I think it's because I resonate with it deeply on one level, but I still find myself not fully agreeing with the advice at the heart of it.

I saw my life branching out before me like the green fig tree in the story. From the tip of every branch, like a fat purple fig, a wonderful future beckoned and winked. One fig was a husband and a happy home and children, and another fig was a famous poet and another fig was a brilliant professor, and another fig was Ee Gee, the amazing editor, and another fig was Europe and Africa and South America, and another fig was Constantin and Socrates and Attila and a pack of other lovers with queer names and offbeat professions, and another fig was an Olympic lady crew champion, and beyond and above these figs were many more figs I couldn't quite make out. I saw myself sitting in the crotch of this fig tree, starving to death, just because I couldn't make up my mind which of the figs I would choose. I wanted each and every one of them, but choosing one meant losing all the rest, and, as I sat there, unable to decide, the figs began to wrinkle and go black, and, one by one, they plopped to the ground at my feet.

For the last eight years, I've made most of my decisions one at a time, evading all decisions entirely that related to long-term commitments.

From this restaurant, I'll take this bus to this city in this new country. Days pass, months pass, and years can pass like this. I didn't decide eight years ago that I would choose a life abroad and only come back to the States for the holidays, or that I would be gone for more than ten years, but now that seems highly likely. Eight years ago, I was simply brave enough to jump through a small window that I found open, and I've stumbled my way around the world one choice at a time ever since. I've given myself far-off goal posts—like a flight home from Hong Kong three months out—and filled the time between with all the right notes, like so many purposefully hollow songs.

These first three-and-a-half years of my travels, documented here, led me to Remote Year, and around two years into Remote Year I started working on this project. When I started writing this, I didn't realize I would end the story where I do—with landing my dream job—but it had to end somewhere. That stretch of my life feels like a complete thought, a fully-formed Act One to be followed by Act Two: Remote Year, responsibility, and getting paid to travel.

Through these eight years of my life abroad I've tried a lot of figs, and I don't think I lost all the rest. Life is long if you're lucky, and someday if I want to go back to the States, buy a house, start a family, run a nonprofit, become a college professor, or start my own bakery for dog treats, I can at the very least still *try* all or some of those figs.

This is something I wish a wiser person would have told me when I was stressing out about choosing my college major. Society, in general, told me something along the lines of: "This is really important, and it'll set the course for the rest of your life."

That's complete bullshit.

It's the same needless stress that every early 20-something-year-old backpacker I met carries around, asking themselves way too many questions about what to do with their life instead of just living it.

Rather than worry about what career path to choose, my suggestion would be to simply worry about what you're going to do later that night and what you'll do tomorrow that will hopefully make it a great day—a day worth remembering. If my math is correct, great days strung together should make for a great life. Worry more about how you show up for the people in your life and less about whether you're impressing them or not. *How did you get here* reveals so much more depth than *where are you from.*

Obviously, you have to make money doing something. But if earning that money is going to take up nearly half of your waking hours, hopefully you're not busy doing something that you fucking hate. If you are, *try a new fig.*

When Brian came to South America, he was in the middle of a one-year pause button he found and then hit before going back to start his "real life" as a fancy accountant, sitting in an office and looking at a computer for eight hours a day for the next forty-some years. I'm guessing that, at the time, most people in his life framed his trip to South America as *one last romp before his "real adult-life" started.* He went to school to be an accountant, *so an accountant he would be!*

Last year, he opened up a little café called *Happy Out* out of a shipping container in his hometown of Dublin, right on the water. He works for himself, doing something he loves—making food that people love. I haven't asked, but I'm guessing it was seeing the world and realizing there are countless options for how to live your life that led to that hard left turn for him. At one point, the only fig he could envision was the accounting fig, and all of a sudden, there's a Bali fig, a Buenos Aires fig, a restaurateur fig, and countless others. If you can't see all those other figs, how can you possibly grab them?

———

When I returned home from Asia for Christmas before embarking on Remote Year, my folks had a pile of mail set aside for me. Sorting through it is part of my yearly homecoming ritual, along with an essential trip to Walgreens and an overpriced STD test. In the pile, I found a hand-addressed envelope from Leslie—my middle school, high school, and post-college sweetheart.

She was inviting me to her wedding.

She was marrying a slightly-older granola guy whom she had met at one of our mutual friends' weddings. This hand-colored dinosaur invitation was letting me know: this fig is gone. For a long while, it was the only one I cared about; it seemed destined for me, but now it was gone, and I felt the permanence of that settle in my heart like a hearty meal sticks to the ribs.

I could feel the multitudes of my future life paths shooting out in front of me, like branches of the green fig tree in Plath's story. Scenes of the last four years flashed through my mind, and I was just as grateful to know my many different options as I was to know, definitively, that Leslie was no longer one of them. I was proud that a new job—a real travel job—was the fig I was currently holding.

I was proud of my heart's reaction to the news as well.

In the end, I can usually pick up the figs that have already fallen to the ground. The figs in the tree I can still grab tomorrow if I decide to, and for those figs that haven't yet ripened, I imagine they'll get there at the right time and place. If they look tasty enough, I'll reach out and pluck them too.

Who knows, maybe a fatherhood fig will grow someday.

It's the not-picking-anything that's the real problem: starving at the base of the tree, lonely in your parents' basement, or feeling stuck in the suburbs; those folks who haven't yet grabbed one they really wanted and tasted the nectar of serendipity, the sweetness of adventure, and the juice of a life well-lived.

————

Save up a little money, give the kids to grandma, take a leave from work, put in a request for sabbatical, lean into the fear of not knowing what awaits on the other side, and buy yourself a one-way flight somewhere far away. I know I said I'd go easy on the advice, but I'm my father's son and really, if you can, *I think you should.* Also, I think you should wear your seatbelt.

The "one-way" part is key, and it brings me back to something I promised a few continents back: the difference between a tourist and a traveler, the recurring, waxing-philosophical hostel conversation. There's a lot more I could say about it, but in essence it comes down to one thing: *how you leave.*

You can be a typical tourist or potentially a proper traveler flying roundtrip. But anyone who flies one-way—with no plan for a return, just days and countries before them—is a proper traveler. Everyone who has ever done that has had their future and the idea of their place in the world altered by it. It's impossible to evade the awakening that true travel forces on you. It's a gift, not a competition, and just leaving on a one-way flight is how it starts.

You could set off in your car, but the riches of new discovery are harder to find, harder to be made uncomfortable by in such proximity to what you already know. A plane or a boat has a far better chance of getting you away to the degree that manifests revelations and growth, getting you somewhere far away enough that it scares you just the right amount.

Dipping into that fear, fully submerging in it, is what will forge your armor, like an icicle growing in size and strength with the uncomfortable melting of each intense morning sun. When the night comes and brings a chill—time to reflect on what you've seen and learned, time to appreciate that you've survived whatever scared you—you'll find yourself sturdier than before. You'll find yourself swelling with life, more resilient, and larger in spirit.

Some people seem certain that traveling *just isn't for everyone.* I don't buy it. Traveling is certainly harder for some than others, but when given the opportunity, it's always an accelerated path to growth, adventure, new connections, and new memories.

If you don't like those things, well then I just don't believe you—or believe that you're being honest with your truest self. I think you might be a bit scared, which is totally fine to admit. Ask anyone who has traveled a lot about when they first started, and if they can't admit that they were a scared young pup to begin with, well, I don't believe them either.

Be brave enough to go see something new, eat something new, meet someone new, and it'll get easier with every new story you make. I'm willing to bet you'll love it—the good and the bad times alike—because surgeries can lead to dream jobs, and one-way flights can lead to the most incredible new futures and the tastiest new figs that you could ever imagine. The world is inviting you to see it, and if you don't accept the invite, if you convince yourself that you can't, then all that's left to say is, *"Never try, never know."*

The hostel friends who helped me fall in love with Melaka.

After the Starbucks and before the Tom Yum soup in Penang.

The waterfall where our rental car keys went swimming.

Behind the scenes at our photo shoot with the wedding photographer.

Margaux and me, cruising around Bali, avoiding the police.

Posing with strangers, as you do, in Uluwatu.

Happy Margaux on our last day together as us.

The Gili Meno Eco Hostel main entrance. I made the "want" sign.

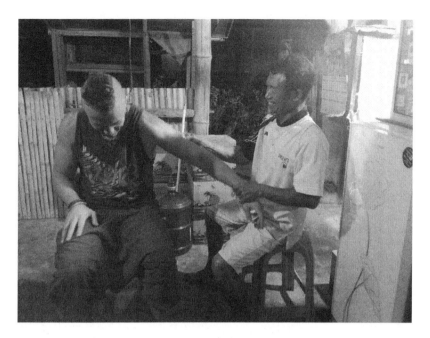

Pak Man giving one of his incredibly deep massages.

My beautiful Argentinian friends and the sign we made for Pak Man.

Right before heading home to find a bunch of paranoid Swiss guys.

My Chilean friends (and crush) during the ride to Komodo.

Dinosaurs with their weird double-dicks.

Bromo, Java's origin story, in the early morning light.

Caving north of Manilla in Sagada

Overly proud of my brick-wall-making skills at Hands On Tacloban.

The chocolate hills of Bohol with Van.

Ol' Norway and me in accidental couple-mode.

The scene during silent breakfast at Mindful Farms.

Putting my wall making skills to work for the farm's vegan restaurant.

This place is something else entirely.

Bagan with Alex and my Norwegian lover. My brain and dick fighting.

Trying to pass the time and to not puke on the slow boat to Mandalay.

Alex and me on our way to Inle Lake.

With our two 16-year-old guides on our final morning of the hike.

The only picture I have of my first visit to the original full moon party.

With my Swedish mates at Angkor Wat.

Margot and me after our first day exploring together.

Showing off my kayaking skills for Margot on Koh Rong.

Back in Wisconsin. Finally, with some good news to tell my Pops.

THE AFTERWORD IN THREE PARTS

———

THE PROCESS & A THANK YOU

So, *some people did ask.*

From about two years into my travels, people back home and others I would meet on the road would occasionally make jokes and soft suggestions like, "When are you going to write your book?" These ranged from someone just giving a unique compliment to a really sincere suggestion from a friend who thought that I should—that I had enough stories and a sufficiently unique voice to write something worth reading.

The idea that I would write a book was romantic, and the urge from others was flattering, but I never took it seriously; I would let it wash over me like a compliment about a new haircut or shirt. Which is why, out of the next few thousand times I opened my computer after first receiving that suggestion, it was never once to start writing a book.

It did float through my head, and I kept a note in my phone called "writing ideas and jokes" for more than four years. And there were some good notes, like how when people take out one earbud for seemingly no reason then put it back in it's because they farted and wanted to know if it was audible (I know this because I caught myself doing it and then more people at an airport doing it the same day I jotted that note down). It was an egg basket of interesting anecdotes that I didn't want to forget, but there wasn't much there.

One day, while working for Remote Year about seven months after my first group finished, I was leading a weekend retreat in 1000-year-old Tavella, Italy, where a total of eight people, one dog, and no WiFi connections live. During a goal-setting session I said, "I want to write a book." I then wrote it down as part of a vision and set a goal to write "one chapter worth reading" by the end of the month. In order to keep myself accountable, I started to tell friends and family and people I cared about that it was something I wanted to do.

I put the wheels in motion, still without ever opening my computer to start writing. One day, I thought of the mediocre first line of the book and repeated it in my mind while walking through Split, Croatia, until I got to the Remote Year workspace to open my computer.

"I just started telling people I was leaving" were the first words I wrote down that led to over 100,000 more, but it really started in that small town in Italy. Once you make a proclamation to the world, it's out there, and as we all learned at a tender, young age: *no take backs.*

When I told everyone that I was going to travel to South America, I eventually felt like I had to. If you want to take the leap and go on a big trip, I suggest you just start telling people you're going to. If you want to write a book, become a yoga teacher, or break a Guinness World Record, do the same. Put that intention into the universe. When I put my goal of writing my stories down into the world, I was either all talk or I was going to write this fucking book.

Over the next three years, as I started to slowly write my stories and thoughts down, I had daily moments of self-doubt. They ranged from *you'll never finish this* and *why do you think anyone cares about your stories* all the way to *what are you doing you ego-maniac, crazy person, wannabe writer—not only are you going to embarrass yourself but also you're going to fuck up your future with all these stories of drugs and bathroom sex!*

———

I went home again last Christmas, making it seven straight holiday seasons that I'd found a way back to Milwaukee by the 24th of December. With my family gathered around the kitchen island, destroying cheese dip and working on our fourth bottle of wine, my Dad sounded off to the whole family—for the third time in just as many hours—*"Man,* that Austin is one heck of a writer!"

He's right—my brother is an amazing writer and has always been objectively smarter. He has degrees from NYU and Harvard to prove it, along with a long list of childhood accomplishments, accolades, and honors classes that far outshine mine.

With the help of my fourth glass of wine, I reminded my Dad, along with my whole family, "You know I'm trying to write a book, right? I know Austin is a good writer, but when you keep saying that it feels a bit like what you're also saying is 'and you're *not* as good of a writer, Travis. *Maybe you should scratch this whole book idea.'"*

My Dad listened, and then cried—because that's what he does—but he heard me and apologized. My Dad is nothing if not supportive of his sons, even if he bungles compliments, accidentally insults us from time to time, and calls me Austin almost as often as he calls me Travis.

The next morning, he read an early draft of the Colombia cocaine-making story. Handing back my laptop, he said, "You're a pretty damn good writer yourself, Trav. I'm sorry if you didn't feel like I was supporting you. Keep going on that book. Just have Austin edit it when it's done." Knowing that my Pops was in support of my writing, drugs or no drugs, also spurred me along. Knowing my brother would eventually edit it didn't

314

hurt either.

———

Besides my Dad's eventual support, I have some ideas about what kept me going—to get here, to have it done. In part, it's certainly that my will is strong, my belief in myself is high, and, more than anything, I'm optimistic as fuck. It's helped me in travel, and it helped me to write about it as well.

It's also in part because I was able to trick myself along the way. I would call it an *"e-book"* and include the caveat, "Even if it's just for my non-existent future grandkids to read so they know how cool grandpa was back in the day..." when explaining what I was working on to friends.

After writing that first sentence in Croatia, momentum also played a role, as well as not wanting to leave something unfinished or the question *What if I did write a book—would it be any good?* unanswered. I was curious enough on my own, but others telling me that they were too was the reason I would set an alarm for 8 a.m. to write under Bali's first sun or spend nights in Lisbon out at a café, alone with my computer open and a glass of port at my side until they closed the restaurant.

Ultimately, I decided that if my Dad, my family, and my closest friends were behind me—regardless of failure or judgment—*then fuck it*. It's my story to tell, and I'm the sharing type.

Thank you very much for reading it. *The first thank you is for you.*

THE ASK

I self-published this book, and outside of my Instagram reach and network of friends and family, I don't really know how to share it with the world. If you did enjoy it, I'd greatly appreciate your telling three friends about it. Maybe bring it up at the next dinner party you attend. Maybe post about it on your social media. Maybe leave a review. *Maybe go fly a kite?* Your help and kindness is the only way others will discover and read it.

Now, the second thank you is for you as well. *Look at that.*

EXTENDED ACKNOWLEDGMENTS

After I started at Remote Year, Trish became my boss, thought partner, and one of my best friends over the next few years. She remains one of my closest friends to this day, but she hasn't been my boss for over a year now. She left Remote Year for new pursuits, and about six months later the COVID-19 pandemic ended the Remote Year dream for the rest of us.

I'm incredibly grateful for my four years at Remote Year, most of which I spent serving as the Director of Community Development. I took on that role after I finished up my lap around the sun as a program leader, cruise director, bandleader, and adult-summer-camp counselor for more than seventy adults on a year-long trip around the world (the role you got a glimpse of me winning at the end of the book). I want to thank Trish, Hannah, Greg, Sam P., Sam Tom, Sam M., Jason, Andrei, Zeke, Elke, Stasia, Jenna, Rose, Sara, Tue, Will, Casey, Omar, Tyler, Kote, Matty, and everyone else with whom I've worked closely over the last four-plus years at Remote Year. It's been a trip, and I was right to want the job so badly.

There are certainly plenty of stories that came with that first trip, with the group that traveled with me as the third Remote Year community (RY Cousteau) and officially became my largest travel family—but those stories aren't for this book. They're for us. In a snapshot, we started as 73 individuals in Cordoba, Argentina, and finished as a family of 53 in Ho Chi Minh, Vietnam, after living in and traveling to twelve cities around the world. I want to thank all 73 of you for letting me lead you, and each of you individually for teaching me something in your own way. I learned more about myself as a leader and a man during that year and in that role than through any other thing life has thrown at me in 36 years.

Side note: As soon as that year finished, Mom Tom (aka Sam Tom, a.k.a. my work wife) and I took ourselves on a lil' honeymoon to Phu Quac, to turn off our brain and notifications and to celebrate a job well done—a family well-formed. From there, I flew myself to Laos, got my Sakura Bar tank top, chugged an opium shake, and barfed off the side of my inner-tube as it carried my lifeless, drug-filled body down the famous-party-lazy-river. Over a full year later, *I finally got my Laos visa!*

Thanks as well to everyone in the Remote Year Nation for putting up with me on Slack and in person. I loved that job and our community deeply—which is in large part thanks to you all. Companies sometimes go under or get bought, but a community lasting is up to its members.

I also want to thank each person that I've met traveling along the way, from when I was a lost puppy up until now—all those who did and did not get written into this book. I would never have kept pushing the adventure forward if it wasn't for being supported, inspired, and simply surrounded by wonderful humans on a daily basis.

Specifically, to those who are scattered around the pages of this book, thanks for making these stories with me. Thanks for being some of my favorite humans. Thanks for making me feel normal when the rest of the world didn't.

Finally, maybe I can add "I am a writer" to my "I am" poem now, which I have many people to thank for. Thank you to all the teachers I had growing up and throughout college and graduate school who would tell me they liked the way I wrote. Without their sincere encouragement, I don't think I would have ever entered into adulthood thinking in the back of my mind, *I can write.* I certainly wouldn't have started on a memoir at age 34. For those in the back: Remember, *we can never know where our words will end up or the steely weight they may hold, so be generous and kind with them.*

When you're gone for a long time, the first assumption you hear is that you're running away from something. For me at least, that could not be further from the truth. It's my family and network back home that lets me feel supported and grounded enough to be so free. Thanks to my family and the boys of Pickerel who make leaving so easy because home will always be there.

Thanks to my brother, Austin, for editing this entire book and covering the cost with a smile—just like he did at my sister's 30th birthday.

Thanks to my partner Maria for being a real *"ride or die"* type. You're the fucking best and were always so patient and supportive in listening to me when I needed to talk about *"the book."* Thanks for loving me as my authentic self (read: when I fart in bed or get good and blacked out) and for letting that exact guy make you so happy. I'm so grateful that I met you when I did. (Also, sorry for all the kinky stories.)

Thanks to Natasha Schwartz, Arestia Rosenberg, Patrick Kolb (aka Marbles), Trish (The Zebra) Kennelly, and Jeanie Linguine, who read and gave feedback about what I was working on, which was always followed by genuine encouragement to keep going.

Thanks to Zoe Bjornson for adding the maps and interior design of this book to her list of 184 projects. Stay young, young Zoe.

Finally, thanks to Lolly Spindler who took what I already thought was a nearly-finished project and squeezed it like a lump of coal, transforming it into something far shinier. I feel lucky beyond measure that you sent me that WhatsApp message.

Lastly, thanks to you, Pops. If I was going to be a chip off of somebody's old block, I'm glad it was your old block...you old, *block*. I love you, and If I'm not dead in a ditch somewhere, I'll see you at Christmas.

PRO TIPS COMPILED

1. If you don't absolutely need to be somewhere, and an airline asks for a volunteer to come to the desk before boarding starts, go up there!

2. Always wear your seatbelt.

3. Always have your own toilet paper.

4. Wet salads and veggies have caused many a chaffed butthole while traveling, so consume with caution.

5. If you're going to travel with a guitar, invest in a travel guitar or guitalele. Most airlines (except punitive-ass Ryanair with their rules) will allow a travel guitar to be stowed in the overhead at no cost as your "extra item" (read: purse, essentially). Almost all airlines will charge well over $50 for a full-sized guitar in a case, which really adds up during extended travel.

6. A.B.C. Always be charging. All of the devices, downloads, apps and maps are only as good as their battery life.

7. Always double check your flight info. Some cities have two airports, and some relationships won't survive that.

8. Southeast Asia is the best place in the world, in terms of quality for value, to get your teeth worked on. I haven't had my teeth worked on anywhere else in the world in the past five years, and I've spent a total of less than $200, without insurance, keeping my pearly whites healthy. Apparently, Colombia is the place to go if you want a new butt or tighter face skin.

9. An overnight bus cancels out the cost of a day's accommodation, so getting comfortable on overnight rides is one of the best things any backpacker on a budget can do to extend their travels.

10. Look into the cheapest airports in each region for cross-continental flights when one-way solo traveling. Hong Kong wins by a mile going from Asia to the States.

ABOUT THE AUTHOR

Travis King is a full-time digital nomad who specializes in community-building within the remote-work movement, cultivating global perspectives, improving location-independent company culture, as well as large- and small-group facilitation and team-building.

After completing his Masters Degree in Nonprofit Management at Marquette University, Travis set out for a solo-travel adventure that turned into four years of working and volunteering across four continents. His solo travels then turned into community travel when he landed a role as a Program Leader for the international work-travel company, Remote Year, where he led a diverse group of 70 adults around the world for a year, helping them to bond as a community, become more culturally aware, and grow both professionally and personally.

Travis was then promoted to the role of Director of Community Development for the entire company where he managed a community of over 2,500 digital nomads, developed new products to bring the community together, and created events to foster bonding, growth, and learning—both virtually and in-person.

Travis is also a travel blogger, a singer-songwriter, a dolphin whisperer, and, after spending time in over 50 countries—he has released his memoir, "Not That Anyone Asked: A Travel Memoir About Sex, Drugs, Love and Finding Purpose."

You can reach him through his website www.traviswking.com or at traviswk@gmail.com for all writing and business inquiries.

Made in the USA
Columbia, SC
23 January 2023

10296915R00198